American Environmental Policy

NEW HORIZONS IN ENVIRONMENTAL POLITICS

Series Editor: Arthur Mol, *Chair and Professor in Environmental Policy, Director, Wageningen School of Social Sciences, Wageningen University, The Netherlands, Professor in Environmental Policy, Renmin University, Beijing*

The New Horizons in Environmental Politics series provides a platform for in-depth critical assessments of how we understand the many changes in the politics of nature, the environment and natural resources that have occurred over the last 50 years. Books in the series question how the environment is (re)defined, debated and protected; explore differences between countries and regions in environmental politics; analyse how actors do and do not collaborate around environment and natural resource conflicts; describe who wins and who loses and in what ways; and detail how to better study, analyze and theorize such developments and outcomes.

The series is designed to promote innovative cross-disciplinary analysis of the contemporary issues and debates influencing the various dimensions of environmental politics. Covering a diverse range of topics, the series will examine the political, economic and ethical aspects of environmental policy, governance and regulation. It brings together cutting edge research on environmental politics worldwide in order to shed light on, and explain current trends and developments.

With oversight from the Series Editor, Professor Arthur Mol – a noted specialist in the field of environmental politics at Wageningen University, The Netherlands – the New Horizons in Environmental Politics series comprises carefully commissioned projects from experts in the field including both academics and professionals. The audience for the series is global, and books in the series are essential reading for students, academics and professionals – in short, anyone with an interest in understanding the vital issues affecting environmental politics in the 21st Century.

Recent titles in the series include:

American Environmental Policy

The Failures of Compliance, Abatement and Mitigation

Daniel Press

Olga T. Griswold Professor of Environmental Studies and Executive Director of the University of California, Santa Cruz Center for Agroecology and Sustainable Food Systems, USA

NEW HORIZONS IN ENVIRONMENTAL POLITICS

Edward Elgar
PUBLISHING

Cheltenham, UK • Northampton, MA, USA

Published by
Edward Elgar Publishing Limited
The Lypiatts
15 Lansdown Road
Cheltenham
Glos GL50 2JA
UK

Edward Elgar Publishing, Inc.
William Pratt House
9 Dewey Court
Northampton
Massachusetts 01060
USA

A catalogue record for this book
is available from the British Library

Library of Congress Control Number: 2014952138

This book is available electronically in the **Elgar**online
Social and Political Science subject collection
DOI 10.4337/9781781001462

ISBN 978 1 78100 145 5 (cased)
ISBN 978 1 78100 146 2 (eBook)

Typeset by Servis Filmsetting Ltd, Stockport, Cheshire
Printed and bound in Great Britain by T.J. International Ltd, Padstow

For Talya

Contents

Figures

Tables

Preface

For over 20 years, I have been teaching environmental politics and policy at the University of California, Santa Cruz. Many of my students come to the subject thinking that policy is a castor oil subject, necessary but unpleasant. Students who last thought of government in a dry high school civics class understandably wonder what they're getting into. Year after year, I have been gratified to find that students actually hunger for exposure to environmental policy once they understand that it is no less imaginative and creative than natural history, art and experimentation.

This book project started off as an effort to put into writing my approach to explaining the successes and failures of American environmental policy. Although it seems far off and unreal for 20-year-olds, I remind them that they will soon enough become important decision-makers. Consequently, I ask them to reflect on the evaluative criteria with which they will judge environmental regulation, rules, laws and voluntary efforts. How will they know success or failure? What trade-offs will be acceptable to them and why? Guiding my students through these questions has taught me as much as it has taught them, I am quite sure, so my first debt of thanks goes to the many hundreds of students who have journeyed along with me in my national environmental policy course.

As the project evolved and I articulated my own evaluative criteria, the book became more critical. I am generally not a polemicist, but had come to feel that too much of American environmental regulation was considered settled and successful. The air and water were cleaner, so regulation today must be superfluous and overbearing. A closer look at commonly praised environmental policies revealed that the successes were more mixed and sometimes temporary. Just as importantly, American political gridlock seemed to discourage reformers from taking a hard look at long established regulatory approaches. After all, without political will for reform, what point is there in discussing new policy designs? Such a view assumes that politics neatly precedes policy; in my experience, the two are locked together and sometimes indistinguishable. And because environmental, social and economic circumstances change, evaluating policy designs should never be off the table.

I cast a fairly wide net in this book; doing so thus required a lot of help.

Many staff members of the US Environmental Protection Agency gave generously of their time and data – I appreciate their doing so especially since I am often critical of the programs that they implement. I hasten to add that I think very highly of federal and state environmental agency personnel. They are some of the most dedicated and hard-working public servants you'll ever meet. At the EPA, I wish to thank Richard Haeuber, Fred Talcott, Bill Kline, Thelma Codina, Tim Antisdel, Velu Senthil, Brian McLean and Jason Lynch. From the California Central Coast Regional Water Quality Control Board, I thank the board chair, Jeff Young, and staff members Lisa McCann, Chris Rose and Matt Keeling. Linda LaMarca, from the US Waterborne Commerce Statistics Center, provided valuable transportation data for the chapter on paper recycling.

Charles Driscoll, from Syracuse University, and Doug Burns, from the US Geological Survey, helped me understand much better how ecologists and biogeochemists currently think about acid deposition. The engineers Phyllis Fox and Ron Sahu, plus staff at the Environmental Integrity Project (Sparsh Khandeshi, John Dawes and Eric Schaeffer) likewise helped me better grasp how emissions factors can or cannot characterize toxic releases.

I received tremendous insights from several people who had long associations with the US paper industry. I thank Glen Johnson, Steven Smith and Ann Jansen, all of FutureMark Paper. I greatly benefited from discussions with Conservatree's Susan Kinsella as well as Maureen Smith and Pam Blackledge (Re-Paper Project). Lee Anderson of the BlueGreen Alliance and Frank Locantore (Green America) had great insights on how improving paper recycling could have important consequences for the US labor market and manufacturing. Mitko Yordanov (from the American Forest and Paper Association), Mark Arzoumanian (from the trade journal *Official Board Markets*) and Robert O. Vos (from the University of Southern California), all helped me gather and understand data on paper recovery.

I received great encouragement and insights from academic colleagues and friends, including my old mentor Dan Mazmanian (of the University of Southern California), Sheldon Kamieniecki (my dean and colleague here at UC Santa Cruz), Dan Fiorino (of American University, formerly at the US EPA), Jim Corbett (from the University of Delaware), and James Hamilton (from Stanford University).

I had the great good fortune of having talented, insightful and creative research assistants. I benefited immensely from Pete Holloran's wondrous mind and astounding ability to go down many rabbit holes, as he would put it, always emerging with great finds. Sophia Zeng and Joanna Ory did a great deal of heavy lifting, research-wise, especially for data collection and literature reviews. I am indebted to Aaron Cole, a gifted cartographer and spatial analyst. Kathleen Bertsche drew the figures I needed for Chapter 3, ones that I had been wishing for every time I taught my class. Unlike just about any other work I have published, I did not raise any external funding to pay all these wonderful assistants, but relied instead on the Olga T. Griswold Chair in Environmental Studies. I thank Craig Griswold for funding the chair; I can't imagine this project without his support. I am also deeply grateful to Alec and Claudia Webster.

Environmental Studies graduate students Peter Brewitt, Sarah Carvill, Annie Drevno and Sara Lewis cheerfully read draft chapters and contributed many valuable comments. I am deeply grateful to the UC Santa Cruz staff, including Yamindira Kanagasundarum (UCSC purchasing) and our marvelous librarians, Lucia Orlando and Jan Becking. If the writing is any good, thank Sarah Rabkin, my wonderful colleague, editor and teacher – if the writing is no good, blame me. I thank Alex Pettifer, of Edward Elgar, for his encouragement and patience, in equal measures. Several anonymous reviewers also provided excellent advice.

And finally, I thank my parents Esther McManus and Richard Press, my wife and muse Sarah Press and my late sister, Talya Press, to whom I dedicate this book.

Abbreviations

AF&PA	American Forest and Paper Association
AIR	Association of Irritated Residents
ANC	acid-neutralizing capacity
ARP	Acid Rain Program
ARPCAIR	Acid Rain Program Clean Air Interstate Rule
AWMA	Air and Waste Management Association
BACT	best available control technology
BAT	best available technology
BPA	bisphenol-A
CAA	Clean Air Act
CAAA	Clean Air Act Amendment (Title IV US Clean Air Act Amendment (CAAA) – also known as the Acid Rain Program (ARP))
CAFOs	concentrated animal feedlot operations
CAIR	Clean Air Interstate Rule
CCS	carbon capture and storage
CEEP	Center for Evidence-based Environmental Policies and Programs
CEMS	Continuous Emissions Monitoring Systems
CEPI	Confederation of European Paper Industries
CERCLA	Comprehensive Environmental Response, Compensation and Liability Act (also known as the "Superfund Law")
CHIEF	Clearing House for Inventories and Emissions Factors
CL	critical load
COE	cost of electricity
CSAR	Cross State Air Rule
CWA	Clean Water Act
C&DW	construction and demolition waste
DEQ	Department of Environmental Quality
DIAL	Differential Absorption Light Detection
DILs	dirty-input limits
DOC	dissolved organic carbon
DPR	Department of Pesticide Regulation
DTSC	Department of Toxic Substances Control

ECHO	Enforcement and Compliance History Online
EIA	Energy Information Administration
EIP	Environmental Integrity Project
EMFAC	California Air Resources Board's Emission Factors
EPA	Environmental Protection Agency
EPCRA	Emergency Planning and Community Right-to-Know Act (also known as SARA Title III)
EPN	Environmental Paper Network
EPR	extended producer responsibility
FGD	flue-gas desulfurization
FIFRA	Federal Insecticide, Fungicide, and Rodenticide Act Amendments of 1972
GAO	General Accountability Office
GJ	gigajoules
HSWA	Hazardous and Solid Waste Amendments
ICC	Interstate Commerce Commission
IEA	International Energy Agency
INGAA	Interstate Natural Gas Association of America
ISRI	Institute for Scrap Recycling Industries
LID	low-impact development
LWC	lightweight coated
MAC	marginal abatement cost
MACT	maximum achievable control technology
MATS rule	Mercury and Air Toxics Standard
mmBTU	million British Thermal Units
MRF	materials recovery facilities
MTBE	methyl tertiary butyl ether
NADP/NTN	National Atmospheric Deposition Program's National Trends Network
NAPAP	National Acid Precipitation Assessment Program
NESHAPs	National Emission Standards for Hazardous Air Pollutants
NG2CP	ratio of electricity-generating costs at natural gas versus coal plants
NIMBY	Not In My Back Yard
NTM	Network for Transport and the Environment
NUE	nitrogen use efficiency
OIG	Office of Inspector General
OIRA	Office of Information and Regulatory Affairs
PAC	polycyclic aromatic compound
PAHs	polycyclic aromatic hydrocarbons
PBT	persistent, bioaccumulative and toxic

PCBs	polychlorinated biphenyls
PIA	Procurement Integrity Act
POPs	persistent organic pollutants
POTWs	publicly-owned treatment works
RCRA	Resource Conservation and Recovery Act
SARA	Superfund Amendments and Reauthorization Act
SCAQMD	South Coast Air Quality Management District
Section 112	Clean Air Act Section 112
SEPs	Supplemental Environmental Projects
SMCRA	Surface Mining Control and Reclamation Act
SRA	Staggers Rail Act – also known as Staggers Act
STB	Surface Transportation Board
TDCPP	chlorinated trisphosphate
TIME	Temporally Integrated Monitoring of Ecosystems
TMDL	total maximum daily load
TRI	Toxics Release Inventory
TSCA	Toxic Substances Control Act of 1976
UST	underground storage tank
VOC	volatile organic compound
WPCA	Water Pollution Control Act
WRAP	British Waste & Resources Action Programme

1. Introduction

> The central problem for twenty-first-century environmental policy is how to develop new strategies for attacking new environmental problems, how to develop better strategies for solving the old ones, and how to do both in ways that are more efficient, less taxing, and engender less political opposition. (Donald Kettl, *Environmental Governance*, 2002, p. 6.)

For scholars and policy practitioners alike, the early 1970s – ushered in by the first nationwide Earth Day celebration – marked the beginning of serious environmental regulation in the United States. Forty years later, Americans with any serious green penchant are engaging in some profound soul-searching about our environmental regulations. Did the nation make enough progress, given the gravity and reach of environmental problems? Did American environmental policy perform as well as that of other developed countries? Were the costs acceptable? Did the extensive American green state – to use Klyza and Sousa's (2008) term – select the most appropriate policy instruments? Were these tools applied properly? More fundamentally, to what extent did American environmental regulation transform the way we manufacture, build, consume and move people or goods?

Until recently, these questions could be raised but not answered, at least not very well. We either had scant evidence with which to explore them or we had not lived with our regulatory programs long enough to see results. The passage of time has reduced both of those obstacles. Accordingly, in this book I am able to show that, despite enormous gains achieved with the regulatory apparatus implemented after 1970, American environmental policy has stalled.

At the same time, a fundamental timidity now characterizes many American environmental regulations. Whether it's pollution abatement or habitat conservation planning, American environmental policy rarely requires or aggressively encourages thorough transformation of environmentally damaging activities. Instead, American environmental regulators commonly do their level best to preserve, intact, the way we produce energy, use land, manufacture goods, build structures and move ourselves around – provided the worst abuses of power are mitigated, reduced or contained. I call this the compliance-abatement-mitigation approach to environmental problems. It accomplished much in the first epoch of modern environmental policy, especially in light of ineffectual 1960s-style pollution abatement, but was predicated on an inherently limited model of transformation. The limits of compliance-abatement-mitigation seemed far off when this approach was first launched, but now threaten to undo hard-won accomplishments and thwart future gains in environmental quality. Although my criticisms will be numerous, my aim in this book is a constructive scrutiny of American environmental policy shortcomings accompanied by insights and proposals for developing truly transformative policy in the 21st century.

Many thoughtful commentators have reached similar conclusions over the years, pointing to the substantial gap between legislative goals and what is actually achieved on the ground (Dryzek, 1997), what Fiorino (2006) calls an "implementation deficit" (p. 82). Environmental policy scholars commonly state that classic American environmental regulation has run its course (Metzenbaum, 1998; Kettl, 2002; Davies and Mazurek, 1998; Fiorino, 2006; Cohen, Kamieniecki and Cahn, 2005; Kraft, Stephan and Abel, 2011; Mazmanian and Kraft, 2009).

Much of the environmental policy literature draws attention to the ebb and flow of political support for environmental policies, the struggle between corporate and environmental interests or the public's understanding of environmental quality. My goal here is synthesis, critique and reform – not theoretical innovation or a political autopsy of failed legislation. I do rely on valuable theoretical frameworks from several fairly disparate literatures, but I am not proposing a new theory of environmental regulation. Fortunately, public policy, political science, economics, industrial ecology, engineering and the environmental sciences provide us with all the conceptual tools needed to make sense of our environmental achievements and shortcomings. Using these tools, I take aim at several of the most problematic environmental policy tools and their implementation, relying on far more of the latest environmental science and engineering than is usually the case in contemporary policy studies. By engaging deeply with several scientific literatures, we can much better appreciate our environmental management successes, failures and limits. We can also see more clearly how specific environmental policies generate particular environmental outcomes. In a regulatory era when the low-hanging fruit has already been picked, an equally important contribution of the book is to articulate an environmental policy approach that employs tools and instruments appropriate to the mature administrative apparatus of the 21st century.

Much of this book analyzes important environmental management tools to illustrate our regulatory shortcomings. These examples are not meant to be exhaustive, but rather to demonstrate some of the more consequential ways in which environmental regulations miss the mark. Before providing an overview of the book's plan, I want to present the working definition of regulatory failure that guides my selection and evaluation of these cases.

WHAT IS REGULATORY FAILURE?

Public administration scholars have filled journals and books with policy evaluation studies and frameworks for analyzing policy catastrophes or successes. Most policy scholars agree that objective, technical, uncontested criteria by which to judge the successes and failures of all policies or regulatory programs simply do not exist and never will. Taken to its extreme, however, a purely relativistic position holds that there are no empirically observable regulatory failures, since "success" and "failure" are simply in the eye of the beholder (Sunstein, 1990, p. 75).

But here I adopt a narrower scope, one that is more amenable to empirical verification. Regulations can be deemed successes or failures to the extent that they produce outcomes called for in their enabling legislation. In its purest, simplest form, environmental law seeks to prevent or reduce pollutant loads, to protect species and ecosystems, and to restore degraded landscapes or waterways. Legislators and their administrative agents often express these goals with numerical standards, so failure can most readily be recognized as a violation of these limits. But defining failure as *any* violation, no matter how small or infrequent, would be absurd.

Instead, the term "failure" should be reserved for regulatory shortcomings that allow or cause exceptional, ongoing danger to public and environmental health (see Table 1), especially when we have examples of alternative policy tools that can work unambiguously. For instance, the rare cases in which the US banned certain compounds outright – like lead in gasoline and paints, phosphorus in detergents, and persistent organic pollutants (POPs), including DDT, dieldrin and PCBs – all demonstrated government's ability to decisively remove public and environmental health threats (Commoner, 1987; Kehoe, 1992; Weimer and Vining, 1999).

In invoking this limited meaning of "failure," I adopt an approach similar to that of Moran's (2001) policy catastrophes topology. He proposed five different kinds of political action or events that led to policy catastrophes, illustrated by ". . .five cases that, at least from the vantage point of 2001, are uncontested catastrophes" (p. 415). By this standard, I propose five forms of regulatory failure in environmental programs, listed in Table 1.1.

Table 1.1   Varieties of failure in American environmental regulation

Varieties of Failure	Examples
Catastrophic harm	Deepwater Horizon oil spill, 2010
Ongoing or chronic harm	Nonattainment with Clean Air Act standards
Detection and information breakdown	Guadalupe Oil Field spill, San Luis Obispo County, California, 1997–2002
Inadequate restoration	Surface mine reclamation under SMCRA
Unintended (usually cross-media) consequences	Methyl tertiary butyl ether (MTBE) in groundwater; recycling as solid waste management rather than industrial feedstock

POSSIBLE MECHANISMS OF REGULATORY FAILURE

How do the regulatory failures in Table 1 happen? The various regulatory literatures tend to organize the mechanisms of failure with respect to the agents of such failures. Thus for example, Cass Sunstein (1990) distinguishes between poor statutory language and bad implementation, thereby blaming legislators and agency officials separately.

A voluntaristic view of implementation failure holds that policymakers deliberately ignore their duties or address problems incorrectly (Bovens and 't Hart, 1996); their actions are thus purposeful and the consequences intended (Stone, 1997). A more deterministic view holds that external forces and constraints unintentionally visit implementation failures upon regulatory programs. However, Coglianese (2012) cautions that we should not reflexively invoke regulatory failure in explaining catastrophes visited upon highly regulated industries, like mining or deepwater oil exploration. Some accidents simply cannot be prevented by even the best regulatory designs.

Market failure, a major preoccupation of the regulatory economics literature (see Anthoff and Hahn, 2010), usually shares this deterministic, mechanical agency: markets are machines that perform as designed, but cause harm unless modified. Many economists view regulation (e.g., one-size-fits-all command and control rules) as a cure worse than the disease (market failure in the form of negative externalities, monopolistic or oligopolistic abuses); thus, failure resides in the original policy tool employed (Alleman and Rappoport, 2005).

Cohen, Kamieniecki and Cahn (2005) situate failure not necessarily in the policy tool, but in the strategic approach (or lack thereof) used to implement regulation. The rare success stories occur at the confluence of

Table 1.2   Regulatory failure mechanisms

Mechanism	Agents	Examples
Negative regulatory slippage over time	Legislators and regulators	The "low-hanging fruit" problem; gradual changes in rule content or enforcement; use of waivers
Obstruction	Regulated community	Capture, information bottlenecks or "filter failure," lawsuits, protests, reduced penalties
Policy instrument mismatch	Legislators, regulators	End-of-pipe controls under high growth conditions; Nonpoint source programs for water quality, MTBE; Deepwater oil drilling; single-stream (commingled) recycling

three factors: the regulated community's capabilities, its motivations and the feasibility of regulations themselves.

Moreover, like any human endeavor, regulations age. As they grow older, some programs succeed at addressing their mandates, developing supportive constituencies along the way even as they impose costs on regulated interests. Other programs evolve toward failure. Either way, there may be little in the way of active human agency involved.

As with the failure typology I developed above, I propose three general mechanisms in Table 1.2 as useful heuristics for explaining how regulatory programs fail. I offer illustrative examples within each general category. I stop short of presenting empirical evidence, except where the literature provides some; instead, this typology of mechanism is designed to guide further theorizing and empiricism.

In some of these mechanisms, failure occurs through intentional obstruction; in others, there is no agent willfully inciting failure, but policy tools may be inadequate to resolve problems, as the following sections suggest.

REGULATORY FAILURE THROUGH SLIPPAGE

Regulatory programs often "slip" or "drift," eventually resulting in implementing agencies facing changed mandates, or at least implementing to fairly different outcomes than the ones in original legislation. Regulatory slippage also has negative consequences for environmental management (Farber, 1999) as well as positive results (see what Klyza and Sousa, 2008, call "green drift"); here I will focus on failures rather than gradual improvements.

In Farber's formulation, negative slippage occurs when either federal or state agencies fail to adopt standards – as mandated by enabling legislation – or when agencies fail to enforce existing rules adequately. Negative slippage also occurs when the regulated community simply doesn't comply with what might otherwise be good rules. These factors are all related, of course. The regulated community will continue flouting rules while administrative agencies fail or refuse to enforce them.

Reasonably strong regulatory programs can also drift ". . .when rules remain formally the same but their impact changes as a result of shifts in external condition" (Mahoney and Thelen, 2010, p. 17). This is a major source of failure in the main pollution abatement laws, which are now entering their fifth decade of implementation. After Congress passed tough amendments to federal clean water and clean air laws, dramatic improvements in pollution abatement occurred very rapidly, in large part because previous standards had been lax or non-existent. In the 1970s it was easy to find side-by-side pictures of smokestacks belching dark smoke before passage of the 1970 Clean Air Act, contrasted with the same smokestacks emitting nearly invisible emissions thanks to the Act's particulate matter controls.

Congress recognized that abatement costs increase the more one tries to remove pollutants, which is why the CAA and the CWA gradually phased in ever more stringent controls, with some astonishingly ambitious end goals. Indeed, the 1972 CWA amendments actually stated that "It is the national goal that the discharge of pollutants into the navigable waters be eliminated by 1985" (33 U.S.C. § 1251).

It makes sense that initial abatement efforts will be relatively easy, while higher costs and quite possibly very different kinds of technological controls will be required to abate the latter fractions of remaining pollution (e.g., from 70 percent to 90 percent removal). The simple s-curve in Figure 1.1 illustrates this "low-hanging fruit" phenomenon.

Regulators understand that technologies for removing, say, the "first" 75 percent of a pollutant stream – e.g., through secondary water effluent standards or flue-gas desulfurization – are likely very different from processes and equipment for removing pollutants at higher efficiencies. Indeed, reaching 100 percent abatement through end-of-pipe controls is really an oxymoron: truly complete abatement can only be achieved through completely redesigning industrial processes.

Moreover, regulators have historically not required the highest removal efficiencies. Instead, the much stricter standards come years or even decades after initial legislation was passed, sometimes as a result of new health findings (which in recent years prompted the EPA to revise most of its ambient air standards). By then, the legislative champions who passed

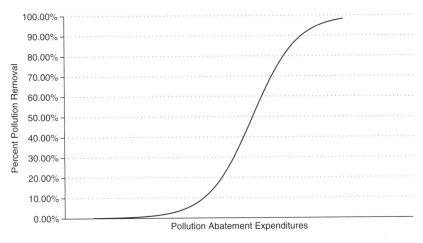

Figure 1.1   Diminishing returns from pollution abatement expenditures

initial laws have long since moved on – in essence, leaving a political vacuum into which arrive well-organized opponents of tougher standards.

Sometimes regulatory programs themselves are to blame for preventing greater pollution abatement. For example, the best available control technology (BACT) approach employed by EPA required very specific technologies and processes for a wide variety of industries. When initially implemented, BACT resulted in improvements (the low-hanging fruit), but also froze abatement performance, technological innovation and change at a specific point in time. Until Congress passed the 1990 CAA amendments, Midwestern power plants had little incentive to exceed SO_2 removal levels mandated by earlier versions of the Act (90 percent removal, which nearly half the plants didn't regularly reach anyway). After EPA implemented the SO_2 tradable permit system, no plants failed to reach the 90 percent removal rates; by 1997 nearly 80 percent of the plants had exceeded 95 percent removal rates (Popp, 2003).

Why is the low-hanging fruit phenomenon a case of *regulatory* failure? It is regulatory failure because policy tools adopted at the onset of regulatory programs cannot force pollution reductions after initial gains have been achieved by picking the low-hanging fruit. Yet, the same policy approaches continue to be applied to the problem, leaving it unsolved (e.g., out of attainment with clean air standards) for decades. The built-in limitations of the end-of-pipe, low-hanging fruit approach make it hard to achieve further gains using the same regulatory approach (Kraft, Stephan and Abel, 2011, p.4). Diminishing returns even apply to recycling if consumption grows faster than materials collection (Geiser, 2001, p.235).

In sum, 1) regulators lack the political support for tougher standards, while 2), pollution removal rates through end-of-pipe controls encounter hard technical limits, and 3) population growth swamps the per-unit improvements, thereby vitiating the end-of-pipe approach.

REGULATORY FAILURE THROUGH OBSTRUCTION

> As a rule, regulation is acquired by the industry and is designed and operated primarily for its benefit. (Stigler, 1971, p. 2)

Many interests oppose regulation and learn to parry regulatory efforts through a variety of mechanisms. I raise here the specter of regulatory capture, but before proceeding any further, I acknowledge that environmental agencies can be unduly influenced at least as much by environmentalists as they can by the regulated community (Wilson, 1980). While environmentalists don't tend to pressure agencies to promulgate weak regulations, their influence can result in regulatory delay, increased costs (beyond what would efficiently reduce the same amount of pollution) and impractical, hard-to-implement programs. California's proposed climate change tradable permit program was delayed longer by environmental groups than industry opponents. In this case, the Association of Irritated Residents (AIR), argued the program would result in pollution "hot spots" concentrated in poor and minority neighborhoods (Egelko, 2011).

What makes capture an instance of failure as opposed to "the workings of an acceptable political process," as Peter Strauss (1991, p. 924) would put it? Strauss's answer is to include only "interest-group transfers masquerading as regulation. . . and. . .[the] inevitable and permanent imbalance of cost and benefit" (p. 923). Similarly, Croley (2008) points out that regulatory failure can be defined by its alternative, "public interested" regulation, which ". . . delivers no rents or, if it does, the gains for those who benefit from the regulatory decision outweigh any losses to the rest of society. . .it is Kaldor-Hicks efficient" (Croley, p. 11). Interest-group transfers occur when regulation is adopted to address a genuine market failure with a policy that does not work very well, but transfers wealth to, or protects the wealth of, powerful private interests. The classic environmental case of this concerns air pollution from power plants. Until the 1990 CAA amendments were promulgated and enforced, Appalachian coal mining companies benefited from rules that pushed sulfur scrubbers onto electric-generating facilities rather than promoting the use of low-sulfur western coal (Sunstein, 1990; pp. 84–85; Ackerman and Hassler, 1981).

In other words, taking statutory language at face value, laws like the Clean Air Act, the Clean Water Act and the Comprehensive Environmental Response, Compensation and Liability Act (the Superfund law) specifically intend to provide environmental protection, but different choices about how to attain environmental quality goals can result in enormous windfalls or costs. For example, oxygenating gasoline with MTBE opens up a huge market for American and Canadian chemical manufacturers; using ethanol provides a windfall to Midwestern corn growers and ethanol producers.

Setting aside instances whereby legislators write their hostility toward environmentalist objectives into statutes, regulations can fail through outright obstruction, which can be overt or quite discreet. A vast literature refers to regulatory obstruction by many names, some of them falling under the "capture" rubric. They can generally be grouped into categories including 1) information capture and filter failure, 2) weakened enforcement, 3) revolving-door appointments, and 4) delay.

Wagner's (2010) anatomy of information capture shows how Congress's well-intended impulse to invite (if not require) a maximum amount of information input to the regulatory process has backfired. Today, environmental regulations require enormous amounts of information, but administrative law does not make clear provisions for managing the flow of such information, especially as to whether and how to filter it, thereby distinguishing between what is useful and legitimate, and what is irrelevant or deliberately provided merely to gum up the works. Stakeholders (especially in the regulated communities) have an incentive to overwhelm administrative agencies and courts with information (Laffont and Tirole, 1991). The result is that decision-making becomes more obscure and very few participants have the wherewithal to manage the information.

Interest-group transfers – Strauss's principal concern with regulatory failure – can be caused when the regulated community engages so deeply in the rule-writing enterprise that it can be fairly credited for authoring the very content of regulations (Rosenbaum, 2011). This has happened with transportation policy (Etzioni, 2009), the underground storage tank (UST) rules that led to methyl-tertiary butyl ether (MTBE) contamination (McGarity, 2004), monitoring leaks on the seals of petrochemical tanks (Wagner, 2010) and the new source review provisions of the Clean Air Act (Barcott, 2004).

Even excellent rules fail if regulators don't enforce them. Makkai and Braithwaite showed that inspectors who had held senior management positions in industry were less "tough" than their counterparts lacking industry experience (1992). This is a finding echoed many times by investigative reporters examining state and federal environmental rule enforcement (see Duhigg, 2009 for a recent multi-part series in the New York Times), scholars tracking variations in state enforcement (e.g., Hunter and Waterman, 1996) and federal watchdog agencies like the General Accountability Office, which demonstrated that funding has not kept pace with inflation and enforcement responsibilities (Forgacs, 2010).

Sometimes enforcement loses its bite when the regulated become the regulators, through what's known as a revolving door between industry and government (Heyes, 2003; Dal Bó, 2006). Many scholars and political observers would agree that the revolving doors are real and that the phenomenon probably has an influence on policy outputs and outcomes. Indeed, the phenomenon is real enough that the federal government restricts former government employees from ever representing their private sector clients on matters in which the former employee "personally and substantially" participated while in government (5 C.F.R. § 2637.201). The Procurement Integrity Act bars, for one year, a former government employee who participated in procurement contracts in excess of $10 million from serving as an employee or consultant with the contractor (48 C.F.R. § 3.104–1–11).

These restrictions still leave a lot of room for mischief, but how should undue influence be measured? If a former government employee goes to work for the industry he or she once regulated, is that a *prima facie* case of undue influence that will result in regulatory failure? Again, investigative reporters have made more headway with this topic than scholars, finding anecdotal evidence for rule-writing by regulated industries, private meetings and lobbying activities by former government officials (see Barcott (2004) for an example).

It's easier to measure regulatory obstruction through what Sunstein (1990) calls "administrative delay and torpor." Kosnick (2005) found that dam operators whose federal licenses were up for renewal made strong efforts to delay the process, most likely because doing so would postpone ". . .costly environmental mitigation requirements that go along with a relicense. The longer the delay, the greater the chance of avoiding the costly requirements altogether–but if nothing else, delay will certainly subject these costs to greater discounting" (pp. 279–280).

Ando (1999) found a similar interest-group influence effect on the Fish and Wildlife Service's endangered species listing process. Generally speaking, when legislators (especially those with Fish and Wildlife Service regulatory and/or budget oversight responsibility) and stakeholders opposed listing species as endangered or threatened, listing decisions were delayed, sometimes to the point of inaction.

Regulation can fail through delay because of rigid procedural requirements that force agencies to spend more time and money developing and issuing rules. (Sunstein, 1990, p. 100). The small community of Los Osos, California, illustrates how due process can stymie rulemaking. This 15,000-resident community on the southern end of the Morro Bay estuary uses septic tanks to treat its municipal sewage. Unfortunately, the small, narrow lots and sandy soils prevent septic tanks from functioning properly, resulting in nitrate groundwater contamination. Although the community has been under orders from the state to stop discharging nitrates into groundwater since 1988, which effectively means building a sewer and connecting residents to it, twenty-five years later, a functioning sewage treatment facility was still a long way off.

Delay also results when agencies face tremendous uncertainties and must work with incomplete information. For nearly a generation, the US EPA failed to regulate air toxics as required by the 1970 Clean Air Act in its NESHAPs program, because of extraordinary complexity in determining risks and setting scientifically defensible air standards that were also technologically feasible.

Ultimately, regulatory capture is a situational phenomenon, which helps to explain the frequent failure of systemic reforms such as limits on revolving door appointments. (Makkai and Braithwaite, 1992).

REGULATORY FAILURE THROUGH MISMATCH

Regulations can fail because particular policy tools simply cannot address problems for which they were not designed. But if the tools don't work, why are they adopted? Deborah Stone's (1997) well-known policy paradox concept helps us see that it has been politically rational for the nation to substantially abate pollution without fundamentally changing industry. Political communities form around specific policy tools, making their adoption and implementation possible – even if such tools cannot possibly solve a problem over the long run.

Worse yet, real environmental policy paradoxes actually cause precisely the opposite of their intended purposes. Sunstein (1990) offers three such examples applicable to environmental policy; I add illustrative cases to each:

1) "To require the best available technology is to discourage technological development" (p. 106). Forced to favor compliance over performance, companies lock in, for example, manufacturing, power generation or pollution abatement technologies rather than pursue innovations (Chertow and Esty, 1997; Popp, 2003).

2) "To regulate new risks in the interest of health and safety is to per-
petuate old ones, and thus to reduce health and safety" (p. 106). As
I'll discuss further in Chapter 3, the Acid Rain Program, adopted to
combat new concerns over surface water acidification and tree mortality in the Adirondacks and Appalachia, likely resulted in differential
health benefits to the public. That's because the program shifted SOx
emissions from relatively under-populated rural areas to more urban-
ized parts of the country, where more people were exposed to these
pollutants (Henry, Muller and Mendelsohn, 2011).

3) "Strict regulatory controls produce underregulation, at least when the
regulator has prosecutorial discretion" (p. 106). American regulators
have at their disposal all the authority they need to curb the most
dangerous hazards, like those posed by some toxics, but very rarely
exercise their discretion because of the damage they might pose to particular industries. The result is that regulators match "wait-and-see"
approaches for far too many risks that really require banning a chemical (e.g., DDT) or practice (e.g., land disposal of hazardous wastes)
outright (see Commoner, 1987 and Kehoe, 1992).

These regulatory paradoxes, along with policy legacies from the
1960s and 1970s, ensure that environmental policy mismatches abound.
Sometimes regulations adequate for one system (shallow water oil drilling)
fail spectacularly in another (deepwater oil drilling, as the country learned
with the BP Gulf oil spill in 2010). In some cases, regulators simply can't
keep up. As Goodin, Rein and Moran (2006) put it, "[p]olicy is simply
sometimes taken over by events. Whole swathes of policy regulating
obsolete technologies become redundant with technological advances"
(p. 26). Rapidly-unfolding booms in new economic activity associated
with technological advances commonly overwhelm regulatory agencies.
Recently, these include deepwater oil drilling, mountaintop mining with
valley fills and hydraulic fracturing for natural gas. In still other instances,
an ambient management approach fails spectacularly to control nonpoint
sources of pollution, as is the case in water quality (Houck, 2002).

The compliance-abatement-mitigation approach favors end-of-pipe
pollution controls based on the assumption that removing nearly all the
pollution from some source will usually be good enough. End-of-pipe controls end up as policy mismatches simply because the number of pollutant
sources grows enough to overwhelm the per-unit emissions or effluent
reductions.

The Los Angeles basin provides a good illustration of this failure. In the
1940s, when the smog problem became well-defined and mobile sources
were implicated in its cause, there were about 2.5 million mobile sources

in the basin; by 2005, the number had grown to more than 10 million (Mazmanian, 2006). Today's cars emit 89 percent less NOx per mile, 96 percent less CO and 98 percent less hydrocarbons, but the LA basin is still far, far out of attainment with ambient clean air standards. A 2010 report by the Environment California Research & Policy Center pointed out that a new car purchased in 1960 could be expected to emit one short ton (2,000 pounds) of smog-forming compounds during 100,000 miles of travel, while today's vehicles emit 10 pounds of pollutants over the same distance. Despite being 99 percent cleaner, vehicles still account for 20 percent of California's smog-forming compounds (Madsen et al., 2010).

In order to eventually comply with ozone standards, the South Coast Air Quality Management District (SCAQMD), charged with enforcing state and federal clean air laws, estimates that daily NOx emissions need to come down by 192 tons by 2014 and 383 tons by 2023 (SCAQMD, 2007). Currently, all on-road mobile sources in the basin (passenger vehicles, light and heavy duty trucks) contribute over 400 tons of NOx per day. Thus, cars and trucks would have to reduce their NOx emissions another 50 to nearly 100 percent if regulators sought attainment through mobile source controls alone.

A big part of the problem is the LA basin's topography, of course, but a larger population of vehicles is also much to blame. Consider the following hypothetical: how many tons of NOx would LA basin mobile sources emit, per day, if the same *number* of cars were on the road today as in 1978 (by which time EPA's mobile source standards had been adopted), but with *today's* emissions standards?

The California Air Resources Board's Emission Factors (EMFAC) model makes this thought experiment possible. EMFAC estimates on-road mobile source emissions using different population and emissions factor inputs using the following:

Emissions factor X correction factor X travel activity = Emissions in tons per day

Using the EMFAC model with actual vehicle populations from 1978–2008, but current tailpipe standards, yields the daily NOx emissions depicted in Figure 1.2. The key difference lies in the daily NOx emissions between the number of vehicles on the road in 1978 (220 tons) and the number of vehicles in 2008 (460 tons).[1] The difference – 240 tons per day – is very close to the emissions reduction target the SCAQMD set *for all*

---

[1] The actual NOx emissions from mobile sources are higher than what this model run estimates, because the model here assumed that *all* mobile sources on the road complied with the latest standards. In reality, there is always a mix of old and new vehicles, so the older vehicles drive up the total emissions burden.

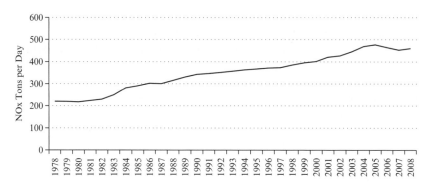

Figure 1.2   *Mobile source NOx emissions in the LA basin with 2009*
                standards

sources between 2014 and 2023. Of course, I am not seriously suggesting
that the LA basin population should not have grown at all between 1978
and 2008, but this model illustrates the hard limits all end-of-pipe control
strategies must reach. Something eventually has to give, either the number
of sources or the basic technology itself.

Recycling in America makes for another of the most disappointing environmental policy mismatches, painfully illustrating the law of unintended
consequences. After 40 years of cultural change, spurred on by legions of
righteous school children and vigorous ad campaigns, Americans have
raised recycling to the level of a moral act. And so, millions of us wheel our
carts out to the curb every week, certain that we are doing our part for sustainability. How ironic, then, that so many of these recyclables are either
too contaminated to reuse or so hopelessly co-mingled that it has become
economically impractical to sort them here in the US. Sadly, much of what
gets recycled at the curb ends up in a landfill or on a slow boat to China.

Municipalities around the country opted for co-mingled curbside recycling as a way of increasing public participation. The public did participate
more, but co-mingled (also known as "single-stream") recycling was the
right policy for the wrong problem (Morawski, 2009). Cities and counties
around the country thought they were going to run out of landfill space,
especially since nobody wanted new landfills in their backyards. States
mandated solid waste diversions, so local governments had real incentives
(albeit negative ones) to reduce trash shipments to their local landfills.

The right problem is not waste, it's running out of materials and the
damage incurred through using materials wastefully (MacBride, 2011).
In the ultimate end-of-pipe mentality, American environmental policy
took a four-decade break from the laws of thermodynamics. We live on

one, finite planet, but consume as if we had many more. Had we thought of waste as a materials management problem, we might have designed recycling programs so that they provided much better industrial feedstock.

We need look no further than Europe for plausible examples of better – not ideal – materials management. Europeans generally do a better job of end-of-pipe recycling and materials management, albeit with a lot of room for improvement. European countries tend to recycle much more container glass than Americans–the average is 65 percent for the EU 15 and as high as 86 percent for Germany in 2005 (OECD Environmental Data Compendium, 2008). Americans only reached 28 percent recycling for container glass in 2006 (Container Recycling Institute, 2011).

Similarly, Europeans recycle high percentages of aluminum containers (63 percent for beverage cans) and more than 90 percent of aluminum used in the building, construction, automotive and transportation sectors (European Aluminium Association, 2011). In 2008, 34 percent of total US aluminum supply came from recycled (secondary) sources; for beverage cans, the figure was about 65 percent in 2011 (The Aluminum Association, 2009, 2012). Ninety percent of automobile aluminum components are recycled (Jupiter Aluminum, pers. comm., 2009).

Plastics recycling is relatively poor all over the world, but again, Germans do better than the US. In 2006, Americans recycled 23.5 percent of PET bottles; Germans recycled 47 percent of all plastics in its waste streams (CRI, 2011; ETC/SRP Working Paper, 2009).

Once American industries recover materials, how well do they recycle them? Chapter 3 reviews the American experience with flue-gas desulfurization (FGD); many other industrialized countries rely on FGD systems. As a result of all this scrubbing, power plants around the country produce vast quantities of what are called "coal combustion products." In 2009, American facilities produced 16.3 million metric tons of FGD gypsum; the EU 15 countries produced about 10.8 million metric tons in the same year. FGD gypsum can be used in agriculture, gypsum panel products, highway construction, mining applications, cement production, water treatment and glass making. FGD gypsum recycling in the US in 2011 was 47.2 percent (American Coal Ash Association, 2012) and considerably higher in the EU 15, at 83 percent (European Coal Combustion Products Association, 2012; www.ecoba.org).

Construction and demolition sites recently became the new frontier for recycling. Demolition, in particular, produces enormous amounts of waste aggregate that can be productively put to use in road building and as fill for other construction purposes. Construction and demolition waste (C&DW) recycling in the EU 15 averaged 20 percent in recent years, but ranged from less than 5 percent in countries like Ireland and Portugal to more than 80 percent in countries like Denmark, the Netherlands and Belgium (cited in del Rio Merino et al., 2011).

The best C&DW recycling data are on cement recycling. According to the Construction Materials Recycling Association, about 140 million tons of cement are recycled in the US every year, which is a greater than 80 percent recycling rate; Germany had an 89 percent recycling rate (World Business Council for Sustainable Development, 2009). Old cement is not primarily used to make new cement, but rather as aggregate for roadbeds and construction fill.

Americans generally lead the world in steel recycling, partly because the US boasts so many electric arc furnace "mini-mills," which rely on scrap steel (of which there is a great amount, given the size of the American economy). In addition, different steel grades can be sorted easily, and the high cost of transporting steel makes regional recycling a cost-effective alternative. Consequently, the US steel industry relies on scrap for 55 percent of its production, much more than any other country (Yellishetty et al., 2010).

In the years since the environmental legislation heydays of 1969–76, older industrial economies greatly increased their recycling rates, but most nations still vary tremendously in their materials recovery patterns. The US, relative to other advanced industrial nations, tends to recycles less, use more energy and produce higher waste per dollar of GDP than the best-performing European countries.

In summary, this chapter has outlined a number of recurring shortcomings in American environmental regulatory process; these serve as the basis for the critique I lay out in Chapters 2 to 5. They can be summarized as:

1) A focus on compliance and technology rather than on performance. This is just as true of scrubbers placed on industrial boilers as it is on best management practices (BMPs) adopted for agricultural pollution prevention.
2) Very limited ability to handle population effects, i.e., most end-of-pipe limits work only if the number of polluting sources doesn't get too large.
3) A failure to connect policy outputs to their consequent environmental outcomes.
4) Very limited incentives to reduce virgin raw material inputs (either through process efficiencies or materials recovery of recyclables).

Old, mismatched regulations fail because the low-hanging fruit has been picked, but polluting sources continue to grow in size and number (Kraft,

Stephan and Abel, 2011), resulting in extraordinarily high marginal costs for further pollution abatement. Our voluntaristic, clearinghouse-based approach to efficiency in general – and materials recovery in particular – hobbles any serious attempts at harmonizing environmental, labor, trade and tax laws into an integrated industrial policy (Fiorino, 2006, pp. 19, 65, 81). Consequently, American industrial efficiency falls further behind that of industrial sectors in other industrialized nations. Cutting across all environmental policies, since administrative agencies lack systematic, long-term indicators with which to establish performance benchmarks and changes, inadequate or anecdotal environmental data collection and reporting hamper reform efforts (Metzenbaum, 1998 and Metzenbaum in Kettl, 2002; Kettl, 2002; NAPA, 2000).

A POLICY TOOLS AND OUTCOMES APPROACH

I adopt a systems-oriented, policy tools and outcomes approach to assessing modern American environmental policy and regulation, one focused on the deterministic failure mechanisms described above (regulatory slippage, policy mismatches). I leave political or ideological obstruction for others to evaluate. In addition to critique, I offer a way forward based on science and altered incentives (see Fiorino, 2006, p. 20).

How does a tools-and-outcomes approach work? A first step is to shift the focus of analysis from government agencies or programs to the policy tools themselves (Salamon, 2002). Taking a cybernetic view of government, we further draw our attention to three control activities common to policy tools: a *director* to set standards or targets, a *detector* to observe state changes relative to adopted goals and an *effector*, which brings a system in line with targets if it swings off limits (Hood, 2007).

These elements require detailed understanding of tool designs and their operating characteristics. Following Salamon (2002), this understanding includes:

> . . . the players [that policies]. . .engage, and how they structure the play. . .how to match tools to the problems being addressed in light of the objectives being sought and the political circumstances that exist. . . and knowledge about how best to operate the new instruments to achieve these objectives in the most effective fashion (p. 39).

Most policy scholars forego any concerted effort to connect environmental regulations (outputs) to their associated bio-physical or other material outcomes. The causal linkages are exceedingly difficult to establish, even with the best data and many years into a regulatory program's life. But policy analysis without outcomes is an unsatisfying endeavor, all critique without consequence. We can know in exquisite detail who struggled to adopt what rules and how they justified their choices without ever learning how this regulatory politics changed our material reality (Hood, 2007, p. 141).

If the work is difficult, it is not impossible, however – especially today. Although environmental data need to improve significantly (a point I develop fully in Chapter 2), we have nearly a half-century of environmental science and indicators that can help us tie policy outputs to outcomes and many models for doing so (Dunn, 1994; Metzenbaum, 1998; Milon and Shogren, 1995; Knaap and Kim, 1998; Hamilton and Cook, 2010; Press, 2007; Michigan Sea Grant and Graham Environmental Sustainability Institute, 2009). Doing so will provide much greater meaning than the conventional wisdom regarding the book's cases: acid rain, nonpoint source water pollution, toxic releases and industrial recycling.

THE PLAN OF THE BOOK

Using case studies, Chapters 2 to 5 show how and why contemporary US environmental regulation falls far short of its mandated goals and its obligations to the American public. Each of these chapters opens with an in-depth examination of the empirical evidence demonstrating regulatory shortcomings. The environmental science, the relevant trade data and long-term monitoring results all confront us with worrisome trends, but what do the data mean? Each chapter answers this question through in-depth interviews and engagement with a wide range of relevant literatures. Chapter 6 proposes policy reforms designed to correct these shortcomings, drawing on regulatory experiments from the US states and overseas.

THE CASES

Chapters 2 to 5 provide an eclectic mix of cases illustrating how compliance-abatement-mitigation fails. Widespread acclaim for the programs or activities discussed in each chapter unites all of these cases. Conventional wisdom holds the Toxics Release Inventory, the Clean Water Act, the Acid Rain Program and paper recycling in high regard, but I will show that these favorites of American environmentalists, regulators and the general public actually perform far less well than widely believed. But if these exemplars of environmental success really don't meet our expectations, then it does not bode well for the many other, generally less well-regarded regulatory programs.

I begin with Chapter 2, "Measuring Pollution," which confronts the state of the nation's environmental information. First-rate, longitudinal environmental data are a necessary element for any good regulatory program. Unfortunately, regulators far too often cannot confidently convey the environmental consequences of their regulatory programs. Consequently, it is exceedingly difficult to hold the policy community–regulators, dischargers and other stakeholders–accountable for their actions.

A big part of the problem here is that environmental regulations do not or cannot avail themselves of evidence demonstrating a causal link between policy instruments and environmental outcomes. There are also pathologies of information use – what Wendy Wagner (2010) calls "filter failure": regulations fail to provide mechanisms to parse information effectively, thereby preventing meaningful participation by a wide range of interests.

Chapter 2 explores the evidentiary problem primarily using the US Toxic Release Inventory (TRI) as the illustrative case. I begin by examining the data – in this case, trends in how toxic releases are estimated. The data show that industries actually measure relatively few of their reported releases, which calls into question what we can confidently say about trends in American toxics. The rest of the chapter answers this question, drawing on various literatures and interviews with respondents from the US EPA, industry and non-governmental organizations.

The next three chapters take up the end-of-pipe theme, each from a different point in the progression from raw material to pollution. Chapter 3, "Failure at the end of the pipe," fully develops the end-of-pipe critique by examining the 1990 US Clean Air Act Amendment's Title IV, also known as the Acid Rain Program (ARP). I selected this program precisely because it is widely considered the model of effective and economically efficient regulation, especially for large, stationary pollution sources (Kraft, Stephan and Abel, 2011; Fiorino, 2006; Davies and Mazurek, 1998). In 2009, the US House of Representatives modeled the landmark Waxman-Markey cap-and-trade climate change bill (HR 2454) on the ARP even though a carbon tax is widely thought to be a better policy tool for curbing greenhouse gas emissions (Nordhaus, 2008). Despite conventional wisdom, the ARP has not ended the acid rain problem and will not do so by further end-of-pipe curbs on coal-fired power generation. As expected, given the thermodynamic limits to emissions scrubbers, further acid deposition reductions will only be achieved by changing the way we generate electric power.

Chapter 4, "Failure when there is no pipe," demonstrates how US regulators and policymakers applied end-of-pipe approaches even to nonpoint sources – that is, cases where there are no highly controllable, distinct discharges (i.e., no pipes). The best examples of nonpoint source failures come from state and federal water quality laws and programs. The Clean Water Act has often been praised for its ambitious application of technology standards and waste discharge permits, along with generous federal largess. These successes notwithstanding, Chapter 4 provides evidence showing that too much of the United States' waters remain heavily polluted. Nonpoint sources of water pollution – urban development, agriculture, logging, mines – now impair the nation's waterways far more than point sources. US waters are literally overwhelmed with toxic chemicals (including pesticides, herbicides and nutrients from fertilizers), metals and sediments, along with nitrates and fecal coliform bacteria from concentrated animal feedlot operations (CAFOs).

Drawing on a wide variety of environmental science, technology, engineering and law literatures, I show that regulators focus far more on how difficult it is to lay the blame for poor water quality on millions of diffuse sources than on truly regulating them. "Nonpoint" has become synonymous with "too complex" and "politically impossible;" in effect, "nonpoint source" has morphed into *not a source at all*. Consequently, regulators treat nonpoint sources as if they were somehow categorically impossible to control with the suite of tools – standards based on performance and technology, outright bans, incentives – long employed for point sources in all media.

My critique of American environmental regulation culminates in Chapter 5, "Failure before the end of the pipe," and focuses on paper recycling, an activity that stirs great pride in Americans and regularly finds its way into grade school classroom activities and lesson plans (Macbride, 2011). Chapter 5 chronicles the missed opportunities for pollution prevention that occur long before the end-of-pipe, that is, in industrial materials use. This chapter faults policymakers for failing to help transform the country's industries in ways that reconcile trade, environmental and employment objectives. I build this argument around industrial materials recovery and reuse trends. A few commentators have already noted that the US, relative to other advanced industrial nations, recycles less, uses more energy and produces high waste per dollar of GDP. Industrial materials recovery provides an excellent example of American regulatory underperformance, or perhaps more fairly, the consequences of going without an integrated, active industrial policy for many decades.

Chapter 5 provides an in-depth analysis of recycling in the US pulp and paper sector, with particular emphasis on the industry's missed opportunity for greater materials recovery and economic growth (including employment). Using data on recovered paper exports and emissions factors for sea, rail and truck freight transport, I examine the environmental consequences of our failure to make substantial use of recovered paper. Drawing on trade, engineering and economics literatures along with in-depth interviews, the rest of Chapter 5 plumbs the reasons for our country's low utilization rate.

Chapter 6 draws on the many findings of the prior chapters to propose a suite of environmental policy reforms, which could either be applied piecemeal to the different media-by-media statutes or in an omnibus environmental bill. Some could also be pursued without new legislation. The reforms include improvements in environmental data collection and reporting, better and wider use of "polluter pays and precautionary principles" (including supplemental environmental projects and performance bonding) and so-called triple bottom line policies that reconcile environmental, economic and labor objectives (Paehlke, 2003).

Common themes unite all of these reforms: an insistence on accountability and evidence, the importance of strategic regulation, and a preference for source reduction and performance-based approaches over end-of-pipe or minimal compliance. Taken as a whole, these reforms comprise what Fiorino (2006) calls a reflexive legal strategy, a set of incentives and procedures ". . .that induce people to continually assess their actions. . .and adjust them to society's goals, for example, by creating less pollution, using fewer resources, or protecting endangered species" (p. 19).

Chapter 6 closes with a brief discussion of the politics of environmental policy reform. Much has changed in the politics of environmental policy-making; what are today's prospects for reform? Today's partisanship and political vitriol creates unprecedented legislative gridlock in American statehouses as well as the US Congress (Sussman, 2004). The American green state does not lack for policy experiments, what Klyza and Sousa call "paths within and around existing rules," but these remain vulnerable and sporadic without statutory reforms (Klyza and Sousa 2008, p.8).

The very purpose of environmental protection is also in flux, in some instances from a focus on environmental protection for personal safety, as Andrew Szasz argues so powerfully in his *Shopping Our Way to Safety* (2007). The consumer safety and environmental movements use voluntarism and labeling, which are widely implemented policy tools, but can be singularly ineffective if they draw attention away from a regulatory response to environmental protection.

Worsening or persistently poor environmental conditions lead to public frustration with government and demands for greater oversight and accountability. But legislative gridlock means that generating political support for new or modified policy initiatives requires shared responsibility. This proliferation of implementing agents, in turn, often creates an unwieldy mode of governance with unclear responsibilities and numerous veto points. These conditions favor policy tools that are relatively invisible, indirect (i.e., implemented by private third parties) and automatic (e.g., tradeable permit systems that use existing stock exchanges) (Salamon, 2002). As Salamon (2002) puts it so well:

> Such tools have the advantage of defusing political opposition to governmental action, recruiting new talents and resources to the tasks of public problem-solving, and avoiding the enlargement of the public sector. At the same time, however, they have the disadvantage of vastly complicating the tasks of public management and risking the subversion of public purposes. In a sense, we seem caught in a vicious circle in which disappointment with public action yields forms of such action that seem most likely to further disappoint. Clearly, the future of collective efforts to respond to public problems will remain gloomy unless this paradox can be resolved (p. 37).

Lest this circle seem too vicious, there are numerous recent instances of every type of policy reform discussed in Chapter 6. Although the particular circumstances in which a state may succeed in innovating – for example, by banning a chemical like the plasticizer bisphenol-A (BPA) – I draw on a large enough set of models to offer some promising political strategies and narratives for reform.

REFERENCES

Ackerman, B. A. and W. T. Hassler (1981). *Clean Coal/Dirty Air or How the Clean Air Act Became a Multibillion-Dollar Bail-Out for High-Sulfur Coal Producers and What Should be Done about It*. New Haven, CT, Yale University Press.

Alleman, J. and P. Rappoport (2005). "Regulatory Failure: Time for a New Policy Paradigm." *Communications and Strategies* 60: 105–121.

Ando, A.W. (1999). "Waiting to be Protected Under the Endangered Species Act: The Political Economy of Bureaucratic Delay." *Journal of Law and Economics* 42: 29–60.

Anthoff, D. and R. Hahn (2010). "Government Failure and Market Failure: On the Inefficiency of Environmental and Energy Policy." *Oxford Review of Economic Policy* 26(2): 197–224.

Barcott, B. (2004). "Changing All the Rules." *The New York Times*. New York, NY.

Bovens, M. and P. 't Hart (1996). *Understanding Policy Fiascoes*. London, UK, Transaction Publishers.

Chertow, M. R. and D. C. Esty (Eds.) (1997). *Thinking Ecologically: The Next Generation of Environmental Policy*. New Haven, CT, Yale University Press.

Coglianese, C. (Ed.) (2012). *Regulatory Breakdown: The Crisis of Confidence in U.S. Regulation*. Philadelphia, PA, University of Pennsylvania Press.

Cohen, S., S. Kamieniecki, et al. (2005). *Strategic Planning in Environmental Regulation: A Policy Approach That Works*. Cambridge, MA, MIT Press.

Commoner, B. (1987). "A Reporter at Large: The Environment." *The New Yorker*. New York, NY: 46–71.

Croley, S. P. (2008). *Regulation and Public Interests: The Possibility of Good Regulatory Government*. Princeton, NJ, Princeton University Press.

Dal Bó, E. (2006). "Regulatory Capture: A Review." *Oxford Review of Economic Policy*, 22(2): 203–225.

Davies, J. C. and J. Mazurek (1998). *Pollution Control in the United States: Evaluating the System*. Washington, DC, Resources for the Future.

Dryzek, J. S. (1997). *The Politics of the Earth: Environmental Discourses*. New York, NY, Oxford University Press.

Duhigg, C. (2009). "Clean Water Laws are Neglected, at a Cost in Suffering." *The New York Times*. New York, NY.

Dunn, W. N. (1994). *Public Policy Analysis: An Introduction*. Englewood Cliffs, NJ, Prentice Hall.

Egelko, Bob (2011). "Cap and Trade Wins California Supreme Court Ruling." *San Francisco Chronicle*, 29 September.

Etzioni, A. (2009). "The Capture Theory of Regulations – Revisited." *Society* 46(4): 319–323.

Farber, D. A. (1999). "Taking Slippage Seriously: Noncompliance and Creative Compliance in Environmental Law." *Harvard Environmental Law Review* 23: 297–325.

Fiorino, D. J. (2006). *The New Environmental Regulation*. Cambridge, MA, MIT Press.

Forgacs, N. (Ed.) (2010). *Enforcing Federal Pollution Control Laws*. New York, NY, Nova Science Publishers.

Goodin, R. E., M. Moran and M. Rein (Eds.) (2006). "The Public and its Policies." *The Oxford Handbook of Public Policy*. New York, NY, Oxford University Press.

Henry, D. D. III, N.Z. Muller and R.O. Mendelsohn (2011). "The Social Cost of Trading: Measuring the Increased Damages from Sulfur Dioxide Trading in the United States." *Journal of Policy Analysis and Management* 30(3): 598–612.

Heyes, A. (2003). "Expert Advice and Regulatory Complexity." *Journal of Regulatory Economics* 24(2): 119–133.

Hood, C. (2007). "Intellectual Obsolescence and Intellectual Makeovers: Reflections on the Tools of Government after Two Decades." *Governance: An International Journal of Policy, Administration, and Institutions* 20(1): 127–144.

Houck, O. A. (2002). "The Clean Water Act TMDL Program V: Aftershock and Prelude." *Environmental Law Reporter* 32: 10385–10419.

Hunter, S. and R. W. Waterman (1996). *Enforcing the Law: The Case of the Clean Water Acts*. Armonk, NY, M. E. Sharpe.

Kehoe, T. (1992). "Merchants of Pollution?: The Soap and Detergent Industry and the Fight to Restore Great Lakes Water Quality, 1965–1972." *Environmental History Review* 16(3): 21–46.

Kettl, D. F. (Ed.) (2002). *Environmental Governance: A Report on the Next Generation of Environmental Policy*. Washington, DC, Brookings Institution Press.

Klyza, C. M. and D. Sousa (2008). *American Environmental Policy, 1990–2006*. Cambridge, MA, MIT Press.

Knaap, Gerrit J. and T. John Kim (Eds.) (1998). *Environmental Program Evaluation: A Primer*. Urbana, IL, University of Illinois Press.

Kosnick, L.-R. D. (2005). "Sources of Bureaucratic Delay: A Case Study of FERC Dam Relicensing." *The Journal of Law, Economics and Organization* 22(1), 258–288.

Kraft, M. E., M. Stephan, et al. (2011). *Coming Clean: Information Disclosure and Environmental Performance*. Cambridge, MA, MIT Press.

Laffont, J.-J. and J. Tirole (1991). "The Politics of Government Decision-Making: A Theory of Regulatory Capture." *The Quarterly Journal of Economics* 106: 1089–1127.

Mahoney, J. and K. Thelen (2010). *A Theory of Gradual Institutional Change. Explaining Institutional Change: Ambiguity, Agency and Power*. New York, NY, Cambridge University Press: 1–37.

MacBride, S. (2011). *Recycling Reconsidered*. Cambridge, MA, MIT Press.

Madsen, T., B. Davis and B. Del Chiaro (2010). *Clean Cars in California: Four Decades of Progress in the Unfinished Battle to Clean Up Our Air*. Los Angeles, CA, Environment California Research & Policy Center.

Makkai, T. and J. Braithwaite (1992). "In and Out of the Revolving Door: Making Sense of Regulatory Capture." *Journal of Public Policy* 12(1): 61–78.

Mazmanian, D. A. (2006). *Achieving Air Quality: The Los Angeles Experience*. Los Angeles, CA, USC Bedrosian Center on Governance and the Public Enterprise.

Mazmanian, D. A. and M. E. Kraft (Eds.) (2009). *Toward Sustainable Communities: Transition and Transformations in Environmental Policy*. Cambridge, MA, MIT Press.

McGarity, T. O. (2004). "MTBE: A Cautionary Tale." *Harvard Environmental Law Review* 28: 281–342.

Merino, M. R., P. Izquierdo Gracia and Isabel Salto Weis Azevedo (2010). "Sustainable Construction: Construction and Demolition Waste Reconsidered." *Waste Management & Research* 28: 118–129.

Metzenbaum, S. (1998). *Making Measurements Matter*. Washington, DC, Brookings Institution.

Michigan Sea Grant and Graham Environmental Sustainability Institute (2009). *Tackling Wicked Problems through Integrated Assessment*. Ann Arbor, MI, University of Michigan.

Milon, J. Walter and Shogren, Jason F. (Eds.) (1995). *Integrating Economic and Ecological Indicators: Practical Methods for Environmental Policy Analysis*. Westport, CT, Praeger Publishers.

Moran, M. (2001). "Not Steering, but Drowning: Policy Catastrophes and the Regulatory State." *The Political Quarterly* 72(4): 414–427.

Morawski, Clarissa (2009). "Understanding Economic and Environmental Impacts of Single-Stream Collection Systems." Culver City, CA, Container Recycling Institute. Accessed July 2011 at http://www.container-recycling. org/.

National Academy of Public Administration (NAPA) (2000). *Environment.gov: Transforming Environmental Protection for the 21st Century*. Washington, DC, The National Academy of Public Administration.

Nordhaus, William (2008). *A Question of Balance: Weighing the Options on Global Warming Policies*. New Haven, CT, Yale University Press.

Paehlke, R. C. (2003). *Democracy's Dilemma: Environment, Social Equity and the Global Economy*. Cambridge, MA, MIT Press.

Popp, D. (2003). "Pollution Control Innovations and the Clean Air Act of 1990." *Journal of Policy Analysis and Management* 22(4): 641–660.

Rosenbaum, W. A. (2011). *Environmental Politics and Policy* (8th ed.). Washington, DC, CQ Press.

Salamon, L. M. (2002). *The Tools of Government: A Guide to the New Governance.* New York, NY, Oxford University Press.

South Coast Air Quality Management District (SCAQMD) (2007). *Final 2007 Air Quality Management Plan.* Diamond Bar, CA.

Stigler, G. J. (1971). "The Economic Theory of Regulation." *The Bell Journal of Economics and Management Science* 2(1): 3–21.

Stone, D. (1997). *Policy Paradox: The Art of Political Decision Making.* New York, NY, W. W. Norton and Company.

Strauss, P. L. (1991). "Sunstein, Statutes, and the Common Law: Reconciling Markets, the Communal Impulse, and the Mammoth State." *Michigan Law Review* 89(4): 907–935.

Sunstein, C. R. (1990). *After the Rights Revolution: Reconceiving the Regulatory State.* Cambridge, MA, Harvard University Press.

Sussman, G. (2004). "The USA and Global Environmental Policy: Domestic Constraints on Effective Leadership." *International Political Science Review* 25(4): 349–369.

Szasz, A. (2007). *Shopping Our Way to Safety: How We Changed from Protecting the Environment to Protecting Ourselves.* Minneapolis, MN, University of Minnesota Press.

Wagner, W. E. (2010). "Administrative Law, Filter Failure, and Information Capture." *Duke Law Journal* 59: 1321–1432.

Weimer, D. L. and A. R. Vining (1999). *Policy Analysis: Concepts and Practice.* Englewood Cliffs, NJ, Prentice Hall.

Wilson, J. Q. (1980). *The Politics of Regulation.* New York, NY: Basic Books.

World Business Council for Sustainable Development's Cement Sustainability Initiative: Recycling Report (2009). Accessed July at http://www.wbcsdcement.org/pdf/CSI-RecyclingConcrete-FullReport.pdf.

Yellishetty, M., P.G. Ranjith and A. Tharumarajah (2010). "Iron Ore and Steel Production Trends and Material Flows in the World: Is This Really Sustainable?" *Resources Conservation and Recycling* 1084–1094.

2. Measuring pollution

Good environmental regulation depends on high-quality data. How much do we really know about environmental quality in this country? More pointedly, can we be reasonably sure that our expensive, complex regulations achieve the desired results? Far too often, regulators cannot confidently convey the environmental bases or consequences of their regulatory programs. Consequently, it is exceedingly difficult to hold the policy community–regulators, dischargers and other stakeholders–accountable for their actions. Policy scholars have not helped much. Those of us writing about policies rely on environmental data without adequately examining their quality.

Chapter 2 explores the evidentiary problem confronting modern environmental regulation, using the US Toxic Release Inventory (TRI) as an illustrative case. In addition to examining problems with the data, this chapter also suggests that policy scholars cannot possibly draw credible conclusions from environmental data collected by others without carefully addressing the data's errors and uncertainties.

The information problem arises largely because environmental regulators do not or cannot avail themselves of evidence demonstrating a causal link between policy instruments and environmental outcomes. There is certainly plenty of information out there, so much that agencies can't possibly handle it all. This is a problem Wendy Wagner (2010) calls "filter failure," meaning that regulations fail to provide mechanisms to parse information effectively, thereby preventing meaningful participation by a wide range of players.

American regulators require copious information from polluters and permit holders and the courts impose high standards of evidence for enforcement and new rulemaking. Very few stakeholders can make sense of even a narrow slice of environmental policy, and just to keep up with a very bounded part of a regulatory program requires full-time, vigilant staff. Most environmental information users therefore often struggle to make sense of what's coming at them. Sometimes, the overwhelming nature of all these data encourages warring parties to argue that their information is better than that of their opponents.

Political struggles over environmental data leave little attention for examining the quality of all this information. It's hard even to talk about data quality, since doing so is often the cornerstone of a legal strategy. Knowing that flawed data can be used to deny a permit or invalidate a proposed rule discourages contestants in regulatory struggles from acknowledging problems. In effect, we are left with a regulatory process in which 1) regulators require data, but don't adequately question the quality of those data, or 2) regulators don't require adequate data, or 3) regulators don't collect the data themselves, generally because of complexity and/or funding obstacles, as in the case of surface water quality.

A FOCUS ON POLLUTION

Notwithstanding bitter battles over spotted owls, wolves, old-growth trees and other objects of high-profile controversy, most American environmental policy is about pollution. Pollution abatement costs much more than any other environmental management domain; it is also complex, controversial and ever changing. The enterprise of managing pollution– developing rules, then monitoring, enforcing, complying and challenging them–employs myriad engineers, analysts, attorneys, activists and scientists. Prompted by tragic, widely-publicized industrial accidents, this policy community has gathered – and wrangled over – data on especially toxic pollutants since the 1980s.

Many readers know that the citizens of Bhopal, India, suffered terribly when the local Union Carbide plant released some 20 tons of methyl isocyanate, a very dangerous chemical used in pesticide and herbicide manufacturing, on the night of 2–3 December 1984. At least 3,000 people died, scores of thousands more were seriously injured (Wolf, 1996). It remains the world's worst industrial accident. But it hardly was unique. Fewer people are aware that less than a year later, the Union Carbide plant in Institute, West Virginia, released gaseous aldicarb oxime (the active ingredient in the pesticide, Temik), sending 11 employees and 135 residents to nearby hospitals (United Press International, 1985).

Just a few years before Bhopal, Congress had passed the high-profile Superfund law, which was set to expire by September 1985; thus, members were already at work amending that law when the disaster hit. Following on the heels of Bhopal, congressional policy entrepreneurs were keen on averting a repetition of its harrowing scenario. In addition to preventing accidents, they wanted to avoid sending firefighters into a dangerous facility without some knowledge of the chemicals they might encounter – so the new version of the law required that most of the country's industrial chemical users keep a detailed hazardous materials inventory.

The Superfund Amendments and Reauthorization Act (SARA) was signed into law by President Ronald Reagan on 17 October 1986. A little-known portion of the act, the Emergency Planning and Community Right-to-Know Act (EPCRA, also known as SARA Title III), for the first time required public disclosure of industrial toxics deliberately or accidentally released from processing and manufacturing plants. At the time, the Toxic Release Inventory (TRI), as it would soon be called, entailed an extraordinary regulatory leap forward. Here was an American Congress telling industries to reveal their releases of some 300 chemicals (the list was later expanded to about 600). Moreover, facilities had to provide lots of information to the public about where these chemical releases were occurring, to what media (i.e., air, water, land), and how–if at all–they were being treated or managed.

The Toxic Release Inventory was pursued with public safety in mind, to be sure, but the architects of the TRI hoped for more. Senator Frank Lautenberg (D-NJ) and Representative Bob Edgar (D-PA) thought the release reports would spur source reductions, mostly because of the bad publicity the inventories would likely cause. Policymakers differed on how the inventories would achieve source reductions. Would the public seize on the new data to advocate for toxics reductions? Or would the release reports alert facilities to wasteful inefficiencies as well as potential hazardous waste management liability? However the process might work, most policymakers considered it imperative to use the momentum of a Superfund re-authorization to add the community right-to-know provisions.

The House debate on the Edgar-Sikorsky amendment (adding a community right-to-know provision in the House version of SARA) focused largely on how onerous the reporting under section 313 would be. Members in both parties worried that this provision would saddle all kinds of small businesses with unreasonable requirements, generating mountains of paperwork. Counties and other public agencies would be flooded with information that was largely useless. Representative Norman Lent (R-NY) exemplified this view: "EPA administrator Lee Thomas has informed us that, under the Edgar amendment here, millions of hardware stores, beauty parlors, gas stations, hospitals, schools, dry cleaners and department stores will have to document the amount of all chemicals, in any amount, that are released. This would be required regardless of the size of the business. This makes little sense" (Library of Congress, Vol. 5, p. 4350).

Senators repeatedly pointed out that "reasonable" emissions estimates could be used where "actual data" were not available (Stafford, Vol. 2, p. 1086; Bentsen, Vol. 2, p. 1088). Members of the House and Senate seemed to feel that any estimate would be better than nothing at all. Legislative overreaching could result in no community right to know at all, so members of both houses bent over backwards to point out that the reporting would be neither difficult nor especially novel. Senator Lloyd Bentsen from Texas stressed how "...[I]t is not the intent of this inventory to generate massive monitoring and data collection efforts. In fact, nothing here shall require the monitoring or actual measurement of quantities of substances or releases beyond that required under other authorities" (Library of Congress, Vol. 2, pp. 1088–89). Ultimately, legislators were decidedly modest in their actual ambitions for the new requirements.

The House champion of the amendment, Representative Bob Edgar (D-PA), assured his colleagues that "[A] workable federal program need not require additional monitoring equipment. In fact, a New Jersey Department of Environmental Protection investigation found that estimates were generally accurate" (Library of Congress, Vol. 5, p. 4194). Although EPCRA's provisions were hotly debated in committee, once a version emerged as part of the much larger Superfund reauthorizations, passage was strongly supported in both houses. The toxics data soon started to roll in.

The TRI became the darling of environmental reporting, not only because it provides so much information, but also because its very existence appeared to spur vast reductions in toxic chemical waste production. Reporters used the TRI to publicize the largest dischargers, especially in the early years of the program. Several analysts in the early 1990s commented that the TRI amounted to "regulation by information or embarrassment" (Wolf, 1996). Shame, fear and embarrassment seemed to work, since *reported* TRI releases quickly declined from the baseline levels reported in the late 1980s and early 1990s.

As Figure 2.1 shows, total on- and off-site disposal and other releases of the chemicals on the original list (called the "1991 core chemicals") decreased from about 2.2 billion pounds in 1991 to a little over 880 million pounds in 2010, an impressive 60 percent decline. During this 20-year period, the US gross domestic product (GDP) grew from $5.99 trillion to $14.52 trillion (in current dollars), an increase of over 140 percent (U.S. Bureau of Economic Analysis, 2012). Had GDP and releases progressed in lockstep, we would have seen 5.4 billion pounds released in 2010. Some of the decrease may be attributable to the US shuttering industrial facilities during these two decades, and indeed, some 4,000 fewer facilities were reporting in 2010 than in 1991, a decline of about 16 percent.

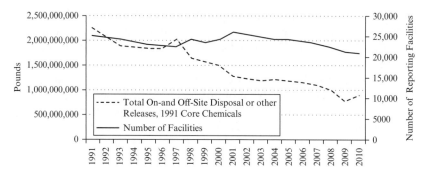

Source: US EPA, 2011.

Figure 2.1   Total disposal and releases reported to TRI vs. reporting facilities, 1991–2010

ARE TRI RELEASE REDUCTIONS REAL?

While the number of reporting facilities may not be going down much, it's possible that toxic releases decline because companies simply don't produce as much from one year to the next. The TRI provides an imperfect measure of this possibility, called the "production ratio" (or also the "activity index"). This number conveys the production change, from one year to the next, of a given chemical. Production ratios usually range from 0.1 to 10, though they can be much larger if companies make batches of chemicals in one year but not another.

Production ratios reported to the TRI vary enormously – and the presence of very large ratios in each of the reporting years suggests some misplaced decimals – but they don't track at all with quantities of chemical releases. That is, correlating changes in pounds of a given chemical released with production ratios for that same chemical reveal no patterns whatsoever (US EPA, 2013).

So if neither production decreases nor plant closures explain release reductions, did the nation's industrial facilities really get much, much cleaner over the last 20 years? The answer eludes us to this day, but not because the data have been ignored. On the contrary, TRI data quickly became a treasure trove for environmental scientists, geographers, sociologists and other policy scholars; now there is a cottage industry in TRI studies (for some of the best, see Hamilton, 2005 and Kraft et al., 2010). Despite all the activity, scholars have made relatively little effort to answer basic questions about the inventory's validity. Instead, researchers started paying particularly close attention to demographic patterns and trends in exposure to toxics. By the mid-1990s, scores of environmental justice studies were coming out, each iteration besting the other with more advanced computing and statistical analysis. Because the TRI's launch coincided with advances in geospatial analysis – what's commonly referred to nowadays as GIS (geographical information systems) – scholars could finally produce maps showing stark inequities in environmental exposure throughout the American landscape.

The 1990s and early 2000s were an exciting time for geographers and environmental justice activists. It seemed that long-suspected patterns of institutional racism could finally be proven.

In part because of occupational safety studies, public and environmental health officials had added risk scores to many toxic chemicals by the 1990s. When the EPA and health specialists added these so-called "risk factors" to the chemical releases, TRI studies became ever more meaningful, reaching further into the funnel of causality to show how emissions led to exposures and in turn, to public health inequities.[1]

So it's no exaggeration to say that whole careers have been made using TRI data, whether in academia, industry or the NGO sector. As of early 2012, Web of Science listed over 300 articles using the TRI since 1988.[2] Several dozen more studies are published in books and in various grey literatures. Given all this interest, we should expect that a lot of attention would be paid to the underlying quality of TRI data. Unfortunately, this has not been the case (de Marchi and Hamilton, 2006, p. 59). As if checking off a box, books and articles using TRI data frequently mention that the data are self-reported and can thus contain errors. Lori Bennear's 2007 study of management-based regulation is typical of this sentiment (and an excellent piece of research in all other aspects). Noting that ". . .real concerns have been raised about the validity of TRI data as measures of environmental performance," (p. 335) she uses the data anyway, asserting that ". . .measurement issues are likely to be common among facilities in all states" (p. 336). At any rate, she goes on, ". . .these data are the only longitudinal data on toxic chemical releases" (p. 336). The absence of equivalent or better data commonly spurs researchers to use the TRI data, *faute de mieux*.

---

[1] Scholars even use the TRI to make inferences about how well firms perform economically. One recent dissertation used the TRI to find that American pulp and paper mills with poorer environmental performance paid a lot more for their debt load (capital) (Schneider, 2008). Powers (2009) argued that counties with more dirty facilities, as measured by the TRI, were less likely to receive new manufacturing plants.

[2] Casting a wider net by looking at both JSTOR and Web of Science, Linda Bui, at Brandeis University, found about 2,000 articles using TRI data between 1987 and 2012 (Bui, 2012).

Thus, an astonishingly small number of published studies (about a dozen, counting peer-reviewed articles and grey literature) make any serious effort at evaluating the TRI data. These few critiques reveal changing concerns over time, as the TRI's novelty wore off and database users became more sophisticated at blending spatial data, statistical analysis, engineering and risk factors.

Although critiques of the TRI were few, they came quickly. At first, watchdogs, journalists and scholars wanted to know whether industry was complying with the TRI and if the public had been spurred to action by all these new data. Early analyses showed that too many firms neglected to send in reports or botched them (Wolf, 1996). Organized interests (labor, environmental justice) pounced on the data releases, demanding reductions by specific facilities, sometimes with impressive results (Hearne, 1996), but the general public did not appear to have learned much about toxic releases (GAO, 1991).

The National Wildlife Federation was one of the first out of the gate, with a June 1989 list entitled "Toxic 500," which simply ranked the 500 largest emitters reporting to the 1987 inventory (Sachs, 2011). The Federation focused on the fact that these 500 facilities had reported 23 percent of the total releases in the 1987 inventory (about 10.4 billion pounds) (Deseret News, 1990). A year later, the Federation used the 1988 inventory to re-examine 29 of the same facilities. The 1990 report, entitled *Phantom Reductions: Tracking Toxic Trends*, made a big splash; its release was widely covered by news media. The authors, Poje and Horowitz, contacted officials at these 29 facilities and asked them to explain how they had achieved impressive reductions in releases and transfers. In a widely cited quote, the authors blisteringly reported that "On the basis of extensive interviews with plant officials, we concluded that most of the largest decreases in toxic emissions resulted from changes in reporting requirements, analytical methods, and production volume, and not from source reduction, recycling or pollution abatement" (Poje and Horowitz, 1990, p.1).

From a contemporary perspective, it's hard to imagine just how seriously major companies took the publicity over TRI reports in those early years. Paul O'Neill, at the time chairman of Alcoa aluminum (and later President George W. Bush's combative Treasury Secretary), actually attended the National Wildlife Federation's press conference in Washington and angrily accused the Federation's president, Jay Hair, of misrepresenting the facts concerning his company's report. O'Neill reportedly jumped up in the press conference and called the Federation's document "a scurrilous attack on our integrity and I'm here to say we resent it" before angrily storming out of the room (Abrams, 1990). At issue had been Alcoa's stated reductions of 763 million pounds of aluminum oxide between 1987 and 1988. In fact, Alcoa argued, non-fibrous aluminum oxide had been taken off the EPA's mandatory disclosure list for the 1988 reporting year. The Federation's president acknowledged that his press release had failed to mention the change in reporting requirements, but added "the fact is that people are breathing 763 million pounds of aluminum oxide. Alcoa, clean up your damned act" (Abrams, 1990).

A year later, in 1991, the General Accounting Office (GAO) produced a fairly detailed analysis of the inventory program. Regarding the TRI's data quality, the GAO noted that EPA ". . .used its limited inspection resources to identify facilities that failed to report data (nonreporters) rather than to examine the quality of data already submitted. As a result, EPA, states, and other users of the data are not assured of the inventory data's quality" (GAO, 1991, p. 43). By the time the GAO conducted its study, EPA had inspected 27 facilities (examining 1987 and 1988 data), finding inaccurate estimates in three of them; however, neither the GAO nor EPA explained the nature of the estimation problems.

A 1993 study, contracted by the EPA, played down the role of estimation methods without actually examining them. Noting that TRI inventories reported decreases between 1989 and 1991 while the number of facilities reporting increased, the three authors posited that these changes could be explained by 1) changes in measurement techniques, 2) production fluctuations or 3) source reduction activities. Accordingly, they surveyed 960 facilities, asking operators to account for the majority of their reported decreases using one or more of these three explanations. According to respondents, nearly 70 percent of the changes in release quantities was attributable to changes in production, followed distantly by source reduction. Changes in how facilities actually measured their emissions only accounted for 15 percent of the difference between the 1989 and 1990 totals. Moreover, these measurement changes resulted in both increases and decreases; the net decrease was only 3 percent of the totals (Riley, Warren and Baker, 1993). This led the authors to conclude that so-called paper reductions probably had little to do with the changes they had observed between the 1989 and 1990 reports.

Oddly, the 1993 study glossed over the nature of estimation methods altogether. Here was a missed opportunity: the study authors had reached 960 facility operators on the phone, but failed to ask anything that would reveal the nature of facility estimations. Did operators attempt mass balance or accounting methods? Did they use emissions factors? Did any operators move from direct measurements (emissions monitoring, stack gas tests) to simpler, easier or cheaper methods? The only glimmer of light authors shed on measurement methods was to comment on a technical guidance document EPA issued in 1990:

...EPA issued technical guidance on the 1990 reporting of ammonia and ammonium sulfate, which had a significant impact on the study results. An estimated decrease or 'paper' change of 250 million pounds is attributed to the technical guidance. Approximately 93 percent of this change is the result of a handful of very large facilities in the chemical industry (SIC 28) taking advantage of this reporting option (Riley, Warren and Baker, 1993, p. 4–16).

Not long after the Riley, Warren and Baker study, the New York NGO INFORM reported in its Toxics Watch that facilities had increased their waste generation between 1991 and 1992. For the 1991 year, EPA had added a category called "production-related waste." This new category allowed analysts to look at a facility's overall waste generation before any in-process recycling or in-house treatment occurred. It was thus an excellent way of assessing the country's net source reduction activities (INFORM, 1995).

INFORM also exploited the existence of other toxics data that might corroborate TRI reports. Specifically, the 1976 Resource Conservation and Recovery Act (RCRA) requires hazardous waste generators to identify, quantify and report hazardous waste shipments sent offsite. This "cradle-to-grave" tracking system consists of a waste manifest. For example, a generator attests that his or her firm handed over 100 drums of spent plating solution, weighing 17 tons, to a registered hazardous waste transporter. The transporter then fills out the manifest attesting that he or she hauled the waste to a permitted hazardous waste treatment facility. That facility might consist of a recycling plant, an underground injection well (e.g., a former oil or gas well), or a special Class I landfill (also known as a residuals repository). The key feature of the waste manifest system is that it consists of real measurement (counting) of named wastes – not estimates or engineering "best guesses."

INFORM went on to mine hazardous waste data that the US EPA compiles from the 50 states in its biennial reports. In 1995 INFORM pointed out that the RCRA biennial reports showed a 9 percent increase in hazardous waste generation between 1989 and 1991 (INFORM, 1995), while the TRI showed overall decreases. No other studies since 1995 picked up on this odd mismatch between RCRA and TRI reports, but what would we find if we extended and updated INFORM's comparison of the two databases?

To do so, we can compare RCRA off-site transfers for chemicals that are also tracked by the TRI. Waste quantities reported to the TRI and RCRA should track very closely, even if the quantities are not the same, because TRI releases to RCRA-permitted facilities should be a subset of the nation's total hazardous wastes tracked by the RCRA manifest system (RCRA hazardous wastes rise to millions of tons; TRI wastes are in the

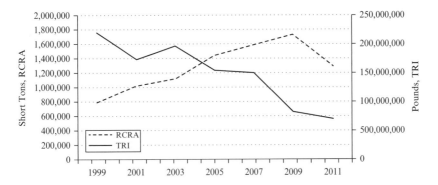

Source: US EPA, 2000–2012.

Figure 2.2 RCRA vs. TRI off-site landfill wastes

millions of pounds). Fortunately, both databases include information on off-site transfers to RCRA-regulated landfills. The TRI provides data on waste quantities shipped off-site to RCRA subtitle C landfills (the ones permitted to handle hazardous wastes). The RCRA biennial reports also provide data on transfers to landfills. In principal the RCRA reports should be more accurate because these hazardous wastes are measured directly – not estimated. A convenient, reliable way for a facility opera-tor to fill out the TRI's category section on waste transfers to RCRA-permitted underground injection or landfills would simply consist of looking up the facility's waste manifests.

Unfortunately, the two databases do not track well at all. Figure 2.2 shows that, with only a single upward bump in 2003, the TRI data trend steadily downwards over the 1999–2009 period, while the RCRA data increase sharply, save for the 2009–2011 period during the recession. Hazardous waste generation usually tracks well with economic cycles, although overall RCRA waste generation (i.e., not just off-site transfers to landfills) actually increased slightly between 2009 and 2011 (US EPA, 2011). EPA officials were at a loss to explain why these data would not track, citing only that RCRA measured wastes while TRI listed chemi-cals, a nuance that shouldn't result in waste shipments trending in differ-ent directions (V. Senthil, personal communication, 1 September 2011; T. Codina, personal communication, 10 August 2011).

None of the EPA's own analyses took advantage of the RCRA data, although the agency did attempt some quality assessments of the TRI program in the late 1990s. In March 1998, EPA released a study of 104 facilities and their 1994/95 reports. Most of the EPA's audits focused on whether facilities were following proper procedures – did they correctly identify thresholds for chemical reporting, were fugitive emissions confused with off-site transfers, and the like. EPA found that facilities were overwhelmingly correct in their threshold determinations and in their use of appropriate methodologies to accurately estimate releases (EPA, 1998a). In December of 1998, EPA followed up with a data quality report for the 1996 reporting year, auditing 60 facilities. Again, the study focused on reporting errors, but was silent on the accuracy of release estimation methods (EPA, 1998b).

On a contract with the EPA, Thomas Natan and Catherine Miller, of the Hampshire Research Institute, also used a survey method to examine TRI release reductions. They called 80 facilities with the largest reductions in production-related waste from 1991 to 1994. Each had reduced its production-related waste by at least 10 million pounds for at least one chemical. Natan and Miller determined that "half of the total decrease arose from paper changes, especially redefining existing activities as in-process recovery." Despite the paper changes, the authors also found many "genuine" reductions in release and disposal, some of these by efficiency gains, others by process changes and some by selling chemical wastes as products (Natan and Miller, 1998, pp. 372A–373A).

By the late 1990s, the scant interest in the TRI's accuracy seemed to have played itself out. For much of the next decade, very little attention was paid to the inventory's estimation problems. James Hamilton, an economist at Duke University, is the one notable exception, publishing his *Regulation through Revelation: The Origin, Politics, and Impacts of the Toxics Release Inventory Program* (Cambridge University Press, 2005). As well written as it is researched, *Regulation through Revelation* provided a thorough history of EPCRA, sharp political analysis and a comprehensive sense of the inventory's impacts. True to his sophisticated, balanced approach, Hamilton's take on the TRI's accuracy was that it ". . . depends on what data elements in the TRI are involved, the degree of precision expected in the reporting, and whether one defines accuracy in part by the conclusions about likely chemical risks the public might make based on the data" (p. 221).

Hamilton's aim in that volume was not to contribute new research on the TRI's estimation methods, but along with his colleague Scott de Marchi, he offered some unsettling findings in a 2006 paper. First, the authors compared ambient pollutant concentrations measured by EPA pollution monitors to air emissions reported in the TRI. Facilities reported drops in lead and benzene emissions (−45 percent and −84 percent, respectively), but these matched poorly with EPA monitored data (−24 percent and −56 percent, respectively). One chemical, ethylbenzene, showed *less* of an improvement than ambient emissions picked up by EPA monitors (de Marchi and Hamilton, 2006, p. 64). How could the ambient monitors and the TRI reports differ so much?

Firms could be overestimating their pollution reductions in order to reap some good will and publicity. Since the EPA doesn't audit for accuracy and the releases are difficult to estimate, erring on the side of greater reductions could be common, rational and uncontroversial. But "fudging" aside, the EPA's monitors could be too far away from facilities to pick up the same emissions rates. Similarly, the averaged figures for the releases de Marchi and Hamilton examined could be due to just a handful of large facilities; ". . .thus, average concentrations measured by a large number of monitors would tend to underreport the influence of large facilities" (de Marchi and Hamilton, 2006, p. 65). And a final possibility is that the ambient monitors are picking up other facilities or mobile source emissions.

The authors use a statistical property known as Benford's Law to see whether the TRI figures make sense – that is, whether they plausibly follow the distributions we'd expect in a sample of numbers. In 1938, the physicist Frank Benford observed that in many numbers drawn from real life (stock prices, population numbers, natural features) the leading digits are distributed non-uniformly. Thus, the first digit is 1 about 30 percent of the time, 2 is first a little over 17 percent of the time and so on, until we reach 9, which is first in a little fewer than 5 percent of number lists.

De Marchi and Hamilton found that the ambient measures of air pollutants listed in the TRI conformed quite well to the expected Benford patterns, but the TRI data did not, especially for lead and nitric acid. TRI releases for these chemicals began with 2s and 5s far more frequently than either the ambient air data or the expected Benford distributions. Noting that facility operators were more likely to leave blank their estimation methods for lead and nitric acid than the other ten chemicals they examined, the authors speculate that "[T]he relatively high levels of regulatory scrutiny and health hazards associated with lead and nitric acid may give plants an incentive to underestimate their releases" (de Marchi and Hamilton, 2006, p. 72).

The only other peer-reviewed work analyzing the TRI's estimation methods published by 2012 consists of Dinah Koehler and John Spengler's 2007 aluminum industry study. Koehler and Spengler chose the US primary aluminum sector, because it had only 23 facilities during the 1990s and early 2000s, thereby making it possible to survey all facilities in addition to examining their reported releases. Moreover, aluminum manufacturing produces some problematic pollutants, so accurate toxics reporting in this industry can really make a public health difference.

Aluminum facilities consume huge amounts of electricity to drive the processes that first release alumina (aluminum oxide) from bauxite, the ore in which it is found, then further separate out elemental aluminum (Al). The Hall–Héroult process, as it is known, also tends to produce significant polycyclic aromatic compound (PAC) emissions. Polycyclic aromatic compounds are quite dangerous and include some of the most heavily regulated air emissions. In this elegant and careful study, Koehler and Spengler show that fluctuations in PAC releases reported to the TRI by these facilities very likely had more to do with new regulations and market forces than with estimation methods or changes in pollution control technology.

Specifically, in 1997, maximum achievable control technology (MACT) standards for primary aluminum manufacturing came into force, prompting many of the 23 primary aluminum plants in the US to conduct stack gas and other direct tests of PAC releases. Ironically, the PAC emissions releases for the next reporting year (1998) shot up, even though most facilities had been using the MACT required for aluminum manufacturers (i.e., dry alumina scrubbers). Poor emissions measurement prior to MACT, followed by better testing, explained the difference in releases.[3]

Fluctuations in aluminum prices and electricity also help explain dramatic changes in TRI releases. In 2000 and 2001, drought conditions in the Pacific Northwest dramatically curtailed hydropower electricity production, a major source of energy for the power-hungry aluminum facilities of Washington, Oregon and Montana. Faced with high energy prices and a glut of Chinese aluminum, four of the six older plants using the Bonneville Power Administration's electricity elected to shut down operations, thereby reporting no PAC releases in 2001. These plants chose to resell their electricity, which they had purchased under long-term contracts, rather than competing in such a tight market (Koehler and Spengler, 2007, p. 303).

Koehler and Spengler, along with the few other scholars questioning the TRI's data, creatively drew on surveys, cross-checks with ambient air quality data, the statistical properties of the toxic releases figures themselves, command-and-control regulation (i.e., the MACT standards) and market forces. All of these factors can help explain reported toxic release reductions; all also point to the fundamental mystery surrounding the TRI estimations themselves.

---

[3] One facility's (the Ormet Corporation) PAC emissions dropped after 1998 when it closed its carbon anode bake plant, electing instead to purchase large anodes from suppliers in South America and Asia (Koehler and Spengler, 2007, p. 302).

ESTIMATING EMISSIONS FOR THE TOXIC RELEASE INVENTORY

As Figure 2.1 (p. 30) shows, some 20,000+ facilities report chemical releases, waste transfers and the like to the TRI each year. These reports document well over 100,000 separate releases, transfers or treatment processes. There's no way that state or federal environmental regulators could perform this task on their own, so facility employees are expected to do their best in estimating releases and transfers.

Imagine the ideal way to estimate a chemical release. Suppose that a smokestack contained probes measuring waste gases as they made their way up and out the top. Properly designed and calibrated, such probes would measure each pollutant of concern on a continuous basis. A data logger could even send information directly to regulators; at a minimum, the equipment could notify facilities when stack gas concentrations exceeded acceptable limits. If the data feed was reasonably tamper-proof, the data could even be used to enforce penalties.

This kind of equipment, in fact, does exist. Called Continuous Emissions Monitoring Systems (CEMS), the devices are standard features in all but the smallest electric generating power plants and many other facilities emitting large quantities of air pollution. But CEMS were developed and required for just a handful of air pollutants – notably, the ones responsible for causing smog and acid rain (sulfur and nitrogen oxides, especially). Smog-forming air pollutants are heavily regulated and CEMS units have thus long been key elements of American air pollution control and regulation. A properly-functioning CEMS is one of the better technical innovations to come out of our compliance-abatement-mitigation approach to regulation.

For all the good data they generate, CEMS are nonetheless costly and fastidious (requiring frequent calibration and maintenance); it's the rare facility that would install a CEMS unless doing so was required in its permit to operate. Logically then, CEMS vendors concentrate on the most heavily-regulated pollutants – CO, NOx, SOx and a few others. The probes and data processing equipment developed for these pollutants have the longest track records and the largest number of competing models and receive the most attention in the form of research and development dollars. CEMS technologies do exist for other dangerous air pollutants, such as various kinds of volatile organic compounds (VOCs), ammonia, metals and polycyclic aromatic hydrocarbons (PAHs), but they are very rarely required; consequently, we have less experience tailoring these technologies to more "exotic" chemicals.

Moreover, CEMS really work best in large air emissions exhausts ("stacks"). CEMS don't make sense for monitoring fugitive emissions from leaky pipe flanges, gaskets, valves or other seals. A complex chemical manufacturing plant or refinery typically maintains thousands of these components, some percentage of which is failing at any given time. So the CEMS ideal – direct, continuous measurement of all pollutants – never happens, either because they are not required or they are ill-suited to the nature of a facility's emissions. CEMS probably cannot help with fugitive emissions, but many stack emissions estimates could be vastly improved by increasing the number of pollutants monitored.

Enter the ubiquitous emissions factor. Initially developed in the mid-1960s by some of the state and regional pioneers in air quality regulation, including Los Angeles's South Coast Air Quality Management District (SCAQMD), emissions factors offered a quick way to estimate sources without requiring frequent, costly measurements. Once the US EPA was up and running, federal regulators turned to the states looking for their best guesses regarding emissions from a wide range of processes, starting especially with combustion sources. These algorithms were gathered into a document, now widely known as the "Compilation of Air Pollutant Emissions Factors, AP-42" (Southerland, 2005). No engineer ever claimed that AP-42 was infallible, or even especially accurate, but it had a whiff of authority since it was maintained and updated by EPA engineers.

There are still other ways of estimating emissions. Barring the CEMS ideal, the EPA has a hierarchy of emissions estimation methods, from best to worst (US EPA, 2006):

a. Continuous Emissions Monitoring
b. Source Testing
c. Materials (or Mass) Balance
d. Emissions Calculating Tools
e. Emissions Factors

As we move from a) to e), measurements become less direct, less frequent and more uncertain; great care should be exercised when employing less direct means.

Although EPCRA never dictated how facilities should estimate their emissions, it does require that companies report their estimation methods in a section of the TRI's form "R." Table 2.1 lists estimation choices, including the reporting codes and their descriptions.

As one reads from the top of Table 2.1 to the bottom, release and transfer estimates become more prone to error and guesswork. The scant literature on the accuracy of TRI estimates claims that "other" or some non-direct estimation is most common (de Marchi and Hamilton, 2006). In Table 2.2, a brief examination of almost 115,000 TRI release records for 2009 confirms what others have suspected: 58 percent of the responses almost certainly involved no direct estimation (35 percent "other" or invalid or unknown responses, 23 percent published emissions factors).

Less than one percent of these estimates (M1) rely on continuous monitoring systems. Periodic or random monitoring can be better than no direct measurements – by definition, they should accurately reflect releases at the time or on the day they are measured, but are not likely to properly scale up from a few measurements to a whole year (Senthil, 2011). Mass balance equations can be quite accurate; unfortunately, these only represented a fifth of estimates in 2009. Focusing on air emissions, estimation methods are not much better (see Table 2.3).

Over two-fifths of the estimates relied on emissions factors, which are algorithms or "recipes" used to predict what releases can reasonably be expected given a particular industrial process. It's likely that many of the "O" category responses also include emissions factors, so the actual use of emissions factors is probably much more prevalent.

Emissions factors help engineers solve a basic compliance problem: how can emissions be estimated and reported without expensive, time-consuming CEMS or frequent stack gas tests? The solution is to come up with a representative value generally expressed as the weight of a pollutant released per unit of industrial activity multiplied by the overall activity. Thus, a power plant burning coal may, on average, release 0.1 pounds of sulfur oxides (SOx) per million BTU of energy produced; if the plant produces 100 million BTU in a given time period, an engineer can report that

Table 2.1   TRI estimation methods and codes reported to Form R

Estimation Code	Description
M1	Continuous monitoring data or measurements
M2	Periodic or random monitoring data or measurements
C	Mass balance calculations, such as calculation of the amount of the EPCRA Section 313 chemical in streams entering and leaving process equipment
E1	Published emission factors, such as those relating release quantity to through-put or equipment type (e.g., air emission factors)
E2	Site-specific emission factors, such as those relating release quantity to through-put or equipment type (e.g., air emission factors)
O	Other approaches such as engineering calculations (e.g., estimating volatilization using published mathematical formulas) or best engineering judgment.

Source: US EPA, 2010.

Table 2.2   Estimation methods for all releases, 2009 TRI data release

Estimation Method	Number of Estimates, Percent of Total
C, mass balance equations	23,563 or 20.5%
E, emissions factors	30,376 or 26%
M1, continuous monitoring	973 or 0.84%
M2, periodic/random monitoring	4,197 or 3.6%
M, continuous *or* periodic monitoring	15,426 or 13.4%
O, other approaches such as engineering calculations	35,286 or 30.7%
X, unknown	3,907 or 3%
N, none	1,141 or 1%

Source: US EPA, 2011.

Table 2.3   Estimation methods for stack or point source air emissions, 2011 TRI data release

Estimation Method	Number of Estimates, % of Total (out of 53,545 reports)
C, mass balance equations	7,070 or 13.2%
E, emissions factors	21,783 or 40.6%
M1, continuous monitoring	459 or 0.8%
M2, periodic/random monitoring	3,510 or 6.5%
M, continuous *or* periodic monitoring	6 or 0.01%
O, other approaches such as engineering calculations	20,705 or 38.6%
X, unknown	5 or 0.01%
N, none	1,141 or 1%

Source: US EPA, 2012.

the facility releases 10 million pounds (or 5,000 US short tons) of sulfur oxides. Engineers can also express the factors as emissions remaining downstream of pollution abatement equipment. The EPA thus offers the following basic emissions factor formula (EPA, 2012a):

$E = A \times EF \times (1-ER/100)$, where:

- E = emissions;
- A = activity rate;
- EF = emission factor, and
- ER = overall emission reduction efficiency (expressed as a percentage).

Examining a specific facility's TRI reports relative to its annual production illustrates both the simplicity and limitations of emissions factors. Consider Rio Tinto Alcan's Sebree plant in Kentucky. Located near the southeastern Indiana border, the plant has a capacity of about 200,000 tons of aluminum per year. For the period of 1998–2010, the plant relied mostly on emissions factors and "other" estimation means to determine its TRI releases.

From 2000 through 2010, the plant reported benzo(g,h)perylene air emissions to the TRI. These are in the same category of dangerous polycyclic aromatic compounds Koehler and Spengler tracked in their 2007 study. Combining the TRI data with facility-level aluminum production data available in SEC filings provide the "E" and "A" in the equation above. In each of those 10 years (minus 2007, for which production data are missing), dividing total releases by production yields *exactly* the same figure, about 0.024 pounds per short ton of aluminum produced.

In using these emissions factors, plant engineers clearly must assume that nothing except production volumes has changed in their production processes – no new equipment or reductions in efficiencies – in relation to the processes in place when the factors were first derived, or to processes at other smelters around North America.

The US EPA's current version of the Emissions Factor Compilation (AP-42) is now quite large, totaling some 20,000 separate algorithms (EPA, 2012). Users can download emissions factors from the Clearing House for Inventories and Emissions Factors (or "CHIEF" – the EPA has always liked catchy, somewhat corny acronyms). Each algorithm in the database includes not only a ratio (that is, pounds per unit activity), but also a particular industrial process to which the factor applies. For example, according to the formulas, we could expect that a power plant burning bituminous coal with pollution abatement equipment will release about half a gram of benzene to the air for every ton of coal burned. But another emissions factor predicts that burning dry wood bark and waste in a boiler with no pollution control device will result in almost four times more benzene releases, about 2 grams per ton of wood burned.[4]

Despite their widespread use, not all emissions factors are created equal. Some factors draw upon multiple stack gas tests all within an identical industry. Others depend on little more than engineering guesswork. Table 2.4 summarizes the EPA's own emissions factor ratings system.

The EPA rates each of the emissions factors in its database (except for those receiving "U" ratings). By the EPA's own analysis, only a fraction of these many emissions factors inspire much confidence. Figure 2.3 provides

---

[4] The factors are 0.0013 pounds of benzene per ton of coal and 0.0042 pounds of benzene per ton of wood, respectively (EPA, 2012a).

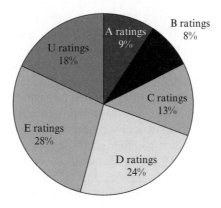

Source: US EPA, 2012a.

Figure 2.3 Emissions factor ratings, all emissions (N = 27,279 ratings)

a breakdown of all the emissions factor ratings available in EPA's database as of 2012.

The EPA characterizes over two thirds (70 percent) of these emissions factors as "below average," "poor" or "unrated." In all fairness, many of the chemical releases reported to the TRI probably don't pose much risk to public or ecosystem health, either because they entail low concentrations, are properly contained and treated, or simply aren't very dangerous. Perhaps, then, more dangerous chemicals should receive more careful attention in the form of better measurements or emissions factors. What might constitute a list of "more dangerous" chemicals? EPA's National Waste Minimization Program has long identified 31 "priority chemicals" that are persistent, bioaccumulative, and toxic (PBT). The EPA explains its choice of priority chemicals thus:

> They are currently being generated in industrial waste and are found in soil, sediment, ground water, surface water, air, and plant, animal and human tissue as a result of past and present releases. Even when released in very small amounts, they accumulate and can cause environmental problems. Many of these organics are difficult to clean up once they get into the environment, resulting in costly clean up efforts (EPA, 2012b).

Quality ratings for emissions factors are available for only 16 of the EPA's priority chemicals,[5] but these fare only somewhat better than chemicals

[5] 1,2,4-Trichlorobenzene, acenaphthene, acenaphthylene, anthracene, dibenzofuran, dioxins/furans (2,3,7,8-Tetrachlorodibenzo-p-dioxin), fluorene, heptachlor, hexachlo-

Table 2.4   The US EPA's emissions factor ratings system

A = Excellent. Emission factor is developed primarily from A- and B-rated source test data taken from many randomly chosen facilities in the industry population. The source category population is sufficiently specific to minimize variability.

B = Above average. Emission factor is developed primarily from A- or B-rated test data from a moderate number of facilities. Although no specific bias is evident, it is not clear if the facilities tested represent a random sample of the industry. As with the A rating, the source category population is sufficiently specific to minimize variability.

C = Average. Emission factor is developed primarily from A-, B-, and C-rated test data from a reasonable number of facilities. Although no specific bias is evident, it is not clear if the facilities tested represent a random sample of the industry. As with the A rating, the source category population is sufficiently specific to minimize variability.

D = Below average. Emission factor is developed primarily from A-, B- and C-rated test data from a small number of facilities, and there may be reason to suspect that these facilities do not represent a random sample of the industry. There also may be evidence of variability within the source population.

E = Poor. Emission factor is developed from C- and D-rated test data from a very few number of facilities, and there may be reason to suspect that the facilities tested do not represent a random sample of the industry. There also may be evidence of variability within the source category population.

U = Unrated. Emission factor is developed from source tests which have not been thoroughly evaluated, research papers, modeling data, or other sources that may lack supporting documentation. The data are not necessarily "poor," but there is not enough information to rate the factors according to the rating protocol.

Source: US EPA, 2012. *Compilation of Air Pollutant Emission Factors, Volume I: Stationary Point and Area Sources (CHIEF).*

in the complete set of factors tracked by the EPA (see Figure 2.4). For these 16 chemicals, CHIEF provides 828 emissions factors, covering many different industries and processes. Fifty-six percent of these were "below average," "poor" or "unrated."

Although new emissions factors appear in the EPA's database every

---

robenzene, hexachlorocyclohexane, gamma (1,2,3,4,5,6-Hexachlorocyclohexane, gamma isomer), naphthalene, pentachlorophenol, phenanthrene, polycyclic aromatic compounds (PACs)/ PAH Group (polycyclic aromatic hydrocarbons), polychlorinated biphenyls (PCBs) and pyrene.

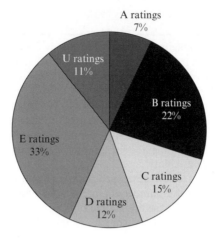

Source: US EPA, CHIEF, 2012a.

Figure 2.4   Emissions factor ratings for 16 EPA priority chemicals (N = 828 ratings)

year, the overall ratings become worse, not better, over time. The EPA's internal watchdog, the Office of Inspector General (OIG), examined emissions factors in 1996 and again 2004. OIG found that EPA had nearly doubled its list of emissions factors, but rated an even greater percentage of factors below average or poor (62 percent) in the 2004 list, 6 percent more than in the 1996 list (56 percent) (OIG, 2006, pp. 8–9). Although discouraging, this trend makes sense. Many of the newer emissions factors address industrial processes or pollutants that have not previously been systematically measured, so one should expect that the initial factors will draw upon fewer sources and will not have been vetted by many engineers. What's more troubling is that the newer emissions factors cover fine particulate matter (widely believed to present some of the greatest risks to human health) or hazardous air pollutants that are exceedingly difficult and costly to adequately sample or measure (Frey, 2007).

VERIFYING AND IMPROVING EMISSIONS FACTORS

Why are emissions factors so flawed? It all boils down to representativeness. Emissions factors are based on samples of facilities, industrial processes, atmospheric and operating conditions (like the wind turbulence above a gas flare). Samples are representative only when their aggregate characteristics closely approximate the aggregate characteristics of the total population in question (Babbie, 1995; Frey, 2007). Equipment design, maintenance, operating temperatures, control device and fuels selection can all cause up to an order of magnitude (ten times) difference in emissions measured between any two sources (Southerland, p. 12).

What would it take to ensure a statistically valid sample for all emissions factors? James Southerland, an EPA veteran who worked for years on emissions factors, offered a thought experiment to estimate the magnitude of this effort. If each of the 250 major source categories in the EPA's AP-42 compilation averaged at least three major processes, then each process should be tested between 10 and 30 times for a valid set of statistical samples. Typical stack gas tests cost upwards of $50,000 each. If each process in the major source categories releases 10 to 20 pollutants of interest, the costs rise to $3–6 billion, so prohibitive as to be nonsensical (Southerland, 2005).

Differential Absorption Light Detection (DIAL)

Advances in remote sensing technology offer completely different approaches to estimating emissions. One of the most promising goes by the acronym DIAL (Differential Absorption Light Detection) and takes advantage of differences in the light absorption properties of gases. DIAL systems can be placed just outside a facility's gates or on aircraft and aimed at stacks, storage tanks and other possible emissions sources. Since 1988, dozens of studies using DIAL show much higher emissions, *by one or more orders of magnitude*, at facilities like petroleum refineries and chemical plants than do inventories based on emissions factors (Cuclis, 2012). Sweden has required emissions measurements at its five refineries rather than estimates since the early 1990s. While Swedish regulations don't specify which methods the refineries must employ, all use DIAL (Cuclis, 2012).

Alberta (Canada) and the Texas Department of Environmental Quality used DIAL to check up on refinery benzene and other VOC releases estimated with emissions factors. The Washington, DC-based Environmental Integrity Project (EIP) pushes for, and publicizes, DIAL results. Reviewing these DIAL studies, the EPA found that British Petroleum's Texas City refinery emissions from flares were six times higher than predicted by emissions factors. DIAL estimates of storage tank emissions, in some cases, were three to seven times higher than emission factor estimates (EIP, July 2012 NOI).

Working for Alberta's Research Council, Allan Chambers and Mel Strosher conducted a DIAL test at a refinery in Alberta, Canada, and concluded that actual emissions from storage tanks significantly exceeded emission factor estimates for benzene and VOCs. The City of Houston's Bureau of Pollution Control and Prevention conducted a DIAL test at the Shell Deer Park facility in 2011, finding that ". . .actual VOC emissions from tanks were underestimated by a factor of 132; actual benzene emissions from tanks were underestimated by a factor of 93; actual VOC emissions from wastewater treatment systems were underestimated by a factor of 108; and actual benzene emissions from wastewater treatment systems were underestimated by a factor of 67" (EIP, July 2012 NOI).

After years of publicizing these DIAL studies and brow-beating federal agencies, the Environmental Integrity Project sued the US EPA in September 2012, arguing that the agency had failed to revise emissions factors for hazardous air pollutants as required under the Clean Air Act. EIP's complaint drew on DIAL studies to demonstrate that many emissions factors used by refineries were deeply flawed (EIP, September 2012).

INFORMATION FAILURE IN THE TOXIC RELEASE INVENTORY

EPCRA's modest reporting requirements suffer from three fatal flaws. First, as the discussion of emissions factors shows, the law allows facilities to use virtually any means imaginable to estimate release amounts. In the original Senate bill (S.51), Senator Frank Lautenberg pushed for a kind of mass balance accounting. Mass balances would be achieved by requiring facilities to provide information ". . . on the quantity of chemical substances transported to the facility, produced at the facility, and transported from the facility as waste or products" (Library of Congress, Vol. 6, p. 5116).

Senators reasoned that:

[such]. . .procedures would provide essential reference data against which to compare TRI data on waste generation and environmental releases. Further, they argued that such mass accounting data also would provide a means of determining whether TRI reporting forms were understood and properly filled out, much as ledger-sheet procedures and data provide valuable checks for financial managers (National Research Council, 1990, p. 1).

Support for mass balance accounting methods was by no means universal in the Senate, even among senators sympathetic to community right-to-know concepts. Indeed, much of the House and Senate debate revolved around how onerous the reporting requirements would be – mass balance accounting was far, far outside the comfort zone of many supporters. In conference committee, the Senate's mass balance approach was quickly dropped in favor of mandating that the National Academy of Sciences conduct a study on mass balance accounting for toxic materials and releases.

Second, the law allows facilities to report ranges, rather than specific estimates, for releases of less than 1,000 pounds (except for a small class of PBT compounds) (EPA, 2007). Senator Lautenberg anticipated problems with reporting ranges rather than actual quantities, noting that ". . .Where volumes are to be reported in ranges, those ranges must be established so the information is valuable and not so broad that it is impossible to determine anything of relevance" (Library of Congress, Vol. 7, p. 5632). Unfortunately, EPA's Form R allows firms to represent a range using a single value (e.g., the range's midpoint), thereby conveying a false sense of specificity (Hutzell and Luecken, 2008, p. 175).

Third, the law requires no uncertainty estimates.

EFPAG's study found that if emissions factors were adjusted to better account for uncertainty, almost all of the 3,600 hot mix asphalt plants in the United States likely would have to recalculate production limits. As a result, some plants would be unable to retain their synthetic minor source status, thus making them subject to the Title V air operating permits program and, as a result, potentially subject to stricter regulations and state or local air toxics rules (EPA, 2006, p. 10).

The typical guidance for emissions factors urges users to rely on them only for averaging many area-wide sources, on the theory that doing so can ". . .mitigate the uncertainty associated with quantifying site-specific emissions" (EPA, 2012a; Frey, 2007). But if everyone is using the same substandard emissions factors without estimating errors or uncertainty, then simply aggregating hundreds or thousands of sources does nothing to improve our estimates of real-world emissions.

Ultimately, we are left with much better ambient air and water quality data than source (emissions, effluent) data. We thus know we have problems – we can readily tell with frequent ambient quality tests – but we have very limited abilities to tie ambient quality to specific sources (and ideally, we would want to know pollutant sources within narrow time windows). This might be the worst of all possible worlds: we know ever more specifically how poor some of air and water quality has become, but we still know too little to assign responsibility where it belongs. As one might expect, the greater the danger seems, the less polluters wish to be blamed.

The more polluters evade detection actively or through neglect, the greater our uncertainties.

The TRI's flaws fit squarely within the Compliance-Abatement-Mitigation policy approach discussed in Chapter 1. Although the law was designed to provide the public with meaningful data about toxics, compliance with EPCRA 313 actually means *submitting a completed Form R* – not providing the best release estimates possible, given reasonable cost and technical constraints. Moreover, EPCRA's premise – that information disclosure would result in source reduction – is untestable. If the release estimates don't reliably report toxics, then year-to-year increases or decreases also mean nothing.

The TRI also shows its age – just like end-of-pipe pollution abatement, which succeeds initially, but becomes overwhelmed by increases in sources. The TRI's woes stem not from growth in the number of reporting facilities, but from a kind of policy fatigue that set in after the program's first decade. By 2000, nearly no studies emerged critiquing the TRI at all; only three (de Marchi and Hamilton; Koehler and Spengler; the EIP) bothered to analyze the estimation methods themselves. The handful of 1990s-era studies claiming "paper reductions" had it right in the first place: everything hinged on whether the data themselves were meaningful; too often, they were not. But Congress did not require (or support) EPA to demand meaningful data; accordingly, EPA cannot impose penalties on a firm for using, say, outdated, poor-quality emissions factors to compute its releases.

Hamilton pointed out that the impacts of the TRI depend on a lot of factors, many of them idiosyncratic to particular facilities. Common sense and careful studies suggest that the nature of surrounding communities significantly affects the overall impact of TRI reports. Better-educated, more politically organized communities, and those with skilled investigative reporters, all tend to increase the probability that a facility will act on its toxic emissions releases (Hamilton, 2005, p. 242).

Hamilton ended up surmising that the TRI probably has had a positive effect on environmental quality. But he was agnostic about the TRI's data quality. For a policy that was all about information, the TRI has not improved the quality of environmental data very much. In effect policymakers picked the low hanging fruit, just as they did in moving from zero pollution abatement to smokestack scrubbers and catalytic converters. When none existed, *any* new information surely looked impressive. Knowing which facilities released toxics (and which chemicals, specifically) improved enormously on previous conditions. The TRI worked best through fear, publicity and lawsuits, not by improving our estimates of toxic releases.

The Toxic Release Inventory thus offers an object lesson in what happens when public policy merely requires compliance through a reporting obligation. At first, fearing the worst from information disclosure, some facilities tighten up their housekeeping; some even change their production processes. The early gains are real and they are significant. Soon enough, however, fatigue and routine set in; people come to realize that their operating permit does not depend on their TRI reports and that the watchdogs have moved on. When that happens, all that is left is a form to file based loosely on some old algorithms.

Many engineers know the old algorithms are flawed and have professional interest in improving them (Sahu, 2012). Since at least the mid-1990s, professional associations (especially the Air and Waste Management Association, AWMA) and the EPA have sponsored conferences and workshops focusing in part on critiquing and improving emissions factors (Southerland, 2005). The state of the art in emissions factors now far exceeds what was available when the TRI was first launched, and includes best practices – facility-specific stack gas tests, adequate replicates for various process and atmospheric conditions, uncertainty estimates – that could vastly improve the country's air pollution estimates.

In contrast to academic engineers and agency scientists, why would operators, facilities or industry associations seek to improve emissions factors? One reason, as engineers have observed, might be to lower permit and related compliance fees. To the extent that the permit fee rate schedule is tied to emissions and emissions factors report high release levels, a firm may be keen to improve its estimates in hopes that they would go down. On some occasions, legal challenges have also forced facilities to improve their emissions factors (Sahu, 2012; Fox, 2012).

Lost revenue can also drive measurement improvements. After all, emissions are not just pollutants; they can also constitute lost product. In a 2003–04 DIAL study at five natural gas plants in Alberta, Canada, authors discovered fugitive emissions ranging from 38 to 342 kg/hour (Chambers et al., 2006). While these leaks represented less than 0.2 percent of each plant's natural gas throughput, they corresponded to real costs – in 2003–04, a 100kg/hr gas loss represented CAN$237,000 in lost revenues (at CAN$5/GJ) (Chambers et al., 2006, p. 5). At a single sour gas plant, operators acting on the authors' findings repaired methane and C_{2+} hydrocarbon emissions, thereby increasing revenues by CAN$730,000 per year. (Chambers et al., 2006, p. 8). Fortunately, many engineers and agency officials recognize that emissions estimates can and should be improved. Shell Oil even markets its remote sensing technologies, heralding the leak detection benefits of using DIAL as well as the superior legal protection afforded by measurements versus estimates (Cuclis, 2012).

Beyond the TRI

When presented with these critiques of the TRI program, a seasoned EPA veteran, Fred Talcott, offered his Talcott Proposition of TRI Irrelevance (TPTI), which bears reproducing here in full:

> By legislative design, TRI contains release reports from only a small fraction of fixed sources of toxic substances. There are still around 300,000 manufacturing facilities in the US, and TRI covers less than 20,000 of them; admittedly among the larger of them, but misses all the small facilities and most of the medium ones. It has most of the petroleum refineries and the more important electric utilities, and many non-coal mining operations. But no drinking water or POTWs or gasoline stations or perc-releasing dry cleaners and some other classes of potential toxic releasing facilities. By design it has none of the transportation toxics sources. Pipelines, ports, rail and truck terminals, as well as the cars, trucks, ships and trains are all excluded. By design it has none of the dispersive toxics releases – glues and surface coatings of new and renovated construction, the painting of lines on highways, household uses of a myriad of chemicals, agricultural, municipal and residential pesticides and fertilizers – all beyond TRI's ken.
>
> Does TRI capture a significant fraction of air toxics releases? No. (F. Talcott, personal communication, 8 August 2011).

Talcott's proposition cautions us not to take the TRI too seriously, since there are so many other pollution sources. And if the TRI's approach to pollution estimation bore no resemblance to what thousands of facilities do for permit compliance, then we could concur that what happens with the TRI can't possibly represent the nation's pollution risks. But facilities use the very same emissions factors that underpin so much questionable TRI data for much of their other regulatory compliance (Frey, 2007). As the GAO put it in 2001, "EPA's data show that, nationally, emissions factors are used for about 80 percent of emissions determinations" (GAO, 2001, p. 3). The US EPA's own Inspector General pointed out that the quality of emissions factors matters not primarily because of their use in inventories (including inventories of greenhouse gas emissions). Their quality matters because facilities use them to develop emissions control and reduction strategies, and it matters because agencies use the estimation results to ascertain whether facilities pollute enough to trigger permitting and regulatory requirements (EPA, 2006, p. 1). In its 2006 study, the EPA Inspector General pointed out that ". . .according to EPA enforcement records, three industries – petroleum refineries, wood products, and ethanol production – operated with insufficient control equipment primarily because emissions limits were significantly underestimated due to the emissions factors used (EPA Office of Inspector General, 2006, p. 8)."

Even permit limits, regulating how much a source can release in a given time period, rely on emissions factors. Along with a regulatory agency's control technology requirements, permit limits are the most crucial and costly components of the Compliance-Abatement-Mitigation approach.

While the TRI should give us pause, because the inventory's failures mirror those of many environmental regulations, we can easily find better alternatives. The Clean Air Act's Acid Rain Program (ARP) offers just such an alternative: CEMS directly measure, in real time, acid rain-forming SOx and NOx emissions (*not* ranges), and engineers understand the uncertainties associated with stack gas probes and related equipment. Coupled with very good pollutant transport models, atmospheric deposition measurements and long-term ecological studies of water and soil acidification, the Acid Rain Program's environmental information is about as good as it gets. In Chapter 3, I turn to what is done with that excellent information, examining regulatory failure at the end of the pipe.

REFERENCES

Abrams, J. (1990). "Alcoa Chief Disputes 'Phantom' Pollution Cuts." *Pittsburgh Post-Gazette*. Pittsburgh, PA.

Babbie, E. (1995). *The Practice of Social Research*. Belmont, CA, Wadsworth Publishing Company.

Bennear, L. S. (2007). "Are Management-Based Regulations Effective? Evidence from State Pollution Prevention Programs." *Journal of Policy Analysis and Management* 26(2): 327–348.

Bui, L. T. M. (2012). "What we Know About What we Know About Toxic Polluter Behavior from the TRI: Evidence from (almost) Twenty Years of TRI Data in The Petroleum Refining Industry." Brandeis University working paper, May 2012. http://www.brandeis.edu/departments/economics/RePEc/brd/doc/Brandeis_WP45.pdf.

Chambers, A., M. Strosher, et al. (2006). "DIAL Measurements of Fugitive Emissions from Natural Gas Plants and the Comparison with Emission Factor Estimates." *15th International Emission Inventory Conference: Reinventing Inventories – New Ideas in New Orleans*. New Orleans, LA.

Codina, T. (2011). US EPA, personal communication.

Cuclis, A. (2012). "Why Emission Factors Don't Work at Refineries and What to do about it." *Emissions Inventory Conference: Emission Inventories – Meeting the Challenges Posed by Emerging Global, National, Regional and Local Air Quality Issues*. US EPA, Tampa, Florida.

de Marchi, S. and J. T. Hamilton (2006). "Assessing the Accuracy of Self-Reported Data: An Evaluation of the Toxics Release Inventory." *Journal of Risk and Uncertainty* 32(1): 57–76.

Deseret News (1990). "Are Firms Emitting 'Trick' Data?" *Deseret News*. Salt Lake City, UT.

Environmental Integrity Project (2012a). "Accident Prone: Malfunctions and Abnormal Emissions Events at Refineries, Chemical Plants, and Natural Gas Facilities in Texas, 2009–2011." EIP.

Environmental Integrity Project (2012b). "On Behalf of Seven Community Organizations, EIP and Earthjustice Sue EPA for Failures to Update Multiple Toxic Emission Standards for Refineries." EIP.

Fox, P. E. (2012). Personal communication.

Frey, H. C. (2007). "Quantification of Uncertainty in Emission Factors and Inventories." *16th Annual International Emission Inventory Conference – Emission Inventories: "Integration, Analysis, and Communications"*. Raleigh, NC.

Hamilton, J. T. (2005). *Regulation through Revelation: The Origin, Politics, and Impacts of the Toxics Release Inventory Program*. New York, NY, Cambridge University Press.

Hearne, S. A. (1996). "Tracking Toxics: Chemical Use and the Public's 'Right-to-Know'." *Environment* 38(6): 4–34.

Hutzell, W. T. and D. J. Luecken (2008). "Fate and Transport of Emissions for Several Trace Metals over the United States." *Science of the Total Environment* 396(2–3): 164–179.

INFORM (1995). Toxics Watch 1995. Accessed at http://www.informinc.org/xsum_tox95.php.

Koehler, D. A. and J. D. Spengler (2007). "The Toxic Release Inventory: Fact or Fiction? A Case Study of the Primary Aluminum Industry." *Journal of Environmental Management* 85(2): 296–307.

Kraft, M., M. Stephan, et al. (2010). *Coming Clean: Information Disclosure and Environmental Performance*. Cambridge, MA, MIT Press.

Library of Congress. Environment, N. R. P. D. and United States. Congress. Senate. Committee on Environment Public Works (1990). *A Legislative History of the Superfund Amendments and Reauthorization Act of 1986 (Public Law 99–499): Together with a Section-by-Section Index*. US Government Printing Office.

Natan, T. E. and C. Miller (1998). "Are Toxics Release Inventory Reductions Real?" *Environmental Science & Technology* 32(15): 368A–374A.

National Research Council (1990). "Tracking Toxic Substances at Industrial Facilities: Engineering Mass Balance Versus Materials Accounting." Committee to Evaluate Mass Balance Information for Facilities Handling Toxic Substances. Washington, DC. National Academy of Sciences.

Poje, G. V. and D. M. Horowitz (1990). "Phantom Reductions: Tracking Toxic Trends." Washington, DC, National Wildlife Federation.

Powers, N. E. (2013). "Measuring the Impact of the Toxics Release Inventory: Evidence from Manufacturing Plant Births." Center for Economic Studies, US Census Bureau Working Papers. Accessed at https://ideas.repec.org/p/cen/wpaper/13-07.html.

Riley, G., J. Warren, et al. (1993). "Assessment of Changes in Reported TRI Releases and Transfers between 1989 and 1990." Research Triangle Park, NC, Center for Economics Research, Research Triangle Institute.

Sachs, J. S. (2011). "What We Want is ACTION." National Wildlife Federation. Accessed at http://www.nwf.org/news-and-magazines/national-wildlife/animals/archives/2011/history-of-national-wildlife-federation.aspx.

Sahu, R. A. E. E. (2012). Personal communication.

Schneider, T. E. (2008). "Is There a Relation Between the Cost of Debt and Environmental Performance? An Empirical Investigation of the U.S. Pulp and Paper Industry, 1994–2005." Paper presented at the School of Accountancy, University of Waterloo.

Senthil, V. E. (2011). Personal communication.

Southerland, J. H. (2005). "An Abridged History of Emission Inventory and Emission Factor Activities." *14th International Emission Inventory Conference "Transforming Emission Inventories – Meeting Future Challenges Today"*. Las Vegas, NV.

Talcott, F. (2011). Personal communication.

United Press International (1985). "OSHA Cites Union Carbide with Neglecting Safety Policy." *Houston Chronicle*. Houston, TX. 1 October 1985, p. 7.

United States Bureau of Economic Analysis (2012). "Current-Dollar and 'Real' Gross Domestic Product." US Department of Commerce.

United States Environmental Protection Agency (1998a). "1994 and 1995 Toxic Release Inventory Data Quality Report." Washington, DC, EPA.

United States Environmental Protection Agency (1998b). "1996 Toxic Release Inventory Data Quality Report." Office of Pollution Prevention and Toxics. Washington, DC, EPA.

United States Environmental Protection Agency (2006). "EPA Can Improve Emissions Factors Development and Management." Office of Inspector General. Washington, DC, EPA.

United States Environmental Protection Agency (2007). "Toxics Release Inventory Form R Toxic Chemical Release Reporting Information Collection Request Supporting Statement OMB Control No. 2070–0093." Washington, DC, EPA.

United States Environmental Protection Agency (2010). "Toxic Chemical Release Inventory Reporting Forms and Instructions, Revised 2011 Version." Washington, DC, EPA.

United States Environmental Protection Agency (2011). "2011 National Hazardous Waste Biennial Report." Washington, DC, EPA.

United States Environmental Protection Agency (2012a). "Compilation of Air Pollution Emissions Factors." Washington, DC, EPA.

United States Environmental Protection Agency (2012b). "Priority Chemicals. Office of Waste." Washington, DC, EPA.

United States Environmental Protection Agency (2013). "Toxic Release Inventory (TRI) Program: TRI Basic Plus Data Files: Calendar Years 1987–2011." Washington, DC, EPA.

United States Government Accounting Office (GAO) (1991). "Toxic Chemicals: EPA's Toxic Release Inventory is Useful but Can Be Improved." Washington, DC, EPA.

United States Government Accounting Office (GAO) (2001). "EPA Should Improve Oversight of Emissions Reporting by Large Facilities." Washington, DC, EPA.

Wagner, W. (2010). "Administrative Law, Filter Failure, and Information Capture." *Duke Law Journal* 59 (Energy Center Research Paper No. 07–10).

Wolf, S. M. (1996). "Fear and Loathing about the Public Right to Know: The Surprising Success of The Emergency Planning and Community Right-to-Know Act." *Journal of Land Use and Environmental Law* 11(2): 217–325.

3. Failure at the end of the pipe, or why acid rain will be a problem as long as we burn coal

The two titans of US pollution law, the 1970 Clean Air Act and the 1972 Clean Water Act, epitomize the best and worst of end-of-pipe regulation. Both acts forced major advances in pollution abatement technology, although there was plenty of pollution management know-how to work with by the late 1960s. At the time these laws were passed, some municipalities around the country had required more than primary treatment of wastewater effluent; similarly, air pollution could be removed with the precursors of today's scrubbers, baghouses and electrostatic precipitators. But most of the nation's largest emitters were not required to operate the very best technologies then available; only three scrubbers were in operation when the 1970 Clean Air Act was passed (Ackerman and Hassler, 1981, p.16). And because so few air polluters were removing particulate matter (soot), smokestack emissions were especially visible reminders of the nation's pollution woes.

The architects of the new US environmental laws drew unprecedented political support for cleaning up air and water pollution, but they faced many uncertainties about how they should proceed. Perhaps the most fundamental choice came down to regulations that would eliminate a pollutant altogether versus reducing it to acceptable levels. Chapter 1 alluded to the first approach, which in some rare instances was followed and led to outright bans (or what Driesen and Sinden, 2009, call "dirty input limits") on the most dangerous or problematic products and processes. Phosphate detergents, DDT and leaded gasoline were simply removed from the US economy altogether. No lead in gasoline meant no lead in tailpipe emissions.

But this kind of transformative policy remains the exception in US environmental regulation (Driesen and Sinden, 2009; Commoner, 1987; Kehoe, 1992; Davies and Mazurek, 1998). Any veteran of the fight against DDT, leaded gasoline and the like would surely note that to achieve these environmental successes required enormous lobbying and movement struggles. The opposition was always much better organized and well funded.

Driesen and Sinden (2009) note two exceptions, including the Toxic Substances Control Act of 1976 (TSCA),[1] which authorizes EPA to ban or limit the production of some toxic substances if the agency deems these dangerous enough, and the Federal Insecticide, Fungicide, and Rodenticide Act Amendments of 1972 (FIFRA),[2] which empowers EPA to ban or limit use of the most dangerous pesticides. Despite the strength these laws conferred on the EPA, the agency has rarely flexed these muscles.

So it should come as no surprise that US lawmakers of 1970 and 1972 concentrated on cleaning up pollution just before it was released into the environment rather than addressing its root causes. Here was the tacit bargain for improving air quality: we won't tell you how to make electricity or some manufactured good unless you remove a lot of soot, smog-forming compounds and acid rain chemicals.

At first, this approach worked spectacularly well. Put a baghouse or an electrostatic precipitator on a coal-fired power plant, and suddenly that smokestack no longer belches forth dark brown or black smoke.

End-of-pipe regulation lies at the heart of the compliance-abatement-mitigation approach. It offers a powerful promise. Technology-enforcing standards require that all sources remove some pollution, even a *lot* of pollution, before it reaches the air or water. Old cars and manufacturing plants ("existing sources") are treated more leniently than new sources based on the common-sense notion that building pollution controls into a new facility or new automobile model is always cheaper than retrofitting one that already exists. As long as dirtier cars come off the road and old power plants close after 20 or 30 years, air quality will get better. Moreover, phasing in technology-based standards on what might charitably be termed "reasonable" timelines ensures that the captains of industry can plan and time their investments with the assurance that regulators will not spring new surprises upon them.

The end-of-pipe abatement approach boils down to a grand political compromise bolstered by technological optimism. As abatement achieves significant gains, proponents can point to impressive changes. Who can argue with a catalytic converter or scrubber that removes 90 percent of air emissions relative to prior technologies?

But as described in Chapter 1, the end-of-pipe approach falls short for three reasons:

---

[1]   15 U.S.C. §§ 2601–2692 (2000).
[2]   7 U.S.C. §§ 136–136y (2000).

1) pollution removal rates through end-of-pipe controls run into serious economic limits long before 100 percent abatement can be achieved, and

2) population growth swamps the per-unit improvements, thereby

3) reversing initial gains in one medium (e.g., air) and generating increasingly problematic pollutants in other media (e.g., soil and groundwater).

The end-of-pipe approach only works when partial abatement results in tolerable pollution levels even if the number of sources continues to grow in the long run.

Using NOx emissions from cars and trucks in the Los Angeles basin, Chapter 1 provided a small thought experiment to illustrate how end-of-pipe pollution abatement fails when emissions sources proliferate. This chapter fully develops the end-of-pipe critique by examining the prospects for controlling emissions under the 1990 US Clean Air Act Amendment's (CAAA) Title IV, also known as the Acid Rain Program (ARP).

The Acid Rain Program grew out of our seemingly endless struggle with coal. Plentiful domestic supplies, low costs and proven power-generation technologies make this energy source exceedingly difficult to resist. The Energy Information Administration conservatively estimates that the US has nearly 200 years' worth of recoverable coal at our current production rate of about one billion short tons per year (United States Energy Information Administration, 2013). But coal is dirty in multiple ways, stressing, air, land and water resources, all requiring expensive and complex pollution controls. Coal consumption confounds regulators as each decade brings new problems associated with it. In the 1970s, regulators treated coal-fired power plants as just another combustion source that released unacceptable levels of soot, carbon monoxide, sulfur and nitrogen oxides. Coal combustion had to be regulated because of human health concerns about smog and soot.

While the US EPA struggled to get power plant emissions down to acceptable levels, new concerns arose over sulfur and nitrogen oxide deposition, especially in the form of acid rain falling over the Eastern US from Appalachia to Maine. After 1990, coal-fired power plants dramatically reduced their SOx emissions and achieved some improvements on NOx emissions. Thanks to the cap-and-trade experiment launched by Title IV, these emissions reductions came at much lower cost than previous abatement efforts. Within just a few years after Title IV went into effect, the conventional wisdom among energy policy analysts held that the acid rain problem was solved, and that this success proved the wonders of market-based policy tools.

Just as it seemed that the country was making headway on this new problem, concerns arose over heavy metals, especially mercury, and other air toxics coming out of power plant stacks. The 1990 CAAA broadened EPA's authority to control air toxics. EPA responded by spending the next decade determining the nature of the connection between power plants and mercury emissions. As it turns out, coal contains trace amounts of mercury and other toxic metals, which are not removed through ordinary abatement techniques (US Environmental Protection Agency, 2012). EPA issued findings in 1997 and a "Utility Air Toxics Study" in 1998. Having taken its time to get there, the agency finally concluded in December of 2000 that it is "appropriate and necessary to regulate coal- and oil-fired electric utilities under section 112 of the Clean Air Act" (Regulations Implementing the Federal Coal Mine Health and Safety Act of 1969, as Amended, 2000). Since section 112 empowers the EPA to regulate hazardous air pollutants, the agency essentially acknowledged its duty to regulate mercury emissions.

In 2004, EPA proposed a two-phase rule for controlling mercury, the first relying on classic end-of-pipe abatement and the second employing a cap-and-trade approach. Perhaps under pressure from the Bush administration, the agency reversed itself in 2006, finding that it is neither necessary nor appropriate to regulate mercury under section 112 of the Clean Air Act, while simultaneously adopting a weak "Clean Air Mercury Rule." This rule was voided by the DC Court of Appeals in 2008. In the spring of 2013, EPA had issued the Mercury and Air Toxics Standard, or "MATS rule," designed to reduce mercury emissions by 90 percent. A year later, in April 2014, the US Court of Appeals for the District of Columbia Circuit upheld the MATS rule, clearing the way for the rule's implementation (Davenport, 2014).

While the Clinton Administration's EPA struggled to comply with its new masters in the Bush Administration, greenhouse gases became the next air pollutant coal-fired power plants would need to control. When it was not denying the need to control greenhouse gases, the Bush Administration hewed to classic end-of-pipe policy designs, favoring carbon capture and storage (CCS) over any serious consideration of reducing coal use.

After regulating soot, SOx and NOx and mercury, and proposing to add CO_2 reductions, the EPA returned in the early 2000s to persistent smog and particulate matter pollution. Despite nearly heroic public health gains, too many states in the Eastern US still failed to meet decades-old ambient air quality standards. Too much pollution in the Midwest blew into New England and the Mid-Atlantic states on strong trade winds. EPA's solution was the Clean Air Interstate Rule (CAIR), which was adopted in 2005 but was held up for years in legal challenges. On 29 April

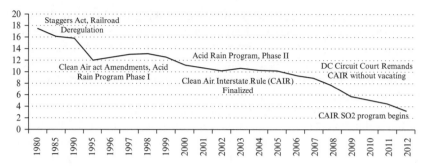

Source: US EPA, 2013.

Figure 3.1   US SO$_x$ emissions from regulated sources (million tons) and major regulatory milestones

2014, the US Supreme Court upheld the EPA's regulations (informally named the Good Neighbor Rule) in a 6–2 ruling, ending a decade of legal challenges that forced the agency to revise its standards twice (Davenport, 2014). CAIR is significant to our story because with it, EPA sought further emissions reductions for public health goals, not because of persistent acidification problems, the original motivation for the Acid Rain Program. Figure 3.1 summarizes trends in SO2 emissions while highlighting relevant regulatory milestones.

Significant emissions reductions came after ARP phases I and II were both fully implemented. That is, from 1980 to 1990, there were only 1.6 millions tons of SOx reductions (a decrease of about 9 percent). Between 1990 and 1999, the ARP started to have a more significant effect, eliminating an additional 3.2 millions tons of SOx emissions (about 20 percent in that decade), but the greater reductions came between 2000 and 2011, with an additional 6.7 million tons, or about 52 percent emissions reductions in that decade. The overall reductions in the period between 1980 and 2011 constitute 12.8 million tons (about 74 percent, well in excess of the CAAA's 50 percent reduction goal).

As if the air quality issues did not pose enough pollution challenges, a 300-million-gallon coal sludge spill occurred at a retention pond operated by the Tennessee Valley Authority on 22 December 2008. The sludge was composed of a 20-feet high wall of the coal burning residue called "fly ash" and water. The vast quantities of coal ash sludge and water stored behind diked ponds or deposited in landfills began to seriously threaten surface and ground waters, prompting calls to regulate these materials as hazardous wastes (Dewan, 2008).

Forty years after the first concerted efforts to transform coal from a dirty to a clean fuel, power plants burning coal still release too many air emissions of all kinds. Each plant also produces hazardous coal ash and withdraws hundreds of millions or even billions of gallons of cooling water, *daily*, to run its condensers. Simultaneously reducing all of these stressors to levels adequately protective of the global climate, human and ecosystem health could theoretically be accomplished, but not at a remotely affordable cost.

Most academic assessments of the ARP by policy analysts focus on the economics of the cap-and-trade program and/or trends in deposition. Doing so almost inevitably leads to an overly positive assessment, because the 1990 Clean Air Act Amendments did result in significant economic savings. Simply put, the cap-and-trade program helped utilities reduce air pollutants at a lower cost than the traditional command-and-control rules previously in place. However, the National Acid Precipitation Assessment Program (NAPAP) reports, issued every five years, and associated environmental science literatures are not nearly so sanguine that the acid rain problem has been solved.

In the compliance-abatement-mitigation approach, policymakers and regulators must set pollution reduction goals for end-of-pipe abatement. In the case of air quality, regulators typically work backwards from their best, most current sense of what constitutes clean air from a public health perspective, then seek end-of-pipe controls that will reduce pollution loads enough to reach their ambient air quality goals. In rare cases like the ARP, public health does not dictate the end-of-pipe abatement goal. As we will see in the acid rain case, Congress based the program's goals on a target that seemed at once ambitious and politically feasible. Emissions reductions were based neither on human nor ecosystem health targets, a fact that continues to plague restoration efforts.

THE ACID RAIN PROBLEM: FROM SCRUBBER TO STREAM

To understand the case of acid rain as an end-of-pipe regulatory approach, it's vital to see how sulfur in Western coal deposits finds its way to waterways in Appalachia and the Adirondacks.

The Powder River Basin of northeast Wyoming and southeast Montana produced 423 million tons of subbituminous coal in 2011, enough to power one out of five homes and businesses in the US, according to the US Bureau of Land Management (2012). Wyoming itself produces about 40 percent of the coal used in US power plants. Subbituminous coal produces between

8,000 and 11,000 BTU per pound, though Powder River Basin coal averages on the low end of this range. Compared to Appalachian coals, Western subbituminous coals have low sulfur content (less than one percent versus as much as four percent), making them ideal for electric power plants that seek air emissions reductions. Sadly, however, Powder River Basin coals typically produce about 30 percent less heat per pound than Appalachian coals, thereby requiring greater quantities to achieve the same power output.

Heavy reliance on western coal for electric power production took off only over the last 25 years. Prior to that, two obstacles discouraged long-range transport and use of these low-sulfur coals. First, railroads used to be highly regulated by the Interstate Commerce Commission (the ICC, whose duties were later replaced by the Surface Transportation Board). Prior to 1980, railroads were required to set rates following tariff guidelines published by the ICC. Railroads were losing freight transport market share to the trucking and airline industries, while passenger ridership had long since declined because of widespread automobile use. Shipping low-sulfur western coal over 1,500 miles to the Ohio Valley or the Atlantic seaboard was prohibitive. Rates were too high, track infrastructure inadequate, loading and unloading too slow. Market forces had transformed freight transportation, but regulation itself hampered the railroad industry's ability to respond competitively.

The second obstacle was also regulatory in nature. The 1977 Clean Air Act Amendments required power plants to gradually install pollution control devices known as "scrubbers." In technical terms, scrubbers provided "flue-gas desulfurization (FGD)," which could remove significant amounts of sulfur dioxide from power plant exhaust streams before these would reach the atmosphere. Specifically, the 1977 amendments set an emissions limit of 1.2 pounds SO_2 per million British Thermal Units (mmBTU) generated, then mandated scrubbers as the best control technology to achieve the emissions limit. The EPA could have mandated coal washing or use of low-sulfur western coal as a control option, but under pressure from eastern members of Congress, ended up favoring eastern coal mining interests (Ackerman and Hassler, 1981).

These obstacles fell away within a decade of each other. First, the 1980 Staggers Rail Act deregulated the railroads, allowing them to compete for business throughout the US and to set their own rates. While the Staggers Act did not transform railroads overnight, as public policies go, the law's effect was very quick. The average cost of carrying coal by all modes peaked in 1981 at an average of $17.65 per short ton. By 2003, coal transport rates had dropped to $12.62 (in constant, year 2005 dollars); by 2010, average rates were $15.54, still not as high as the early 1980s (United States Energy Information Administration, 2012).

Railroads dropped unprofitable routes, including a lot of passenger lines, modernized and upgraded their tracks and aggressively competed for bulk commodities (mostly grains and minerals) hauled over enormous distances. Liberalized freight rates allowed the railroads to write attractive contracts with utilities, who, in turn, found low-cost ways to modify their boilers. In short order, utilities converted their boilers from bituminous coal-burning to the lower-sulfur sub-bituminous coal coming out of western mines (Schmalensee and Stavins, 2013).

Today, about 40 percent of the cost of coal, delivered, is in transportation (United States Energy Information Administration, 2012).[3] Coal at the mine mouth in the Powder River Basin costs about \$10–15 per short ton. Coal arrives at power plants in huge trains, easily numbering 100 or more cars containing 100 tons each. A power plant thus pays \$150,000 for the coal at the mine, but with transportation, faces a total bill nearly twice that amount. A large power plant can run through an entire trainload of coal in a little over a single day! (United States Energy Information Administration, 2012).

By the late 1980s, western mines could compete for power plant contracts in the East, but utilities were still locked into the 1977 Clean Air Act's requirements, which powerfully favored eastern coal suppliers. Enter the 1990 Clean Air Act's Acid Rain Program, which also forced reductions in SO_2 and NOx emissions from power plants in the Midwest, but granted these facilities great latitude for determining how to achieve the reductions. Since Powder River Basin coals contain as little as one quarter of the sulfur contained in eastern coals, many facilities found it far cheaper to buy their coal from western supplies even if they had to ship their fuel many hundreds of miles and actually burn more coal because of the considerably lower heat output per ton. Depending on each facility's emissions allowances, utilities could decide to use scrubbers in conjunction with low-sulfur coal, buy extra allowances or incur the extra emissions and cost of scrubbing higher-sulfur eastern coal. Many power plants have to operate scrubbers, even if they burn low-sulfur coals: "At higher sulfur levels, wet scrubbers typically became the de facto technology selection" (Dickerman and Sewell, 2007).

Coal-fired power plants typically pulverize their fuel so that it burns more quickly, hotter and more uniformly. Like any fossil fuel, coal never burns perfectly. That is, the carbon can be completely consumed, but other constituents, including particulate matter, oxides of sulfur and nitrogen and some metals, end up in the exhaust stream. After leaving the

---

[3] For a fascinating account of coal transport, see John McPhee's *Uncommon Carriers*. New York, NY, Farrar, Strauss and Giroux, 2006.

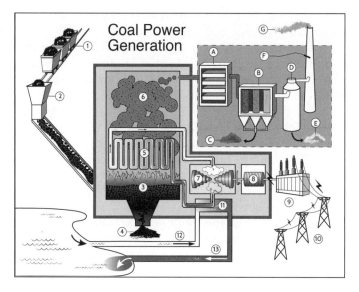

Power Generation

1. Coal Train
2. Pulverizing
3. Burner
4. Ash
5. Steam Generation
6. Flue Gas
7. Turbine
8. Generator
9. Transformer
10. Power Distribution
11. Condenser
12. Cold Water Intake
13. Warm Water outflow

Pollution Controls

A. SCR
B. Baghouse/Electrostatic Precipitator
C. Fly ash
D. SO2 Scrubber
E. Gypsum
F. Continuous Emissions Monitoring
G. Emissions

Source:　Illustration by Katie Bertsche.

Figure 3.2　A typical coal-fired power plant

furnace, these all travel to pollution control devices, including FGD and some kind of particulate removal followed by devices that reduce nitrogen oxides (see Figure 3.2).

FGD systems commonly spray a slurry of limestone and water ("slaked lime") into the exhaust before it is released up the stack. The sulfur dioxide reacts with water to produce sulfurous acid, which then dissociates to sulfite. The slaked lime binds to the sulfite, resulting in calcium sulfate, commonly known as gypsum. The gypsum sludge is dewatered and either landfilled or recycled as a construction material.

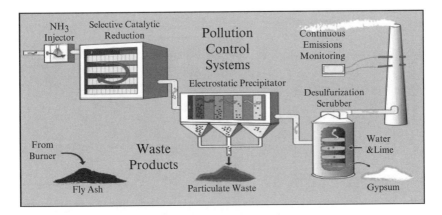

Source: Illustration by Katie Bertsche.

Figure 3.3   Pollution controls in coal-fired power plants

Although this chemistry is fairly simple, making it work reliably for vast emissions loads is expensive and fraught with nettlesome trade-offs. First, it takes enormous quantities of lime – 3,650,000 metric tons in 2011, nearly 20 percent of all the lime consumed in the US. The lime alone costs over $400 million (Miller, 2013). Second, running the scrubber equipment itself saps some of the very same energy the plant is designed to produce, from 0.7 percent to 3 percent (Lange and Bellas, 2006). In 2007, the National Petroleum Council estimated that this "parasitic load" rose to 3 gigawatts, a power generation capacity about equal to that of the state of Nebraska (National Petroleum Council, 2007a, b). If power plants will be required to sequester carbon dioxide and capture mercury in future EPA rules, abating high percentages of these pollutants will add even more parasitic load.

Those 3.6 million metric tons of lime became 22.6 million metric tons of gypsum from FGD in 2011. Not quite half of these "coal combustion products" ended up being recycled, mostly into drywall panels and other construction applications (American Coal Ash Association, 2012). Between 2011 and 2012, recycling of all coal combustion products actually fell, from 56.6 million tons to 51.9 million tons. The major trade association representing coal combustion recycling, the American Coal Ash Association, claimed that recyclers had been spooked by the prospect that these waste by-products might be classified as hazardous, thereby greatly increasing their handling, treatment and disposal costs (Quiñones, 2013). And as Chapter 1 indicated, the US recycling rate is only about half that of the European trend and has actually declined over the last decade. Most

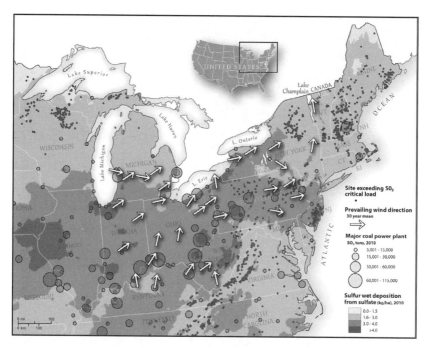

Source: Map by Aaron Cole.

*Figure 3.4   Coal-fired power plants, prevailing winds and sulfate
            deposition in the northeastern US*

of the scrubber material that isn't recycled goes to ordinary landfills, with
potentially serious consequences for groundwater quality.

Figure 3.3 (p. 65) shows the various environmental control technologies
currently required in coal-fired power plants as well as additional ones
necessary to meet EPA rules that will come into force by 2020. These technologies are expensive. In a relatively small coal-fired plant (300 MW),
a selective catalytic reduction unit that can remove NOx costs $50–60
million, activated carbon injection (for mercury) and baghouses (for particulate matter add another $30 million, and sulfur scrubbers run around
$100 million (Celebi et al., 2010).

Despite the efficiency of modern scrubbers, coal plants emit between
three and four million tons of sulfur dioxide every year. After pollutants
go through the pollution abatement equipment, remaining emissions
travel up smokestacks from which they are released into the atmosphere.
In 2011, the General Accountability Office (GAO) found that 284 tall
smokestacks – those rising 500 to 1000 feet above the plant – were operat-

ing at 172 coal power plants in 34 states. Of critical importance to the acid rain problem, about a third of these tall smokestacks are concentrated in five states along the Ohio River Valley (see Figure 3.4). Tall smokestacks disperse pollution more widely than shorter stacks, which is what made them appealing in the first place. Wider dispersion meant better quality near power plants. Unfortunately, tall stacks also provide emissions more residence time during which they can form secondary pollutants like ozone and particulate matter (GAO, 2011). Emissions from tall stacks at the Ohio River Valley power plants are quickly pumped into the prevailing westerly winds and work their way eastward to the Adirondacks, Catskills and Appalachian Mountains, and further on to Maine and Nova Scotia.

As the winds rise over these mountains, the sulfur-containing air cools and its moisture condenses into clouds until these, in turn, reach saturation. The clouds then release an especially acidic rain. Most atmospheric acid deposition occurs as wet deposition of sulfuric and nitric acids, in the form of rain, snow or fog. As recently as 1997, wet deposition in the US Northeast had an average pH of 4.4, which is about 10 times the acidity of normal background conditions (Driscoll et al., 2001). A relatively small percentage falls as dry deposition in the form of gas and particulate matter.

Very few aquatic species can tolerate acidified waters. Whereas unimpaired, neutral waters have a pH of seven, at a pH of six snails and rainbow trout begin to die. Frogs, crayfish and mayflies succumb around a pH of five, hardy Brook Trout vanish at a pH of 4.5, and all fish die at a pH of 3.0 (Lovett et al., 2009).

The acid rain story can be told so comprehensively because the data are so remarkable, especially relative to other programs such as the self-reported toxic releases discussed in Chapter 2. Extensive data all along the environmental policy continuum and a 20-year record make the ARP especially amenable to connecting a policy program to its eventual environmental outcomes, certainly for sulfur dioxide loadings. These data allow us to work from the problem's origins to its consequences and on to its remedies, as an acid rain program veteran, Anthony Janetos, put it in 2007 (Janetos, 2007).

As discussed in Chapter 2, nearly every single electric generating unit fired by coal has a CEMS measuring emissions in real time. Some 200 stations operated by the National Atmospheric Deposition Program's National Trends Network (NADP/NTN) monitor wet deposition throughout the United States; 80-some stations measure dry deposition (Driscoll et al., 2001; Greaver et al., 2012). In the case of SO_2, Title IV recognizes that the overwhelming majority of emissions come from power plants east of the Mississippi. CEMS measure stack gases after these have been scrubbed by pollution abatement equipment (e.g., FGD) and report their concentrations to air quality regulators in real time. Taken together, the CEMS and deposition data provide a good picture of what is leaving power plants and returning to the earth.

The acid rain program benefits from further data. Some 80 sites annually are evaluated by the EPA's Temporally Integrated Monitoring of Ecosystems (TIME) program. TIME's long-term monitoring program has tracked a subset of especially acid-sensitive lakes and streams since the 1980s. Almost none of these data were available when the Clean Air Act amendments were being written in 1989–90.

So regulators know, down to the pound, how much SO_2 these sources load into the atmosphere. Thirty years of atmospheric models and deposition studies further show quite precisely where these emissions go and how much sulfate falls as rain, snow or fog. Hydrologists with universities and the US Geological Survey regularly measure several key water column indicators throughout the eastern US; these provide very reliable surface water acidification trends. Soil scientists and aquatic ecologists describe the ultimate acidification effects by showing how soil chemistry has changed and/or how plants, vertebrates and invertebrates respond.

A CLOSER LOOK AT THE ECOLOGICAL DATA

During debates over an acid rain program for the Clean Air Act, Congress recognized that much more and better ecological data could inform the new amendments, even though members benefited from almost a decade of National Acid Deposition Program reports (created in 1980), and valuable ecosystem science and ecology by people like Gene Likens at the Hubbard Brook Experimental Forest in New Hampshire. Congress was willing to accept the notion that acid deposition in Appalachia and the Northeast was caused largely by Midwestern power plants burning coal, though the exact mechanisms, loadings and even effects were not well specified (Likens et al., 2005). The House report took a fairly simplistic view of acid deposition, stating that ". . .it is reasonable to expect that. . .the roughly 40 percent reduction in sulfur oxide emissions required. . .will result in a roughly 40 percent reduction in acid deposition" (Library of Congress, Vol. 2, p. 3384). The Clean Air Act's legislative history suggests a similar, one-to-one relationship between deposition and ecosystem effects.

In fact, there wasn't much reason to think that such a linear relationship existed. Ecologists suspected that what went up a tall smokestack came down in rain, fog and snow, but establishing the relationship took a good 20–30 years of long-term monitoring. When he came back to the EPA during President Reagan's first administration, William Ruckelshaus commissioned a study to ascertain how many lakes were acidified (McLean, 2013). As for soils, ecosystem scientists were even further behind in characterizing acid rain effects.

If Congress had known more about soil acidification and buffering capacity in 1989, how different might the acid rain program's targeted emissions reduction have been? As it was, many soil scientists didn't expect acid rain to be a problem for soil chemistry, simply because they knew that soils served as enormous pools of base cations (that is, K^+, Ca^{2+}, Mg^{2+} and Na^+), which were continually replenished by rock weathering (Weathers and Lovett, 1998). Indeed, acid deposition falling on watersheds rich in carbonates can actually increasing river alkalinization by speeding up weathering, a pattern that is well-documented in the Northeastern US (Kaushal et al., 2013). But research in the 1980s and 1990s demonstrated quite unequivocally that sulfate adsorption resulted in a net acidification of soils, most importantly by leaching base cations and sometimes mobilizing aluminum (Weathers and Lovett, 1998; Lovett et al., 2009).

Aluminum is widely abundant in soils but not very mobile at a normal pH. Acidified soils release aluminum where it can be toxic to roots and also find its way to surface waters. Fish and other aquatic organisms have very low tolerance for aluminum (Greaver et al., 2012; Lovett et al., 2009). Al^{3+} competes with base cations on the exchange sites of soil organic matter (Driscoll et al., 1996). When they lose base cations, soils become less and less buffered, setting in motion a sort of acidification spiral. After a long time, soils become so depleted that they cannot quickly recover their pH balance even if contemporary acid deposition decreases significantly (Driscoll et al., 2007a). Losing base cations also robs plants of important nutrients like calcium, potassium and magnesium (Lovett et al., 2009), while simultaneously accumulating sulfur and nitrogen in soils. Astonishingly, some Northeastern forest soils receive more nitrogen deposition than trees can use for growth, reaching a sort of "nitrogen saturation" (Driscoll et al., 2007a). In addition to causing eutrophication, excess nitrogen can cause changes in plant, diatom, lichen and mycorrhizal communities (Pardo et al., 2011).

Similar waterbodies can also react differently to acidification depending on dissolved organic carbon (DOC). A lower pH can reduce DOC concentrations in lakes, resulting in higher clarity (Monteith et al., 2007). More light penetrating further into lakes allows macrophytes and benthic algae to grow on lake bottoms. Increased visibility can change the relationship between predators and prey in a lake, though acidity may affect the two differently (Effler et al., 1985; Lovett et al., 2009). And since dissolved organic carbon can bind aluminum, thereby making it less toxic, lowered DOC levels contribute to increased aluminum toxicity (Lovett et al., 2009).

More recently, ecologists have added mercury to the list of acid rain stressors. The same winds carrying sulfur and nitrogen oxides also carry trace quantities of mercury. Mercury is especially toxic in its methylated form. Until the late 1990s, conventional wisdom had it that mercury accumulated in animals only by moving up the chain. Now, however, it appears that anaerobic conditions in soil and waterbodies facilitate the production of methylmercury, thereby providing another deadly route for mercury to enter the food chain (Driscoll et al., 2007b).

Soil acidification may be impressive, but only biogeochemists tend to be witnessing the below-ground drama. Forests, on the other hand, visibly demonstrate acid rain damage. Acid deposition is widely blamed for the decline in red spruce across the northeastern US and sugar maple mortality in Pennsylvania (Driscoll et al., 2007a). More than half of the large canopy red spruce trees in the Adirondacks that were present in 1960 have now died; a quarter of those trees in the White Mountains of New Hampshire have disappeared (Driscoll et al., 2001).

Acid rains, mists or fogs appear to leach calcium from tree leaves and needles, leaving them more vulnerable to freezing damage (Driscoll et al., 2001), while direct acid deposition leads to leaf wax degradation. As soil pH decreases, molybdenum, an essential micronutrient, becomes less available, while manganese becomes more soluble, possibly rising to toxic levels. In addition, plants will change their energetic budgets if their roots need to reach further down to avoid acidified zones of soils.

Aquatic species have suffered terribly from acid deposition. Fish exposed to high acidity and increased levels of dissolved aluminum suffer from salt and water imbalances in their blood, which cause their red blood cells to rupture. The resultant increases in blood viscosity lead to lethal heart attacks (Driscoll et al., 2007a). Macroinvertebrates in streams are especially sensitive to acidity and aluminum; their communities can take a long time to recover. In recent surveys of 200 western Adirondacks streams, decreasing acid deposition was strongly correlated with improvements in pH, but 66 percent of the waterbodies surveyed still had toxic levels of aluminum. In a subset of 36 study streams, 44–56 percent of macroinvertebrates were moderately or severely impacted (Baldigo et al., 2009).

Ecologists and biogeochemists understand the aquatic effects of acid deposition best of all, having access to long-term data and having developed well-documented, properly quantified indicators (Greaver et al., 2012). Acid deposition impairs surface waters in three ways. The obvious first effect is lowered pH (increased acidity). The second is by decreasing acid-neutralizing capacity (ANC). ANC is a waterbody's ability to neutralize strong acids and is measured in microequivalents per liter (μeq/L).

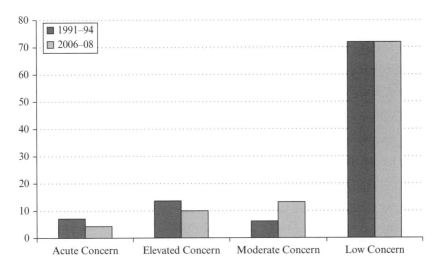

Notes:
Acute concern: Less than 0 meq/L.
Elevated concern: 0 meq/L to less than 50 meq/L.
Moderate concern: 50 meq/L to less than 100 meq/L.
Low concern: Greater or equal to 100 meq/L.

Source: Reproduced from Burns et al., 2011.

*Figure 3.5   Acid-neutralizing capacity in EPA-monitored northeastern
lakes, 1991–94 vs. 2006–08*

Many surface waters in the Northeast still have ANC values at or below
0 μeq/L, classifying them as chronically acidic. At 0–50 μeq/L, waters are
considered sensitive to episodic acidification; at greater than 50 μeq/L,
they are considered relatively unimpaired and less sensitive to acidification
(Driscoll et al., 2007a). A third way in which surface water impairment
occurs is via a rise in dissolved inorganic aluminum concentrations.

The National Acid Deposition Program staff report general improvements in ANC between 1990 and 2008. Most of the improving sites monitored for ANC were in the Adirondacks and the northern Appalachian
plateau (in Pennsylvania and southern New York), but only 12 percent
of the lakes monitored in Maine and Vermont, and 12 percent of streams
in Virginia, showed ANC improvements (Burns et al., 2011). Figure 3.5
aggregates all of the TIME monitoring sites, showing just modest overall
improvements in ANC between surveys conducted in 1991–94 versus
2006–08 (Burns et al., 2011).

The most recent summary assessment, the ARPCAIR 2011

Environmental Health Report (released in 2013), reported that only 15 percent of monitored streams in the Central Appalachians showed a decreasing sulfate trend, ". . .while sulfate concentrations in 12 percent of monitored streams actually increased" (United States Environmental Protection Agency, 2013, p.16). Over the long term, these highly weathered soils can't keep storing large amounts of deposited sulfate. As power plant emissions decrease, the sulfur budget of many northeastern watersheds will shift. Instead of inputs coming mostly from atmospheric deposition, biogeochemists expect the greater share will consist of what might be called legacy sulfur. As sulfur deposited years ago mineralizes, watersheds will receive continued sulfate inputs for years to come (United States Environmental Protection Agency, 2013; Mitchell et al., 2011). Variations in ANC trends illustrate the challenge in summarizing the ARP's effects. The Acid Rain Program caps emissions on power plants; it doesn't direct more emissions to fall on well-buffered, less weathered soils than others.

THE CRITICAL LOADS CONCEPT

Although acid deposition rarely find its way into the news, it receives a lot of attention from ecologists, biogeochemists and environmental scientists. Decades of assessments tell us that, while substantial recovery has been achieved, ccosystems continue to be stressed by acid deposition (Greaver et al., 2012; NAPAP, 2011, p. 72). But what does it mean for an ecosystem to recover? To answer that question, biogeochemists and ecologists increasingly invoke the *critical load* concept.

A critical load is ". . .a quantitative estimate of exposure to one or more pollutants, below which significant harmful effects on specific sensitive elements of the environment do not occur according to present knowledge" (Nilsson and Grennfelt, 1988). The concept was developed in Europe to help frame negotiations over sulfur and nitrogen deposition reductions. In contrast to the 50 percent emissions reduction target mandated by the 1990 Clean Air Act Amendments (CAAA), which Congress settled on apparently because it seemed politically feasible, a critical load concept requires that emissions reductions are driven by ecosystem effects.

Although the 1990 CAAA neither mandated nor authorized a critical load (CL) approach to managing acid deposition, North American scientists developed and applied the concept to numerous Northeastern watersheds and a recent partnership between the US EPA's Clean Air Markets Division and other federal agencies is making progress towards a database of national-scale critical loads, a necessary first step before these can be used for subsequent rule-making (Blett et al., 2014). A typical

CL analysis draws on water and soil chemistry, along with deposition rates, to derive a mass balance model that can account for acid inputs and outputs. Biogeochemists use either empirical data or models to determine what changes in sulfur and nitrogen deposition rates would allow plant, invertebrate or vertebrate species in sensitive soils and waters to recover (Burns et al., 2008; for an example, see Sullivan et al., 2008, applying the CL approach to future sulfur and nitrogen deposition in Virginia's Shenandoah National Park).

Duarte et al. (2013) applied a steady-state mass balance model to over 4000 regional and national soil and vegetation plots in the US. In over 45 percent of the plots they included, their model showed critical load exceedances for acid deposition. Combining all regions within the eastern half of the US, the Acid Rain Program's CAIR 2011 report concluded that ". . .the percent of water bodies. . .receiving levels. . .that exceed the critical load. . .decreased from 42 percent in the 1989–91 observation period to 23 percent in the 2009–11 observation period" (ARPCAIR, 2013, pp. 17–18).

The most authoritative, recent document for policy guidance is the 2011 National Acid Precipitation Assessment Program report to Congress (Burns et al., 2011). That assessment is unequivocal, stating that "additional emission reductions are still needed for ecological recovery, especially in acid-sensitive areas" (p. 71). Drawing on a critical load analysis, authors of the assessment pointed out that dramatically reducing the number of lakes classified as waters of acute concern would require reductions ". . .of SO_2 and NOx below 1.1 and 0.44 million tons per year from the power sector, respectively" (p. 71). Are those reductions plausible? By the EPA's own calculations of what appears technically possible, adoption of the Cross-State Air Rule would result in a drop in SO_2 emissions of 73 percent from 2005 levels; NOx emissions would go down by 54 percent. Those would result in emissions of 2.4 million tons of SO_2 and 1.2 million tons of NOx (http://www.epa.gov/airtransport/), still far from meeting what's necessary for critical loads. The authors of the NAPAP modeled different scenarios to reach further emission reductions, but never intended to take on the technical feasibility of reaching these levels (Haeuber, 2011).

More recent EPA assessments show great regional differences in critical load exceedances over time. Table 3.1 shows that EPA's critical loads models tell an encouraging story for ecosystem recovery, but only to a point. The base-poor soils and low weathering rates of Appalachian sites make surface waters in that region especially susceptible to acidification and persistently so (Burns et al., 2011).

American environmental policy

Table 3.1   Regional critical load exceedances, 2000–02 and 2010–12

Region	Number of Water Bodies Modeled	Water Bodies in Exceedance of Critical Load				Percent Reduction
		2000–2002		2010–2012		
		Number of Sites	Percent of Sites	Number of Sites	Percent of Sites	
New England (ME, NH, VT, RI, CT)	1,298	273	21%	147	11%	46%
Adirondack Mountains (NY)	341	160	47%	70	21%	56%
Northern Mid-Atlantic (PA, NY, NJ)	784	263	34%	155	20%	41%
Southern Mid-Atlantic (VA, WV, MD)	1,690	1,070	63%	745	44%	30%
Southern Appalachian Mountains (NC, TN, SC, GA, AL)	773	308	40%	192	25%	38%
Total	4,886	2,074	42%	1,309	27%	37%

Source: EPA, 2014a.

THE FUTURE OF COAL

Could coal-fired power plants reduce their SOx and NOx emissions enough to meet critical load requirements for the eastern US? The NAPAP and EPA assessments suggest that the technical limits of emissions reductions are over critical loads by about one million tons of SOx and NOx, each. So it seems that the end-of-pipe approach would reach its technological limits before ecosystems in the eastern US could recover, though the reductions might get close. It's much less economically plausible that the utility sector could drive its emissions down to the technological limits.

What, then, are the economically affordable emissions caps? Unfortunately, we don't have as good empirical data for the economic dimensions of low-hanging fruit limits. The environmental economics literature doesn't offer much empirical work illustrating the low-hanging fruit phenomenon and the end-of-pipe limitations, largely because proprietary reasons prevent researchers from having access to actual marginal abatement cost (MAC)[4] curves for real facilities (see Harrington, Morgenstern, and Nelson, 2000; Newell et al., 2003; Islas and Grande, 2008; Becker, 2005).

There are a few notable exceptions to the lack of information on abatement costs. In their analysis of abatement costs for NOx emissions from coal-fired utility boilers, Vijay et al. (2010) provide steeply accelerating MAC curves that clearly show increasing costs per ton of NOx abated as removal efficiencies go up. For example, their results suggest costs of about $1,112 per ton at 80 percent removal and $1,497 per ton at 94 percent (the current technical limit), a per-unit increase of 34 percent.

Similarly, in a series of field tests of mercury removal at three commercial coal-fired utilities with wet flue-gas desulfurization (FGD) systems, Srivastava et al. (2006) estimated steeply rising marginal abatement costs. For example, at 50 percent mercury removal, capital costs run about 0.1 mills/kWh for a halogenated powdered activated carbon sorbent system; costs at 90 percent removal are about five times that level (which, it should be noted, is not prohibitive compared to other air pollution control costs).

Whether coal plant emissions could be abated much more for an acceptably low cost depends partly on a utility's alternatives. Coal-fired power has always been attractive because of its low cost, but what happens if coal plants have to significantly reduce their CO_2, mercury and smog-forming emissions – all at once? Lincoln Pratson and his colleagues at Duke University tackled this question with an elegant study using power production and pollution abatement cost data for 304 coal plants (95 percent of current US coal-fired capacity) and 358 natural gas plants (representing 70 percent of US natural gas-fired capacity).

Observing that the ratio of electricity-generating costs at natural gas versus coal plants (NG2CP) was about 1.42 in 2012, Pratson and his colleagues showed that the cost of electricity in natural gas plants was rapidly coming down to meet that of coal-fired facilities. By 2012, natural gas was competitive with coal largely on fuel costs, because of vast new domestic sources coming online with hydro-fracking technologies. If EPA implements the MATS, CAIR and particulate matter rules, electricity costs for coal will quickly shoot upwards. Pratson et al. project that the total cost of electricity (COE) with maximum environmental controls would jump

---

[4] MAC curves are used to describe how different pollution abatement approaches result in different costs, at the margins, i.e., for each additional increment of pollution control.

from an average of about $28/MWh to as much as $98/MWh. More specifically:

> In this case, the NG2CP can reach 4.3 before a majority of coal capacity has a COE less than that of the cheapest natural gas capacity. . .[T]he NG2CP has averaged >3.5 since January 2002, but continued high production rates of shale gas are predicted to keep the NG2CP <2.8 until 2035. . .[S]hould this prediction hold true, then natural gas capacity would remain cost competitive with coal capacity for at least two decades (Pratson et al., 2013, p. E).

Industry analysts and energy economists speak with one voice on this question: were EPA to implement all of its new air emissions standards at once, coal-fired power plants would be much less competitive with natural gas plants. In 2013, the country's 1400+ coal-fired power plants had about 343 GW of electricity generating capacity. The Union of Concerned Scientists estimates that about three-quarters of all coal-fired plants ". . .have outlived their 30-year life span – with 17 percent being older than half a century" (UCS, 2012, p. 1). From 2010 to 2013, no fewer than ten major finance and power industry analyses predicted that a combination of new standards under the Clean Air Interstate Rule, the Mercury Air Toxics Rule and greenhouse gas limits would likely prompt between 25 and 76 GW of plant retirements by 2020, about 7–22 percent of total coal-fired capacity (Celebi et al., 2010; Shavel et al., 2010; M.J. Bradley et al., 2011; Eggers et al., 2010; North American Electric Reliability Corporation, 2010; The INGAA Foundation, Inc., 2010; Crooks, 2010; Deutsche Bank Climate Change Advisors, 2010; Salisbury et al., 2010; Miller, 2013). In November 2013, the Tennessee Valley Authority announced a second wave of coal plant retirements, targeting eight large plants collectively responsible for emitting 14.1 million tons of CO_2. The agency aims to drive its coal use from about 80 percent in 1971 to 20 percent after all of the announced plants close (Wines, 2013).

Retiring a fifth of coal plant capacity is impressive, but 177 GW (over 50 percent) of coal capacity in the US came online between 1999 and 2004, far more than what is projected to retire (Miller, 2013). Moreover, the US will be burning coal to make electricity for some time to come, especially given its huge reserves. In 2013, as natural gas and electricity consumption both increased, the US Energy Information Administration projected that US coal consumption would rise from 890 million tons in 2012 to 966 million tons in 2014 (Quiñones, 2013b).

Two developments, one market-driven and another arising in policy changes, will likely ensure that natural gas no longer waits in the wings. First, by 2010, hydro-fracking – a technique that uses explosives to free up gas reserves in very deep formations – created an enormous US natural gas supply. Second, in 2013 and 2014, the Obama Administration proposed rules for new and existing power plants that impose aggressive limits on greenhouse gases (US EPA 2014b). Thus, instead of trying to wring very expensive emissions reductions out of coal plants, utilities will simply retire their oldest, least efficient power plants and switch fuels as they design and build replacement facilities.

CONCLUSION

Richard Schmalensee and Robert Stavins view the acid rain program as a grand and deeply ironic policy experiment (Schmalensee and Stavins, 2012). It is ironic because the program's human health benefits far outperformed the ecological restoration policymakers had intended. Schmalensee and Stavins call this "doing the right thing for the wrong reason," noting that analysts estimate the ARP's annual benefits – 95 percent of which are in the form of human health gains – at $59 to $116 billion compared with annual costs of only $0.5 to $2 billion (Schmalensee and Stavins, 2012, p.5).

The Clean Air Act's ambient air quality standards are designed to protect the health of those who are most vulnerable, such as children, the elderly and people suffering from respiratory ailments. Heaping one irony upon the other, the ARP's human health benefits were probably distributed in inequitable ways. In 2011, David Henry and his colleagues argued that, all else being equal, firms or facilities located in non-attainment counties would face higher marginal abatement costs, because additional abatement is likely to be required of firms in non-attainment areas. Firms in non-attainment areas face tougher standards for all kinds of pollutants; moreover, abatement tends to be more expensive, on a per-ton basis, after the low-hanging fruit has been picked.

Rural power plants situated in attainment areas would be the ones with relatively lower abatement costs. Air quality there is better and regulators require less stringent abatement. When a program like the ARP allows trading, abatement moves from high- to low-abatement-cost sites. This is cost-effective for the utilities, but means that emissions move from low-cost sites to those facing higher costs. In effect, rural plants start to control their emissions more, while urban plants do less. However, if it so happens that marginal damages are higher in urban areas where abatement costs are higher (and lower where costs are lower), the net effect will be an increase in damage, because emissions are migrating toward higher abatement cost sites (Henry et al., 2011). Simply put, emissions trading allows urban power plants to lower their pollution control levels, thereby exposing more people to increased pollution. Since urban residents often already face worse air quality than their rural counterparts, the ARP could be, ironically, leading to poorer public health.

Furthermore, should the Acid Rain Program even get so much credit for reducing acid deposition when railroad deregulation prompted power plants to buy low-sulfur coal from western mines? Schmalensee and Stavins argue that deregulation, not the ARP's tradable permits experiment, was responsible for emissions reductions of "...about one third in the early years" (p.7) (see Figure 3.1, showing emissions changes after deregulation occurred).

The ARP undeniably spurred technological innovation. Although many power plants complied with the acid rain program simply by switching to low-sulfur Western coal, many others invested in superior pollution control equipment. Writing in 1981, when sulfur scrubbers were much less advanced, Bruce Ackerman and William Hassler pointed out that "...early scrubbers were prone to frequent breakdown – operating less than half the time" (Ackerman and Hassler, 1981, p. 16). Conditions in the exhaust systems of power plants were very harsh; there might be frequent variations in sulfur content and chlorine impurities, rendering the scrubbing process itself a moving target. By the early 1990s, the average sulfur removal rate rose only to about 85 percent.

All that changed with sulfur allowances and the acid rain program's tradable permit system. Now utilities could save money or even earn greater profits by having more allowances than their facilities needed. Better scrubbing meant lower emissions; lower emissions meant more allowances to sell. That simple incentive changed the kinds of innovations equipment vendors sought. Under the command-and-control approach employed prior to 1990, most new plants had to install scrubbers that would achieve 90 percent sulfur reductions. They were thus motivated to reduce operating costs, not scrubbing rates. After 1990, patent activities show vendors innovating more on sulfur removal rates than on operating costs, since every additional percent of sulfur a power plant could remove translated into not only compliance, but additional emissions allowances. Any surplus allowances could be sold or banked for future use (Popp. 2003). Today's new scrubbers achieve 96–98 percent removal. Those gains may not seem like much, but in the early 1990s, power plants in the ARP were emitting 10+ million tons of SOx, so a 10 percent scrubbing improvement translates into one million tons per year.

In 1988 and early 1989, as Congress debated the new acid rain provisions for an amended Clean Air Act, legislators ended up targeting a 50 percent reduction in SOx emissions, but not because of any environmental science or critical load. Members of Congress from New England introduced scores of bills designed to deal with acid rain between 1980 and 1988; however, these were going nowhere. When Senator George Mitchell, from Maine, took over as majority leader from West Virginia Senator Robert Byrd, Senate leadership went from a coal-producing state to an acid deposition-receiving state. President George H. W. Bush was also from Maine and favorably disposed towards addressing the acid rain problem. Adding favorably to the geographic politics, Representative Phil Sharp (D-IN), then chair of the House Energy and Power subcommittee, brought along not only a powerfully supportive voice from an emissions-sending state, but also a government professor's sensibilities and attentiveness to evidence (McLean, 2013). Ultimately, the 50 percent reductions number was selected because it was the larger of the percentages sought in the various bills making their way through committee in 1988–89, and had crucial environmentalist support from the Environmental Defense Fund. The utilities were not happy about a cap on emissions, but as long as many facilities were covered and the new law offered greater flexibility for compliance (e.g., by scrubbing emissions, buying low-sulfur coal or buying allowances), they were willing to go along (McLean, 2013; Chan et al., 2012).

Brian J. McLean, the former director of EPA's Office of Atmospheric Programs, pointed out that, shortly after the CAAA was passed, staff learned that 50 percent SO_2 reductions would not be enough to recover aquatic ecosystems in the Northeast. Subsequently, Senator Daniel Patrick Moynihan (D-NY) introduced a bill for another 50 percent SO_2 reduction, but it was 1999. Going into a general election, the Clinton Administration didn't support the bill. Several years later, President George W. Bush's Clear Skies proposal had a 65 percent SO_2 reduction (on top of the original 50 percent), but the bill floundered with environmentalists seeking to include CO_2 while industry wanted to repeal new source review rules (McLean, 2013).

The data on utilities and evidence from decades of environmental science show us that first, the ARP, along with railroad deregulation, successfully reduced emissions (especially of SO_2) by almost the theoretical maximum. Second, large, further reductions are required for environmental and public health – this is the US Environmental Protection Agency's conclusion and its justification for the Cross State Air Rule. Third, the power generation industry will not be able to meet the Cross State Air Rule's new requirements without retiring a large amount of coal-fired capacity. Fourth, rules limiting CO2 emissions from large new power plants to 1,100 pound of CO2 per megawatt-hour are too onerous for coal-fired generation without very costly and largely unproven carbon sequestration technologies. Consequently, a sizable percentage of the nation's power generation capacity will switch from coal to natural gas, with unknown and potentially serious environmental consequences, given potential contamination from gas extraction methods.

The ARP and the Cross State Air Rule thus illustrate two forms of environmental regulation failure: reaching the end-of-pipe limits (i.e., it's technologically impossible for the existing coal-fired capacity to reduce emissions enough, at least at a remotely affordable cost) and potential unintended consequences (the air and water pollution associated with natural gas obtained through hydro-fracking).

Ecosystems of the Appalachians and Adirondacks may some day recover from decades of acid deposition, once again supporting large, diverse and resilient aquatic and terrestrial biotic communities. But the finish line will not be reached through end-of-pipe measures. By the time congressional staffers and biogeochemists could figure out critical acid deposition loads for the eastern US, much environmental damage had been done and the political window for doing more intervention had closed tightly. End-of-pipe abatement rules from the 1970s to the 1990s acted like a kind of ratchet. With each click, new standards specified tighter emissions limits for more kinds of pollutants, while the network of actors in this policy system became further committed to existing pollution control regimes. Only the fortuitous convergence of further human health-related rules (CAIR), new rules controlling a "new" pollutant (carbon dioxide) and new natural gas supplies will unseat King Coal and eventually ease the acid rain problem in the US.

In terms of policy design, carbon dioxide emissions limits and hydro-fracking will have achieved the same as a ban, by completely replacing coal – the dirty input – with natural gas, the cleaner substitute. But the US natural gas boom will offer only a pyrrhic victory for environmental quality if hydro-fracking causes another, less desirable substitution, namely surface and groundwater contamination for better air quality. Whether this happens depends in part on how well regulators design non-point source pollution controls, a subject to which we turn in Chapter 4.

REFERENCES

Ackerman, B. and W. Hassler (1981). *Clean Coal/Dirty Air: or How the Clean Air Act Became a Multibillion-Dollar Bail-Out for High-Sulfur Coal Producers.* New Haven, CT, Yale University Press.
American Coal Ash Association (ACAA) (2012). "2011 Coal Combustion Product (CCP) Production & Use Survey Report." Farmington Hills, MI, ACAA.

Ard, E., P. Tesoriero, et al. (2010). "New Clean Air Rules Take Markets on a Detour." *Evolution Markets* 39.

Baldigo, B., G. Lawrence, et al. (2009). "Impacts of Acidification on Macroinvertebrate Communities in Streams of the Western Adirondack Mountains, New York, USA." *Ecological Indicators* 9(2): 226–239.

Becker, R. A. (2005). "Air Pollution Abatement Costs under the Clean Air Act: Evidence from the PACE Survey." *Journal of Environmental Economics and Management* 50(1): 144–169.

Black & Veatch (2010). "What will be the North American Energy Industry's 'New Normal?'" Webinar, 17 November.

Blett, T. F., J. A. Lynch, et al. (2014). "FOCUS: A Pilot Study for National-Scale Critical Loads Development in the United States." *Environmental Science and Policy* 38: 225–236.

Bradley, M., S. Tierney, et al. (2011). "Ensuring a Clean, Modern Electric Generating Fleet while Maintaining Electric System Reliability." Concord, MA, M. J. Bradley & Associates. Accessed at http://www.mjbradley.com/sites/default/files/MJBAandAnalysisGroupReliabilityReportAugust2010.pdf.

Burns, D., T. Blett, et al. (2008). "Critical Loads as a Policy Tool for Protecting Ecosystems from the Effects of Air Pollutants." *Frontiers in Ecology and the Environment* 6(3): 156–159.

Burns, D. A., J. A. Lynch, et al. (2011). "National Acid Precipitation Assessment Program Report to Congress 2011: An Integrated Assessment." U. E. C. A. M. Div. Washington, DC, National Science and Technology Council: 114.

Celebi, M., F. Graves, et al. (2010). "Potential Coal Plant Retirements under Emerging Environmental Regulations." The Brattle Group, Inc. Accessed at http://www.brattlegroup.com/_documents/UploadLibrary/Upload898.pdf.

Chan, G., R. Stavins, et al. (2012). "The SO2 Allowance Trading System and the Clean Air Act Amendments of 1990: Reflections on Twenty Years of Policy Innovation." National Bureau of Economic Research. Accessed at http://www.nber.org/papers/w17845.

Commoner, B. (1987). "A Reporter at Large: The Environment." *The New Yorker*. New York, NY. 15 June 1987: 46.

Crooks, E. (2010). "Wave of Closures Set to Hit US Coal Stations." *Financial Times*, 18 October.

Davenport, C. (2014). "Justices Back Ruling Limiting Coal Pollution." *The New York Times*, 30 April. New York, NY.

Davies, J. C. and J. Mazurek (1998). *Pollution Control in United States: Evaluating the System*. Washington, DC, RFF Press.

Deutsche Bank Climate Change Advisors (2010). "Natural Gas and Renewables: A Secure Low Carbon Future Energy Plan for the United States. Deutsche Bank Group." Accessed at http://www.coga.org/pdf_studies/NaturalGasAndRenewablesExecSumm.pdf.

Dewan, S. (2008). "Coal Ash Spill Revives Issue of its Hazards." *The New York Times*, 24 December. New York, NY.

Dickerman, J. and M. Sewell (2007). "Is it Time to Rethink SO2 Control Technology Selection?" *Power Engineering* 111(11): 132–135.

Driesen, D. and A. Sinden (2009). "The Missing Instrument: Dirty Input Limits." *Harvard Environmental Law Review* 33(1): 65–116.

Driscoll, C. T., C. P. Cirmo, et al. (1996). "The Experimental Watershed

Liming Study: Comparison of Lake and Watershed Neutralization Strategies." *Biogeochemistry* 32(3): 143–174.

Driscoll, C. T., Y. Han, et al. (2007b). "Mercury Contamination in Forest and Freshwater Ecosystems in the Northeastern United States." *BioScience* 57(1): 17–28.

Driscoll, C. T., K. F. Lambert, et al. (2007a). "Acidic Deposition: Sources and Ecological Effects," in *Acid in the Environment: Lessons Learned and Future Prospects*. G. R. Visgilio and D. M. Whitelaw (Eds.). New York, NY, Springer Science+Business Media.

Driscoll, C. T., G. B. Lawrence, et al. (2001). "Acid Rain Revisited: Advances in Scientific Understanding Since the Passage of the 1970 and 1990 Clean Air Act Amendments." *A Science Links Publication*, Hubbard Brook Research Foundation.

Duarte, H., L. Pardo, et al. (2013). "Susceptibility of Forests in the Northeastern USA to Nitrogen and Sulfur Deposition: Critical Load Exceedance and Forest Health." *Water, Air, & Soil Pollution* 224(2): 1–21.

Effler, S. W., G. C. Schafran, et al. (1985). "Partitioning Light Attenuation in an Acidic Lake." *Canadian Journal of Fisheries and Aquatic Sciences* 42(11): 1707–1711.

Eggers, D., K. Cole, et al. (2010). "Growth from Subtraction: Impact of EPA Rules on Power Markets." Credit Suisse. Accessed at http://op.bna.com/env.nsf/id/jstn-8actja/$File/suisse.pdf.

Evolution Markets (2010). "EPA Proposes Interstate Emissions Transport Rule." Accessed 6 July at http://www.evomarkets.com/desks/emissions/post/5719.

Fichthorn, N. W. and E. C. C. Clements (2010). "Fixing CAIR: EPA Embarks on a New Rulemaking for Interstate Pollution." *Natural Resources & Environment*, 24(4): 12–15. American Bar Association. Accessed at http://www.hunton.com/files/Publication/5051a1df-52fc-44c9-9ee5-4116e8e79b5b/Presentation/PublicationAttachment/bbb014cd-7082-4b7f-a2db-931942da09d0/Fixing_CAIR_4.10.pdf.

Greaver, T., T. Sullivan, et al. (2012). "Ecological Effects of Nitrogen and Sulfur Air Pollution in the US: What Do We Know?" *Frontiers in Ecology and the Environment* 10: 365–372.

Haeuber, R. (2011). Chief, Assessments and Communications Branch, Clean Air Markets Division, US EPA, personal communication.

Harrington, W., R. D. Morgenstern, et al. (2000). "On the Accuracy of Regulatory Cost Estimates." *Journal of Policy Analysis and Management* 19(2): 297–322.

Henry, D., N. Muller, et al. (2011). "The Social Cost of Trading: Measuring the Increased Damages from Sulfur Dioxide Trading in the United States." *Journal of Policy Analysis and Management* 30(3): 598–612.

Herrick, C. and D. Jamieson (1995). "The Social Construction of Acid-Rain – Some Implications for Science Policy Assessment." *Global Environmental Change – Human and Policy Dimensions* 5(2): 105–112.

Islas, J. and G. Grande (2008). "Abatement Costs of SO2-Control Options in the Mexican Electric-Power Sector." *Applied Energy* 85(2–3): 80–94.

Jaffe, S. D., A. P. Kahn, et al. (2010). "EPA Proposes Transport Rule to Address Interstate Air Pollution. Foley Hoag LLP News and Resources." Accessed 13 July at http://www.foleyhoag.com/publications/alerts-and-updates/2010/july/epa-proposes-transport-rule-to-address-interstate-air-pollution.

Janetos, A. (2007). "Lessons Learned from the Acid Deposition Research

Experience: An Historical Perspective," in *Acid in the Environment: Lessons Learned and Future Prospects*. G. R. Visgilio and D. M. Whitelaw (Eds.). New York, NY, Springer Science+Business Media.

Kaplan, S. M. (2010). "Displacing Coal with Generation from Existing Natural Gas-Fired Power Plants." Congressional Research Service. Accessed at http://assets.opencrs.com/rpts/R41027_20100119.pdf.

Kaushal, S. S., G. E. Likens, et al. (2013). "Increased River Alkalinization in the Eastern U.S." *Environmental Science and Technology* 47: 10302–10311.

Kehoe, T. (1992). "Merchants of Pollution?: The Soap and Detergent Industry and the Fight to Restore Great Lakes Water Quality, 1965–1972." *Environmental History Review* 16(3): 21–46.

Keller, A. (2010). "Credibility and Relevance in Environmental Policy: Measuring Strategies and Performance among Science Assessment Organizations." *Journal of Public Administration Research and Theory* 20(2): 357–386.

Lange, I. and A. Bellas (2006). "Policy Innovation Impacts on Scrubber Electricity Usage." National Center for Environmental Economics.

Library of Congress. Environment, N. R. P. D. and United States. Congress. Senate. Committee on Environment Public Works (1993). "The Legislative History of the Clean Air Act Amendments of 1990, Together with a Section-by-Section Index, U.S. Senate." Washington, DC, US Government Printing Office, Supt. of Docs., Congressional Sales Office.

Likens, G. E., D. C. Buso, et al. (2005). "Long-Term Relationships between SO2 and NOx Emissions and SO42- and NO3- Concentration in Bulk Deposition at the Hubbard Brook Experimental Forest, New Hampshire." *Journal of Environmental Monitoring* 7(10): 964–968.

Lovett, G. M., T. H. Tear, et al. (2009). "Effects of Air Pollution on Ecosystems and Biological Diversity in the Eastern United States." *Annals of the New York Academy of Sciences* 1162 (Year in Ecology and Conservation Biology 2009): 99–135.

M. J. Bradley & Associates (2011). "MJ Bradley & Co-Authors Report Showing Electric Power Industry Can Maintain System Reliability While Reducing Air Pollution Emissions." Accessed at http://www.mjbradley.com/news_20100809_00.html.

McGuire Woods Consulting (2010). "Beyond CAIR: EPA Proposes Tough New Transport Rules." Legal Updates, McGuire Woods LLC. Accessed 3 August at http://www.mcguirewoods.com/Client-Resources/Alerts/2010/8/Beyond-CAIR-EPA-Proposes-Tough-New-Transport-Rules.aspx.

McLean, B. (2013). Former Director Office of Atmospheric Programs, US Environmental Protection Agency, personal communication.

McPhee, J. (2007). *Uncommon Carriers*. New York, NY, Farrar, Straus, and Giroux.

Miller, M. (2013). "2012 Minerals Yearbook: Lime." US Department of the Interior, United States Geological Survey. Accessed at http://minerals.usgs.gov/minerals/pubs/commodity/lime/myb1–2012-lime.pdf.

Miller, P. (2013). "A Primer on Pending Environmental Regulations and their Potential Impacts on Electric System Reliability." Boston, MA, Northeast States for Coordinated Air Use Management.

Mitchell, M., G. Lovett, et al. (2011). "Comparisons of Watershed Sulfur Budgets in Southeast Canada and Northeast US: New Approaches and Implications." *Biogeochemistry* 103: 181–207.

Monteith, D., J. Stoddard, et al. (2007). "Dissolved Organic Carbon Trends Resulting from Changes in Atmospheric Deposition Chemistry." *Nature* 450: 537–540.

Morris, L. (2010). "EPA Transport Rule Sets Fast-Track for Compliance." *Power-Gen Worldwide*. Accessed 8 July at http://www.power-eng.com/articles/2010/07/epa-emissions.html.

Morris, L. (2011). "Is Coal-Fired Generation Ready to Face Retirements?" *Power Engineering*. February 1. Accessed at http://www.power-eng.com/articles/print/volume-115/issue-2/features/is-coal-fired-generation-ready-to-face-retirements.html.

National Petroleum Council (NPC) (2007a). "Hard Truths: Facing the Hard Truths about Energy." Accessed at http://www.npchardtruthsreport.org/.

National Petroleum Council (NPC) (2007b). "Electric Generation Efficiency." National Petroleum Council. Accessed at http://www.npc.org/study_topic_papers/4-dtg-electricefficiency.pdf.

Nelson, G. (2010). "EPA Unveils Rules on Smog-Forming Emissions from Power Plants." *The New York Times*, 7 July. New York, NY.

Newell, R., W. Pizer, et al. (2003). *Estimating the Gains to Emission Trading*. Washington, DC, Resources for the Future.

Nilsson, J. and P. Grennfelt (1988). "Critical Loads for Sulphur and Nitrogen. Miljorapport." Stockholm, Sweden, Nordic Council of Ministries.

North American Electric Reliability Corporation (2010). "Special Reliability Assessment: Resource Adequacy Impacts of Potential U.S. Environmental Regulations."

Pardo, L. H., M. E. Fenn, et al. (2011). "Effects of Nitrogen Deposition and Empirical Nitrogen Critical Loads for Ecoregions of the United States." *Ecological Applications* 21(8): 3049–3082.

Popp, D. (2003). "Pollution Control Innovations and the Clean Air Act of 1990." *Journal of Policy Analysis and Management* 22(4): 641–660.

Pratson, L. F., D. Haerer, et al. (2013). "Fuel Prices, Emission Standards, and Generation Costs for Coal vs Natural Gas Power Plants." *Environmental Science and Technology* 7(47): 4926–4933.

Quiñones, M. (2013a). "As Recycling Tonnage Falls, Industry Blames EPA." *Greenwire*, 15 November.

Quiñones, M. (2013b). "Use for Power Generation Continues to Rise." *Greenwire*, 11 July.

Richardson, N. (2010). "Death of Cap and Trade?" Weathervane: A climate policy blog from Resources for the Future. *Resources for the Future*.

Salisbury, B., M. de Croisset, et al. (2010). "Coal Retirements in Perspective – Quantifying the Upcoming EPA Rules." FBR Capital Markets. Accessed 13 December at http://www.jlcny.org/site/attachments/article/388/coal1.pdf.

Schmalensee, R. and R. Stavins (2013). "The SO$_2$ Allowance Trading System: The Ironic History of a Grand Policy Experiment." *Journal of Economic Perspectives* 27(1), Winter.

Shavel, I. and B. Gibbs (2010). "A Reliability Assessment of EPA's Proposed Transport Rule and Forthcoming Utility MACT." Washington, DC, Charles River Associates. Accessed 16 December at http://www.lexecon.co.uk/upload-edFiles/Publications/CRA-Reliability-Assessment-of-EPA%27s-Proposed-Transport-Rule.pdf.

Shuster, E. (2012). "Tracking New Coal-Fired Power Plants, National Energy Technology Laboratory." Accessed at http://www.netl.doe.gov/coal/refshelf/ncp.pdf.

Srivastava, R. K., N. Hutson, et al. (2006). "Control of Mercury Emissions from Coal-Fired Electric Utility Boilers." *Environmental Science and Technology* 40(5): 1385–1393.

Sullivan, B., J. Cosby, J. R. Webb, R. L. Dennis, A. J. Bulger and F. A. Deviney Jr. (2008). "Streamwater Acid-Base Chemistry and Critical Loads of Atmospheric Sulfur Deposition in Shenandoah National Park, Virginia." *Environmental Monitoring and Assessment*, 13: 85–99.

The INGAA Foundation, Inc. (2010). "Coal-Fired Electric Generation Unit Retirement Analysis." Accessed 10 June at http://www.ingaa.org/Foundation/Foundation-Reports/Studies/10369/10372.aspx.

Union of Concerned Scientists (UCS) (2011). "A Risky Proposition: The Financial Hazards of New Investments in Coal Plants." Accessed 9 March at http://www.ucsusa.org/clean_energy/smart-energy-solutions/decrease-coal/financial-hazards-of-coal-plant-investments.html.

United States Bureau of Land Management (2012). "Powder River Basin Coal." Accessed at http://www.blm.gov/wy/st/en/programs/energy/Coal_Resources/PRB_Coal.html.

United States Department of Labor (2000). "Regulations Implementing the Federal Coal Mine Health and Safety Act of 1969, as Amended." Federal Register: 79920–80107.

United States Energy Information Administration (2012). "Coal Transportation Rates to the Electric Power Sector." Accessed at http://www.eia.gov/coal/transportationrates/trend-coal.cfm.

United States Energy Information Administration (EIA) (2013). "How Large are US Coal Reserves?" Accessed at http://www.eia.gov/tools/faqs/faq.cfm?id=70&t=2.

United States Energy Information Administration (EIA) (2013b). "Coal 2013." Accessed at http://www.eia.gov/coal/.

United States Environmental Protection Agency (2009). "Acid Rain and Related Programs: 2008 Emission, Compliance, and Market Analyses. Acid Rain Program." Accessed at http://www.epa.gov/airmarkt/progress/ARP_2008_ECM_Analyses.pdf.

United States Environmental Protection Agency (2009). "Acid Rain and Related Programs: 2008 Emission, Compliance, and Market Analyses – Spreadsheet with Data." Accessed at http://www.epa.gov/airmarkt/progress/ARP09_2.html.

United States Environmental Protection Agency (2009). "Acid Rain and Related Programs: 2008 Environmental Results – Spreadsheet with Data."

United States Environmental Protection Agency (2009). "Acid Rain and Related Programs: 2008 Highlights."

United States Environmental Protection Agency (2009). "Appendix A: Acid Rain Program – Year 2008 SO2 Allowance Holdings and Deductions."

United States Environmental Protection Agency (2010). "Acid Rain and Related Programs: 2009 Emission, Compliance, and Market Analyses."

United States Environmental Protection Agency (2010). "Acid Rain and Related Programs: 2009 Emission, Compliance, and Market Analyses – Spreadsheet with Data."

United States Environmental Protection Agency (2010). "Acid Rain and Related Programs: 2009 Environmental Results."

United States Environmental Protection Agency (2010). "Acid Rain and Related Programs: 2009 Environmental Results – Spreadsheet with Data."

United States Environmental Protection Agency (2010). "Acid Rain and Related Programs: 2009 Highlights – 15 Years of Results, 1995–2009."

United States Environmental Protection Agency (2010). "Acid Rain and Related Programs: 2009 Highlights – 15 Years of Results, 1995–2009 – Spreadsheet with Data."

United States Environmental Protection Agency (2010). "Fact Sheet: Proposed Transport Rule Would Reduce Interstate Transport of Ozone and Fine Particle Pollution."

United States Environmental Protection Agency (2011). "Fact Sheet: Proposed Mercury and Air Toxics Standards."

United States Environmental Protection Agency (2011). "Reducing Toxic Air Emissions from Power Plants: Regulatory Actions."

United States Environmental Protection Agency (2011). "Regulatory Impact Analysis of the Proposed Toxics Rule: Final Report."

United States Environmental Protection Agency (2012). "Clean Power Plants." Accessed at http://www.epa.gov/hg/control_emissions/decision.htm.

United States Environmental Protection Agency (2013). "Clean Air Interstate Rule, Acid Rain Program, and Former NOx Budget Trading Program Environmental and Health Results Report." Washington, DC.

United States Environmental Protection Agency (2014a). "2012 Progress Report: Clean Air Interstate Rule, Acid Rain Program and Former NOx Budget Trading Program." Accessed 23 June 2014 at http://www.epa.gov/airmarkets/progress/ARPCAIR12_02.html.

United States Environmental Protection Agency. (2014b). "Carbon Pollution Standards." Accessed at http://www2.epa.gov/carbon-pollution-standards.

United States Government Accountability Office (2011). "Air Quality: Information on Tall Smokestacks and Their Contribution to Interstate Transport of Air Pollution." Washington, DC.

University of Massachusetts, Political Economy Research Inistitute, J. Heintz, et al. (2011). "New Jobs, Cleaner Air: Employment Effects under Planned Changes to the EPA's Air Pollution Rules, Ceres." Accessed at http://www.eenews.net/assets/2011/02/08/document_gw_01.pdf.

Vijay, S., J. F. DeCarolis, et al. (2010). "A Bottom-Up Method to Develop Pollution Abatement Cost Curves for Coal-Fired Utility Boilers." *Energy Policy* 38(5): 2255–2261.

Walke, J. (2010). "EPA Proposes Rule to Cut Smog and Soot Pollution from Power Plants in the Eastern and Midwestern US." Switchboard: NRDC staff blog.

Weathers, K. C. and G. M. Lovett (1998). "Acid Deposition Research and Ecosystem Science: Synergistic Successes" in *Successes, Limitations, and Frontiers in Ecosystem Science*. M. L. Pace and P. M. Grossman (Eds.). New York, NY, Springer-Verlag.

Wentz, J. (2010). "The EPA's Proposed Transport Rule: Implications for Climate Change Regulation." Center for Climate Change Law, Columbia Law School. Accessed 28 July at http://blogs.law.columbia.edu/climatechange/2010/07/28/the-epas-proposed-transport-rule-implications-for-climate-change-regulation/.

Wines, M. (2013). "A Push Away from Burning Coal as an Energy Source." *The New York Times*, 14 November. New York, NY.

4. Failure when there is no pipe

The [Clean Water Act's] technology standards – despite their subsequent compromises, litigation delays, loopholes, and enforcement lapses – worked remarkably well. What no one anticipated was that nonpoint sources would come along to eat up the gains. – Oliver Houck.

INTRODUCTION

The lead federal law controlling water pollution, the Clean Water Act of 1972, has often been praised for its ambitious application of technology standards and waste discharge permits, along with federal largesse. This chapter shows that the Act launched a successful regulatory program for reducing point-source discharges of easily controlled water effluent (i.e., organic wastes and solids), but that too many of the United States' waters remain polluted by nonpoint sources or degraded by dredging and filling.

Nonpoint water pollution sources – urban development, agriculture, logging, mines – now impair the nation's waterways far more than point sources. US waters are literally overwhelmed with toxic chemicals (including pesticides, herbicides and nutrients from fertilizers), metals and sediments, along with nitrates and fecal coliform bacteria from concentrated animal feedlot operations (CAFOs) (Andreen, 2004; Duhigg, 2010). For its failed efforts to control nonpoint sources, the Act has been scorned by environmentalists, while Congress has not responded to calls for reform in nearly 30 years. As in end-of-pipe regulation, nonpoint source water pollution regulation employs the compliance-abatement-mitigation approach, but with generally worse results. The Clean Water Act fails because it treats nonpoint sources as if they were *not sources* of pollution, focusing on how difficult it is to lay the blame for poor water quality on millions of diffuse sources rather than truly regulating them. True progress will require far more willingness to bring nonpoint source dischargers into the regulatory fold and much better information tying diffuse sources to water quality outcomes.

REGULATORY AMBITIONS FOLLOWED BY SLIPPAGE

In 1948, Congress addressed water pollution for the first time, passing the Water Pollution Control Act. This first federal effort asserted that water quality was the responsibility of the states – President Eisenhower would later say that water pollution was a "uniquely local blight" – but also authorized very modest federal sewage treatment loans to cities around the country. Each loan was capped at $250,000 with a 2 percent interest rate. Congress authorized a total of $90 million in subsidies for 1949–52, but few cities and states requested funds, so appropriations totaled only $3 million, ensuring that the law had little effect on sewage treatment capacity.

Municipal sewage plants right after World War II mostly treated to a primary standard, simple settling and screening of solids and removal of floating debris. Secondary treatment, in which the dissolved oxygen balance is restored, usually through anaerobic digestion along with some disinfection, had been developed and proven but served only one third of the US population (EPA, 2000). Tertiary treatment, which removes far more nitrogen and phosphorus, was nonexistent.

The 1948 Act did set in motion successful partnership programs between the states and the US Public Health Service by requiring the Surgeon General to partner with cities and states in planning sewage treatment programs and crafting uniform water pollution control laws. The Public Health Service and state partnerships were successful enough that Congress extended the 1948 activities into the mid-1950s. A 1955 Senate report credited the Water Pollution Control Act for spurring more than half the states to establish better pollution control legislation and water resource protection programs. And in a preview of technologies that would come 20 years later, the Senate noted that some municipalities were reacting to tough state water quality standards by requiring secondary sewage treatment, although this was not very widespread (Milazzo, 2006).

The law was amended again in 1956 (PL-84–660), with changes pushed through by Congressman John Blatnick (D-Minnesota), chairman of the House Rivers and Harbors Subcommittee. In his youth, Blatnick had worked for the Civilian Conservation Corps and saw how the New Deal had helped his constituents in Minnesota; he was a fan of federal spending for infrastructure in great part because of the benefits for local labor markets.

Blatnick was not an especially ardent environmentalist, and resisted suggestions to frame water pollution control as a public or environmental health issue rather than a vital economic input. He was concerned that water pollution might some day degrade valuable surface and ground-water resources that were needed more for higher purposes (drinking, irrigation) than as sinks for sewage. Blatnick thus sold his congressional colleagues on sewage treatment plants primarily as a public works issue, valuable for communities and labor in the same ways as were roads and schools (Milazzo, 2006).

The 1956 Act looked a lot more like a public works bill than previous versions. It authorized grants, rather than loans, for constructing waste-water treatment facilities, and Congress actually appropriated funding for the program, though not much. In contrast with the much more gener-ous, multi-billion dollar 1972 Clean Water Act, Congress earmarked only $150 million for the life of the program. Further cementing its pecuniary reticence, Congress also stipulated that no more than $50 million could be spent per year and that individual grants could not exceed 30 percent of the reasonable cost of construction, or $250,000, whichever was smaller (EPA, 2000). These were very modest sums, even by the standards of the day.

Congress struggled with tensions between state sovereignty and federal control in the 1956 Act. To obtain a sewage treatment grant, a project had to conform with plans prepared by state water pollution control agencies and approved by the Surgeon General. The Feds thus held a crucial veto.

The 1956 law's enforcement provisions revealed what would be lasting problems with this states-first approach to water quality. Congress only provided ". . .federal enforcement authority to interstate waters and tribu-taries thereof, excluding any watercourse that did not flow across or form part of state boundaries" (Milazzo, 2006). To file a claim against a water polluter required a lengthy, convoluted process.

First, the Surgeon General could only address pollution that endan-gered public health in a state other than that in which the discharge originated. The Surgeon General could then notify polluters and relevant state agencies, specifying how long a discharger could have to abate their pollutant releases. Next, the Surgeon General had the option of convening a public hearing board that could recommend "reasonable and equitable measures" to achieve abatement. If a polluter ignored the public hearing board's recommendations, the US Attorney General could bring suit against the polluter, but only if the state where the discharge originated gave its consent! "In sum," observes Paul Milazzo, "anyone seeking to enjoin a particular polluter on interstate waters faced a rather ponderous bureaucratic procedure, a state veto, and a considerable burden of proof before the judiciary. Carried through to the end, the entire process could take four years" (Milazzo, 2006, p. 20).

Although quite ineffective at reducing water pollution, federal water policy had remained unchanged, consisting of small financial incentives and a lot of pleading, for a generation. The modern era of federal water quality regulation began when President Nixon, in a rare departure from his usual endorsement of ambitious new environmental legislation, vetoed the Act. In a swift and nearly unanimous rebuke from Congress, his veto was overturned in one day. The President was spooked by the Clean Water Act's cost, no less than $24 billion in federal spending over five years for municipal sewage treatment plants, and an equivalent amount for industries to either pre-treat their wastes before sending them on to treatment facilities or building and running their own systems. The lure of federal money was backed up with a big stick: water pollution was henceforth illegal unless accompanied by a "national pollutant discharge elimination system" (NPDES) permit. And the law required rapid, ambitious compliance. New treatment plants were required to meet secondary waste treatment levels within five years. The maximum permissible loads for the secondary standards were 30 mg/L biochemical oxygen demand (BOD) and 30 mg/L totals suspended solids. BOD is a measure of how much oxygen is consumed by breaking down organic material from sewage, food processing, wood pulping and animal waste. Another way to state the secondary standard is that treatment must remove BOD by 85 percent.

Congress had good reasons to focus on sewage treatment. From the 1930s onward, cities around the country slowly, steadily built sewage treatment plants to handle mostly residential needs, but by 1972, close to a third of all Americans were still not served by publicly-owned treatment works (POTWs). Thousands of communities released raw sewage into the nation's waterways (US EPA, 2000). Only 29 percent of industrial facilities treated their wastewaters before releasing them to POTWs or the nation's river, lakes and coastal waters (US DOI, 1969).

Congress acted forcefully with its 1972 amendments (more commonly known as the Clean Water Act), which reinvigorated the feckless 1948 statute, and endowed the young Environmental Protection Agency (EPA) with broad new powers and far more water quality funding than it ever had before. For a few years, the Act worked as a classic pork barrel program, picking up the tab for 75 percent of municipal sewage plant construction costs in every nook and cranny of the country. The public investment amounted to $61 billion ($160 billion in 2014 dollars) in federal construction grants disbursed from 1972 to 1996 (US EPA, 2000) and another $27 billion ($45 billion in 2014 dollars) in low interest loans from 1988 to 2008 (US EPA, 2008a).

But the pork barrel was soon empty as the grants program fell victim to federal budget concerns. Between 1983 and 1995, federal largess dropped to 55 percent of wastewater treatment construction costs, then disappeared altogether by 1996. Today, revolving loan funds substitute for the generous construction grants.

In its 1977 amendments, Congress relaxed the secondary treatment requirements for POTWs discharging to oceans, thereby explicitly espousing a dubious (but very popular) maxim, "the solution to pollution is dilution." Congress was convinced that the nation's coastal zones are so vast that primary treatment provides protection enough, a sentiment no longer prevalent among elected officials, especially those from coastal states. Today, there are still 37 plants providing only primary treatment in coastal zones under what are termed 301(h) waivers. Most are relatively small. Perhaps the most controversial is San Diego's Point Loma facility, releasing 175 million gallons per day of effluent treated to the "advanced primary" standard.[1]

States wishing to push 301(h) facilities into secondary treatment face long, protracted battles as water regulators are forced to show why new findings regarding effluents' potential marine impacts justify overturning their own, earlier permits.

Congress last amended the Act in 1987, adding a new section for stormwater pollution prevention and control (§402(p)) that dramatically increased NPDES coverage – from 60,000 permitted POTWs and industrial point sources to 500,000 cities, campuses and industries in 11 separate categories (NAS, 2009). State water quality regulators could barely keep up with all these new permittees, many of whom hardly knew how to properly comply, so early results from the stormwater program were dismal (NAS, 2009). In Minnesota, from 2001–2007, builders either had no Construction Stormwater Permits (CSP), were late with their permits (or violated them), failed to include proper Best Management Practices (BMPs) and frequently neglected record-keeping requirements (Alsharif, 2010).

As if these new mandates were not enough, in 1988, President George H.W. Bush declared a new "no net loss policy" for the nation's wetlands, signaling his intention to invigorate the Clean Water Act's "dredge and fill" proscriptions under section 404. Section 404 prohibits draining and otherwise destroying wetlands without a permit. Permits, in turn, require mitigation or protection of new wetlands. Somehow the Act would, by presidential fiat, henceforth reverse annual losses of 50,000+ wetland acres

---

[1] Advanced primary treatment uses coagulants such as ferric chloride and organic polymers as settling agents for solids in wastewater. These coagulants make it possible for a treatment facility to remove more solids than the usual mechanical means that rely on settling and screening. Advanced primary treatment also captures some of the soluble organic matter that would normally pass through the first stage and thus require biological (secondary) treatment.

in the US. After 1989, presidents of both parties were largely silent regarding water quality issues.

THE CLEAN WATER ACT'S RECORD: POINT SOURCES

The Clean Water Act looks best if we focus on waste discharge permits for point sources, i.e., clean water policy *outputs* (regulations, permits, dollars spent, employees hired) rather than policy *outcomes* (dissolved oxygen, metals, sediment and nutrient loads, aquatic ecosystem health). The one, big exception is sewage effluent, which is treated so well that many "receiving waters" have indeed improved dramatically since 1972.

Aquatic species require dissolved oxygen (DO) to survive; water quality regulators commonly use 5.0 mg/L (higher for larvae and juvenile fish) as minimum safe DO levels. Although regulators seek healthy ambient DO levels, they write wastewater discharge permits (NPDES) in terms of BOD. Prior to the 1972 Act, municipal wastewater from both industrial and residential sources had so degraded major urban river systems and coastal zones – such as the Cuyahoga, Schuylkill, Monongahela, Allegheny and Chattahoochee Rivers and New York Harbor – that they routinely experienced fish kills (if they still supported fish at all). Dissolved oxygen (DO) levels in urban river systems before the 1972 CWA amendments averaged 1.0–4.0 mg/L.

No urban waters in the US had escaped these trends, so the CWA's first success was in nationalizing sewage treatment. EPA's latest data (from 2008) show that more Americans than ever are served by POTWs (226.4 million, or 73.7 percent of the population), secondary treatment (92.7 million or 30.2 percent) and greater than secondary treatment (113 million or 36 percent) (US EPA, 2008b). A negligible few release untreated sewage; some 37 primary treatment plants release to coastal waters.

All this treatment resulted in a lot more BOD load (a 35 percent influent increase between 1968 and 1996), but all this sewage was now going to treatment plants instead of surface waters. Moreover, treatment efficiencies improved tremendously throughout the 20th century, increasingly so after passage of the CWA (US EPA, 2000). By the late 1990s, many major urban river basins in the US exhibited extraordinary progress in DO levels. After conducting an exhaustive sampling effort in 2000, the EPA could conclude improvements at all spatial scales, including river reaches (which average ten miles in length), catalog units (the sampling name for watersheds) and major river basins. At each level, DO below POTW outfalls improved in 69–73 percent of samples, and "after the CWA; none of the major river basins had any statistically significant degradation in worst-case DO" (US EPA, 2000).

Moreover, the nation achieved these improvements at a reasonable cost, while actually contributing to the economic growth (Andreen, 2004). Indeed, the EPA recently estimated that "20,000 – 60,000 jobs are created for every $1 billion in federal investment in wastewater infrastructure" (US EPA, 2008a).

THE CLEAN WATER ACT'S RECORD: NONPOINT SOURCES

The Clean Water Act performs poorly when regulators turn ". . .their attention on incidental dischargers whose water pollution is usually unplanned, unpredictable, and indirect" (Drelich, 2007). These are non-point sources, and on nearly every available metric, trend data show that they degrade the nation's waterways more every year.

To make matters much worse, achieving clean water appears to be a rapidly moving target, which explains why Congress has heaped so many more mandates on the CWA. Take, for example, sediment pollution, typically released by urban stormwater, agriculture, logging and mining. The CWA and many state clean water laws prohibit any sediment releases that impair beneficial uses, but violators routinely express amazement when state regulators fine them for moving dirt around, since most people don't think of it as pollution. And yet, human activities are responsible for billions of tons of sediments released into US surface waters every year, resulting in disastrous aquatic habitat changes and drinking water impairment.

Increased urbanization and new land use practices add ever more sediments to water bodies each year. For example, Appalachian coal miners vastly increased their mountaintop mining and valley fill (MTM-VF) practices in the last twenty years (Copeland, 2013). Based on dredge-and-fill permits issued between 1992 and 2002, 1,944 km of headwater streams have been buried during that decade. The EPA estimated that this buried stream length doubled to almost 4,000 km in the following decade (EPA 2011).

In an unusually critical policy forum piece for *Science*, Palmer et al. called the CWA's posture toward MTM-VF a "failure of regulatory policy and enforcement" (Palmer et al., 2010). They noted that selenium concentrations in 73 of 78 West Virginia streams were above the 2 mg/L threshold for toxic bioaccumulation. Sulfate concentrations were similarly unacceptable; soils in mitigated sites typically contain less organic and nutrient content and allow for poor infiltration rates (Palmer et al., 2010). In its 2009 assessment, the EPA echoed all of these findings, concluding that MTM-VF permanently degraded springs and streams, and significantly damaged macro-invertebrate and fish communities (US EPA, 2011). A novel study linking the ecological integrity of West Virginia streams with human health found the highest cancer incidence with the most impaired streams, which were the ones located near coal mines (Hitt and Hendryx, 2010).

Blowing apart mountains to get at the coal, then filling up valleys with the overburden is dramatic, but pales in comparison to the stresses posed by urban stormwater. In its comprehensive review of stormwater pollution, the National Research Council could not be more forceful regarding the impacts of runoff: "Urban stormwater is listed as the primary source of impairment for 13 percent of all rivers, 18 percent of all lakes, and to 32 percent of all estuaries. Although these numbers may seem low, urban areas cover just three percent of the landmass of the United States, and so their influence is disproportionately large" (NRC, 2009, using year 2000 data). Urban stormwater carries pathogens, sediments and chemical toxins into urban waterways, wetlands and estuaries.

Even the nation's vast ocean resources are suffering terribly from non-point source pollution. Dead zones in the Gulf of Mexico (GOM) and other coastal oceans occur when excess nutrients cause waters (salt or fresh) to become oxygen depleted, or "eutrophied" (Howarth, 2008; Diaz et al., 2008; Robertson and Vitousek, 2009). Huge blooms of algae and vegetation die and become decomposed by microbes on the sea floor. This rapid and large-scale microbial respiration causes a reduction in dissolved oxygen levels. Death of bottom-dwelling organisms begins when dissolved oxygen falls below 2ml of O_2/liter (Diaz and Rosenberg, 2010). A dead zone has occupied the GOM since the 1970s, reaching its greatest extent in 2002, at 20,000 km^2 (Rabalias, 2007; EPA, 2013).

The size of the dead zone in the GOM is directly related to nutrient levels entering from the Mississippi River Basin, with the May-June nitrogen load explaining 47 percent of the variability in the size of the hypoxic zone (Bianchi et al., 2009). Agricultural fertilizer and manure use from Minnesota to the Gulf are responsible for the vast majority of nitrogen (N) and phosphorous (P) loading in the GOM, and over 65 percent of nutrients entering the GOM are from non-point sources (Brown et al., 2011; Bianchi et al., 2010).

Since 1985, scientists have been measuring the size of the hypoxic zone of the GOM. Recent calculations estimate that the average flux of nutrients into the GOM is 1.2 million metric tons of nitrogen and 0.15 million metric tons of phosphorous (Aulenbach et al., 2007). Total N fluxes into the GOM peaked in 1993 at over 1.6 million metric tones and total P fluxes have remained relatively constant (Aulenbach et al., 2007; Turner et al., 2007). The peak N fluxes in the early 1990s correspond with five years of above average size of the GOM dead zone from 1993–97 (EPA, 2013a).

July 2012 measurements showed the zone to be around 10,000 km^2 (EPA, 2013a). In 2012 it was significantly smaller than in previous years (only half its 2010 size) due to 2012 summer drought conditions in the Mississippi River Basin that limited stream-flow and nutrient flux into the GOM (EPA, 2013a). Even at this reduced size, the 2012 zone was still twice as large as the target set by the Mississippi River/Gulf of Mexico Watershed Task Force for the year 2015. To achieve a 5,000 km^2 zone by 2015, the Task Force's Action Plan calls for reducing the N load by 30 percent (Turner et al., 2007).

The water at US beaches is also generally quite poor. During the 2012 swimming season, contaminants caused over 20,000 days of beach closures or advisories in the nation's 30 coastal states. More than 80 percent of the beaches were closed because coastal waters exceeded public health standards for dangerous bacteria (NRDC, 2013). In 2008, coastal waters sickened ten percent of all beachgoers, according to the Centers for Disease Control and Prevention (Dorfman and Rosselot, 2009). Although fewer beaches get closed during drier rainy seasons, these numbers don't represent any significant improvement on recent years.

Water quality trends in rural areas show similar impairment. The proportion of hyper-eutrophic lakes, the most oxygen-depleted, declined from 49 percent of those surveyed in 1972 to 34.9 percent of those surveyed in 2007; however, lake eutrophication is still intractable. In 2007, 26.9 percent of lakes surveyed were classified as "eutrophied," up from 16 percent in 1972 (US EPA, 2009).

The EPA's carefully-designed wadeable streams assessment, conducted on 1,392 random shallow waterway sites between 2000 and 2004, estimated that 42 percent of US stream miles are in poor condition, 25 percent in fair and 28 percent in good condition. Wadeable streams provide unique habitat conditions, flood control functions and recreation. Major stressors include nitrogen, phosphorus and streambed sediment loads along with riparian disturbance (US EPA, 2006a). Streams receiving poor ratings barely support benthic macroinvertebrates, including the small creatures attached to rocks, clinging to woody debris or burrowed in waterway bottoms.

The nation's wetlands continue their long decline as well. The Corps's enforcement of "dredge and fill" permits under section 404 of the Act helped slow the rate of annual wetland loss in the US. Annual losses between 1986 and 1997 were 80 percent lower than in the previous 200 years, but "[G]iven more recent data on declines in area. . .and changes in type, it is clear that the nation is not meeting its policy goal of no net loss" (Zedler and Kercher, 2005, p. 46). Indeed, "no net loss" is only meaningful if one counts created wetlands and/or preserved, existing wetlands against wetland losses. The total wetland area within the US declined by about 62,300 acres between 2004 and 2009, with high losses among estuarine, marine and forested wetlands (Dahl 2011). Acreage losses are exacerbated by losses in wetland quality. Function and ecological health are even harder to maintain than area, and wetland function cannot be easily recaptured, even through restoration (Moreno-Mateos et al., 2012).

Water quality regulators respond to wetland loss through one of three basic policy options: avoidance, impact minimization or impact compensation. "Avoidance" in wetland terms is analogous to a dirty input limit or product ban: in other words, preventing the damage before it happens. It is the environmentally preferable alternative, of course, but also the least implemented option, falling far behind various forms of minimization or compensation.

Minimization and compensation most frequently employ some sort of damage mitigation. Mitigation options include restoring old wetlands, enhancing existing wetland functions, creating new wetlands, preserving existing wetlands, or some mix of all these choices (Gardner et al., 2009). In the early 2000s, Jessica Wilkinson and Mark Smith estimated that restoration, which varies enormously in effectiveness, was the most common type of mitigation nationwide (35 percent of total acres of mitigation), followed by enhancement (30 percent), creation (20 percent) and preservation (15 percent) (Wilkinson and Thompson, 2006).

Landowners and regulators both prefer "compensatory mitigation," in which permit applicants agree to some donation of existing or future wetland areas in exchange for permission to dredge and fill. Regulators can thereby focus on negotiations over the amount of compensation, which is much less contentious than denying a landowner's original request to destroy a wetland on their property (Robertson and Hough, 2011). Unfortunately, compensatory mitigation has a spotty record, according to the EPA's own Inspector General. In a sobering 2014 report, the Office of the Inspector General found that the nation's "no net loss" of wetlands was based on faulty assumptions, most notably by counting future restoration efforts in its projected wetland acreage totals without knowing how many actually succeed (Snider, 2014).

To make matters easier for permit applicants, a cottage industry in wetland mitigation banking sprang up in the last 30 years. In this arrangement, a private entrepreneur buys a parcel of land containing wetlands, such as vernal pools, bogs, fens or marshes. These wetlands may be restored or, as is the case with many vernal pools in California, already exist in a pristine state. After undergoing a multi-agency review led by the Corps, the wetland owner sells mitigation credits to other landowners wishing to dredge and fill wetlands on their properties, usually in an over-ratio of 1.8 or more preserved wetland acres to 1.0 destroyed wetland acre. With this transaction, 1.8 wetland acres remain where previously there were 2.8. Even though the 1.8 remaining acres enjoy strong legal protections, calling the mitigation "no net loss" means nothing. Moreover, if restored and newly-created wetlands do add to the nation's overall wetland acreage, they rarely add high-quality wetland functions, since most such efforts fail spectacularly (because plants die or pools dry out) or receive inadequate long-term management to ensure their viability into the future (Gardner et al., 2009).

NONPOINT SOURCE REGULATION IN ACTION: CALIFORNIA'S REGIONAL WATER BOARDS

In the Clean Water Act, Congress gave the EPA strong mandates but weak tools to control nonpoint source pollution stemming from every imaginable activity. At the heart of the CWA's nonpoint scope are the total daily maximum load (TMDL) requirements, implemented by the EPA and the states through sections (303(d)) and the stormwater programs in section (402(p). The Army Corps of Engineers (Corps) shares responsibility with EPA to limit and mitigate wetland losses (404). If the compliance, abatement and mitigation approach fares poorly with point sources, it achieves even worse results with nonpoint sources. Examining some of the nation's persistent nonpoint source water quality challenges illustrates just how tough it is, in practice, to successfully regulate these stressors using the tools that this country has employed for nearly a half-century.

From 2002 through 2008 I served California as a member of the Central Coast Regional Water Quality Control Board (hereinafter referred as the "Water Board"). Drawing on a progressive-era model, the state launched the water boards as part of the 1969 Porter-Cologne Act, a wide-ranging water quality bill named after its two legislative sponsors. Unlike most states, California is so vast that it elected to divide itself into nine water quality regions. Even so, most of the regional boards cover a large territory, generally distributed in ways that encompass major watersheds. In California's Central Coast area, the region 3 water board covers an area the size of Maryland, from the Santa Cruz-San Mateo county border in the north to as far south as the tip of Ventura County, about an hour and a half north of Los Angeles.

The US Environmental Protection Agency delegates to the states a great deal of implementation authority for the major pollution laws. The states, in turn, often regionalize environmental regulation. This all makes sense in a federalist system as a way of respecting state sovereignty, avoiding a huge, centralized bureaucracy and binding agency officials to their neighbors in the regulated community. The State Water Resources Control Board ("State Board") serves as the statewide oversight agency, with five appointed members. The State Board acts as a general policy-making body and quasi-appellate court.

The regional water quality control boards are independent regulatory commissions. As such, they are a peculiar, typically American institutional invention. Born out of the progressive era distrust of political cronies, the independent regulatory commission pairs administrative expertise with citizen oversight. A professional staff of civil servants writes and enforces water quality discharge permits, initiates compliance actions against violators and crafts watershed basin plans. Seven members of the public, appointed by the governor and ratified by the state Senate, hold much of the decision-making authority.

The regional water boards have quasi-judicial and -prosecutorial powers, which confer on them an unusual, hybrid mix of duties and authority. Usually, US political institutions scrupulously separate such functions. With their prosecutorial powers, staff can initiate enforcement actions (for administrative civil liability, not for criminal charges) without going to the district attorney. The appointed members serve in roles similar to those of administrative law judges. This arrangement allows the boards to move from quasi-indictment to penalties relatively quickly, but also draws fire for perceived conflicts of interest, since regional boards house staff acting as prosecutors as well as appointed members acting as judges.

TOTAL MAXIMUM DAILY LOADS (TMDLs)

The CWA's section 303(d) provides the Act's lead on nonpoint source controls through its TMDL requirements. As a huge state, California delegates TMDL implementation to its nine regional boards. In smaller states, environmental agencies retain the TMDL function on their own. When Congress wrote the 1972 CWA, states had grown used to a water quality standards approach to regulation that contrasted sharply with the technology-based approach adopted in the new Act. In the old approach, states determined the best uses of their waters, monitored water quality, and then abated pollution loads as necessary to reach preexisting goals. Technology standards started by specifying effluent limits and the processes or equipment needed to ensure that effluents are clean enough. In section 303 of the Clean Water Act, Congress retained a vestige of the old water quality approach (Houck, 2002).

To understand how the TMDL process works, let's consider the San Lorenzo River in Santa Cruz, California. The San Lorenzo originates in the Santa Cruz Mountains, flowing about 30 miles before it reaches the sea, bisecting the city at its mouth near the historic boardwalk. A major impairment source is sediment, so this illustration will focus on that pollutant even though this river, like many others, is also impaired by other stressors. Anthropogenic sediment loads in the San Lorenzo come from timber operations, farms, quarries, unpaved roads and construction sites bordering the river as it flows from forested mountains to the Pacific Ocean. Suspecting a nonpoint source-related impairment, water quality regulators launched a TMDL process that takes place in five steps.

First, state water regulators survey their waterways, including the San Lorenzo, on a host of indicators, typically including pathogens, mercury and other metals, fertilizers or other agricultural chemicals, sediment, oxygen depletion and dangerous chemicals such as polychlorobiphenyls (PCBs). Waters that cannot meet their beneficial uses through ordinary, point source effluent limitations, which are controlled with technology standards in NPDES permits, get added to the so-called 303(d) impaired waterways list. As of 2013, the states had come up with a list of about 41,500 impaired waters. Sediment is in the top five impairment causes identified in the 303(d) program, with 6,162 US water bodies listed as sediment impaired in 2013 (US EPA, 2013 TMDL program).

Second, regulators estimate how much sediment each source contributes to the upper San Lorenzo. This lengthy exercise requires careful study, modeling and historical review to derive pollutant load assessments. For the San Lorenzo sediment TMDL, the studies themselves sparked considerable controversy when they were completed in the early 2000s. The Santa Cruz Mountains are famous for their many fault lines and earthquakes. Because the top of the San Lorenzo watershed is constantly being frittered away into the river's many tributaries, everyone is inclined to blame sediment releases on natural processes instead of road use, logging or mining.

If the TMDL is for a mass load, it will specify the target levels in, say, tons. Regulators can also express the TMDL in terms of a concentration of some water pollutant, often equal to a water quality standard (Rose, 2013). Thus, the third step for agency officials developing a mass load TMDL is to assign a number of sediment tons that the San Lorenzo can handle on a daily basis without impairing its beneficial uses as habitat, drinking water and recreation. This number is the Total Maximum Daily

Load. By 2013, the states had adopted, and received approval for, nearly 50,000 TMDLs (EPA 2013).

Fourth, regulators must decide how much each sediment source must reduce in order to meet the TMDL. Fifth, and lastly, regulators must prompt the required reductions from responsible parties. At this crucial juncture, regulators can first try a "lighter, gentler" application of non-point source controls by merely requiring industries and other sources to adopt best management practices (BMPs), on the somewhat circular reasoning that if a sediment-control practice is truly a "best" one, the ensuing sediment releases will be tolerable or maybe even negligent. If self-implemented practices don't happen or don't work, regulators can take a second tack, possibly encouraging cities and counties to adopt innovations and demonstration projects. In the sediment case, this might mean novel stormwater and road erosion controls principally carried out by city or county officials.

A third, much tougher TMDL enforcement approach would specify not only numeric load reductions, but also *when* these had to be reached. In effect, this would mean requiring NPDES permits for nonpoint sources that had previously been granted waivers. What would such permits look like in the nonpoint source setting? Officials don't specify the means of compliance, but exert some influence by virtue of approving or denying proposed controls in a NPDES permit. Regulators might, for example, approve large riparian setbacks for logging operations and deny proposals to cut timber during winter, when storms cause the greatest erosion to hill-sides and riverbanks. Such measures could be accompanied by stringent and possibly expensive monitoring requirements, placing on dischargers the burden of proof that they have achieved reductions. In essence, a regu-latory body would treat nonpoint sources very much like point sources, complete with permits, technology standards, monitoring and reporting requirements.

The nation is very far from completing this five-step process. The best that can be said is that some states have developed many TMDLs, based on reasonably scientifically defensible impairment assessments, while many others are still dragging their feet. The basis for listing impaired waters varies tremendously from state to state, and in too many cases, states base assessments on poor and/or inadequate data (Keller and Cavallaro, 2008). The CWA gives the EPA little in the way of enforcement powers to compel states (Garovoy, 2003), while the courts are as likely to adopt an "any-progress-is-sufficient-progress" approach to TMDL development as they are to overturn EPA's approval of weak state plans (Seaburg, 2007).

A small handful of studies suggest that states and some industries have begun to implement TMDLs in ways that might improve water quality. Sampling 138 TMDLs in six states (Illinois, Indiana, Minnesota, Michigan, Ohio and Wisconsin), Norton et al. (2009) found that a little less than 80 percent of the TMDLs were partially implemented, but none at all in another 20 percent. Less than three percent of the sampled TMDLs were fully implemented.

As of 2013, the California State Water Resources Control Board analyzed about a fifth of the state's 180 approved TMDLs.[2] Of the 35 TMDLs assessed, only eight percent (three waterways) had achieved water quality targets. Another 40 percent showed improving conditions, 20 percent of the Board's assessments were inconclusive, and the remainder still needed much improvement (CA SWRCB, 2013). Similarly, a 2013 Government Accountability Office study that closely analyzed 25 long-established TMDLs found that most could not show that ". . .addressing identified stressors would help attain water quality standards" (US GAO, 2013). Half of the TMDLs were vague on what actions needed to be taken or by whom; two-thirds of the TMDLs lacked landowner participation and adequate funding (US GAO, 2013). The latter finding is especially damning, since EPA and the states generally lack authority to compel landowners responsible for nonpoint source pollution to take recommended actions.

It's exceptionally difficult to tell whether states have taken an aggressive approach to the fifth step – the one that actually results in improved water quality. That's partly because it is so hard to trace nonpoint source pollution back to its diffuse origins, but also because TMDLs generally rely on existing statutory tools to achieve their reductions. Those tools do a poor job delivering monitoring results that can connect ambient water quality to the actions of diffuse dischargers. In the case of sediment in the San Lorenzo River, the Water Board will try everything it can – including inaction – before requiring individual nonpoint source dischargers to obtain permits where none were required before. Doing so would mean writing permits for literally thousands of diffuse sources, a task well beyond the capacity of this agency.

Ultimately, the TMDL program fails because it cannot turn nonpoint sources into point sources without using the policy tools that worked so well for end-of-pipe problems. Congress never endowed the Clean Water Act with that authority. TMDLs emphasize ambient-based management, an approach that Oliver Houck points out ". . .has not worked well in any media. . .it requires enormous amounts of data. It requires analysis that is rarely definitive and nearly always litigable. It launches a process that

---

[2] California had established some 1,600 TMDLs, but only 180 were approved as of 2013.

never ends." (Houck, 2002). Potentially responsible parties vigorously fight all efforts to assign them with responsibility for discharges, and when they are "fingered," they appeal to courts, legislators and popular opinion for relief from what many consider unreasonable demands.

In 1999, the California legislature sought a way to improve on the awkward TMDL process by changing state law rather than attempting to modify how the regional boards implement the federal Clean Water Act. California lawmakers revisited a long-held assumption about the state Porter-Cologne Water Quality Control Act, that nonpoint sources should automatically be excluded from the Act's scope. Senate Bill 390 mandated that the regional boards examine the waivers they had so long granted to various nonpoint sources, including timber harvesting and agricultural operations. The state legislature did not actually require the regional boards to regulate nonpoint sources in the same way they governed sewage treatment plants and other point dischargers. Instead, the state instructed the regional boards to review their waivers and make new findings about nonpoint sources of water pollution. Those findings had to examine the degree to which nonpoint sources might be responsible for surface water quality impairments. The regional boards would then use the new findings, in turn, to *condition* the waivers of permits, also known as waste discharge requirements. A conditional waiver literally excuses a discharger from obtaining a waste discharge permit (WDR). Individual WDRs are so onerous and expensive that permittees will always prefer a conditional waiver, even if the conditions involve cumbersome BMPs, monitoring and reporting. Waivers would have to be renewed every five years.

In SB 390, the legislature steered a middle course between bringing the full weight of the permit process down on nonpoint source dischargers and the status quo ante, which consisted of a pass on requirements with any teeth. SB 390 created a lot of work for the Central Coast Board, especially in the areas of timber and agriculture.

Timber

The Central Coast Board took up timber waivers first. A little over 100,000 acres of commercial forest, primarily coast redwoods (*Sequoia sempervirens*), covers the Santa Cruz Mountains, just south of San Francisco. One commercial mill remains and a handful of commercial forest owners harvest modest amounts of timber, almost all of it redwood used for decking, siding and fencing. In recent years, loggers have cut some ten million board feet in Santa Cruz County, about a half percent of the state's annual totals (CA State Board of Equalization, 2013).

Redwoods are well adapted to California's foggy coast, collecting significant amounts of their moisture needs from fog drip. Redwoods are especially happy next to streams. Not only do they get more water; trees growing next to fish-bearing streams can receive surprising amounts of their nutrients from fish that have swung back upstream to spawn and die.[3]

Naturally, loggers like to harvest the big trees by the creeks, streams and rivers. Moreover, in a hilly setting, it's easier to build logging roads that closely hug watercourses in their valleys and gulches. Unfortunately, building logging roads and landings close to these water bodies can destabilize stream banks, causing landslides. Removing the trees at a stream's bank opens up the canopy, allowing more sunlight to fall directly on the water and raise its temperature. These activities jeopardize populations of anadromous fish, which need cool, clear water with woody debris that make good spawning beds possible.

Environmentalists and loggers are thus locked in a constant struggle over what happens at a water body's edge. Environmentalists would like to have wide riparian setbacks, maybe as far as 100–150 feet. Setbacks that wide on every creek, stream and river in Santa Cruz County would easily lock up 15 percent of available timberland, costing the industry upwards of $1 million per year.[4]

Regional boards thus have to balance seemingly incompatible values. All the water board's permit activity for nonpoint sources had to achieve similar water quality outcomes. To do so, the board's permits had to affect landowner behavior just enough to prevent water pollution, but no so much that they impose crushing costs. By and large, we can distinguish between more and less protective management practices – there really is a best way to cross a forest stream with a heavy vehicle. A properly installed bridge made out of a boxcar floor will almost always work better than a galvanized steel culvert set into the stream channel.

But the greater challenge lies in accountability to the public. How can

---

[3] James Helfield and Robert Naiman, both at the University of Washington, examined ratios of nitrogen isotopes in trees and shrubs bordering areas in two southeastern Alaska watersheds. Greater nitrogen 15 to nitrogen 14 ratios are associated with marine species. Helfield and Naiman were able to determine that up to 22–24 percent of foliar nitrogen in the Sitka spruce, ferns and Devil's club they measured came from marine derived nutrients (MDN) (Helfield and Naiman, 2001).

[4] I am indebted to Aaron Cole for these calculations. Using a vegetation layer of forests in Santa Cruz County, he identified 104 mi.² of timberland and 299 miles of streams. A 150-foot setback on these waterways would result in about 16 mi.² of unavailable timberland, about 15% of the total. Timber companies have logged about 10 million board feet, mostly redwood, from Santa Cruz forests in recent years. At a price of $700 per thousand board feet of redwood, losing 15 percent of available timber would result in $1,050,000 per year of foregone revenues.

the water board assure the public that permit holders did what they were required to do and that these required practices were adequately protective of water quality? Just as continuous emissions monitors are the gold standard for securing environmental data from smokestacks, we can imagine ideal ways of monitoring activity in the forest, the farm or the quarry.

Timber activity in the Santa Cruz Mountains is fairly small; about a dozen timber harvest plans come before the Water Board every year. The vast majority of these occur during the dry season, from about mid April to mid October. Imagine what it would take for a water quality regulator to attest, firsthand, that timber harvest activities were adequately protective of waterways. First, staff would need to participate on pre-harvest inspections, physically walking a proposed timber harvest site and providing input on roads, landings, actual trees to be cut and the like. If the public wished to have real time monitoring, that staff person would have to be present during the timber harvest as well. Timber harvest permits require post-harvest activities, so our hard-working staff person would have to be back a third time for a post-harvest inspection.

Our peripatetic regulator could now confirm whether best management practices had been followed. But more would be needed to actually tell whether water quality declined, improved or stayed the same after a timber harvest. In the geologically busy Santa Cruz Mountains, who is to say that any given pulse of sediment released into a creek, stream or river is caused by a timber harvest? At a minimum, one would have to measure turbidity upstream of a timber harvest and again downstream, ideally for some time before harvest activity begins so that baseline data can be gathered, then again during and after storm events. Presumably, a properly protective timber harvest would result in relatively insignificant differences between the upstream and downstream readings, all else being equal.

It's easy to take up- and down-stream readings on a calm, sunny day. With a modern, portable turbidity meter, anyone can grab a sample and get a reading within seconds. Unfortunately, doing so reveals very little about a timber harvest's potential impact on soils and streams. The real action comes during heavy rainstorms. That's when an unstable stream bank will slough off into the water or when a dirt road will wash out. In-stream turbidity measurements tell us the most if taken at the height of a rainstorm or shortly after the rainfall has peaked. This can be in the middle of the night, on a weekend or holiday and in hazardous conditions.

Since no one seriously proposed sending foresters or landowners out into the woods under hazardous conditions, the Water Board considered requiring some form of continuous, in-stream turbidity sensors that could automatically log water quality data. After an impressive presentation by Brian Dietterick, a forest hydrologist at the California Polytechnic University, San Luis Obispo, board staff and members dropped the idea of requiring each timber harvest to automate its water quality monitoring. Reporting on his studies of sediment releases into forest streams and creeks during rainstorms, Dietterick showed that 1) sediment monitoring is only informative if done during rainstorms, 2) in-stream data loggers do exist, but 3) they are expensive[5] and prone to damage. Ironically, automated equipment is most likely to be damaged by debris and rocks when the information is most needed, i.e., during storms.

Lacking the staff necessary to attend pre-harvest, harvest and post-harvest activities, the Water Board opted for a conditional waiver that relies heavily on best management practices and photo-documentation. The Board's regulatory program also tries to accommodate differences in forests sites and individual timber harvest plans. Logging on a steep slope or a part of the forest with a relatively large amount of surface water potentially can release more sediment than flatter, dryer areas. Similarly, a section of forest that has been extensively logged or otherwise disturbed is also more susceptible to erosion. Logging during the winter is inherently more disturbing for soils than in the summer, given coastal California's Mediterranean climate, so regulators may not grant permits for winter operations if slopes are too steep or soils unstable.

To accommodate all of these differences and to bring transparency and predictability to its waiver conditions, the Board set up four categories, or tiers (I-IV), into which any given timber harvest plan would fall. Moving from tier I to higher tiers, best management practices as well as monitoring and reporting requirements become more stringent (see Figure 4.1). At the highest tier (IV), landowners visually inspect their sites in order to demonstrate compliance, but also provide "forensic monitoring." In forensic monitoring, a discharger documents and reports instances of pollution contamination or nuisance. For example, if a stream crossing or culvert fails, the responsible landowner would have to report that to the Water Board immediately while taking steps to correct the problem. While a landowner could forego doing so, a subsequent inspection would result in very stiff penalties.

To provide certainty about what will be required of them, and some level of automaticity, permittees fill out worksheets determining their

---

[5] For example, a device commonly used by forest scientists interested in the relationship between land disturbance and water quality is an OBS-3+ sensor, distributed by Campbell Scientific. The sensor and associated data logger and cables easily cost $3,000 or more. Moreover, a proper before-and-after-impact analysis designed to isolate the sediment load from a specific timber harvest would likely require two or more continuous turbidity arrays in order to gauge the sediment contributions from upstream sources.

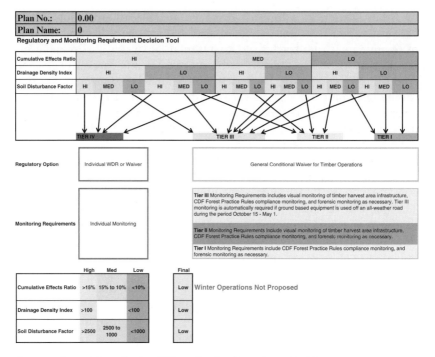

| Plan No.: | 0.00 |
| Plan Name: | 0 |

Regulatory and Monitoring Requirement Decision Tool

Source: Central Coast Regional Water Quality Control Board, 2012.

Figure 4.1   Central Coast Regional Water Quality Control Board timber harvest conditional waiver eligibility matrix

placement in one tier or the other. The "cumulative effects ratio" uses the size of the timber harvest plan (in acres), the number of acres harvested in the last five and 14 years, whether there is a 303(d) listed stream on site and so on. Similarly, the "drainage density index" is derived from the timber harvest slope and distance from streams. The "soil disturbance factor" has more to do with the type of logging operations than with site features. These kinds of scoring methods can show environmentalists and permittees how regulators arrive at their decisions, but are only as good as the data and underlying assumptions about soil erosion.

As of July 2012, Water Board staff had conducted onsite post-harvest inspections on 23 of the 61 enrolled THPs, concluding that BMPs were being well implemented (CCRWQCB, 2012, timber waiver staff report). That assessment was based on inspecting timber harvest sites long after logging was completed, not on water quality measurements during rain events. While there is no reason to doubt either a registered professional forester's

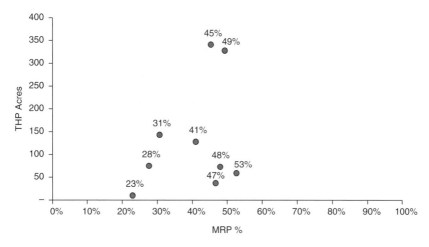

Figure 4.2   Distribution of sample sites used for revised monitoring tier determination

(RPF) or a Water Board staff member's competence, the timber waivers ultimately provide the public only with *post hoc*, indirect assessments. Therefore, the timber waiver remains very much a compliance- and BMP-based approach that does not generate replicable, high-quality data. This ensures that stakeholders will squabble over whatever evidence does exist instead of confidently assessing the timber waiver's successes and failures.

Agriculture

In contrast to its small timber industry, the Central Coast region hosts extensive, economically important agricultural activity. The region boasts some 435,000 acres of irrigated land (about 8 percent of the region's total area) farmed by about 3,000 different agricultural operations. The Water Board first adopted a general waiver of waste discharge requirements for agricultural operations in 2004.

In the months preceding adoption of the first agricultural waiver, farmers in the Central Coast were quite anxious. They had enjoyed an exemption from state and federal water quality regulations for decades; now it seemed that draconian measures might be imposed on all farms because of a few careless or inconsiderate operators. In public hearings and workshops, farmers impressed upon the board how economically marginal their operations were and how even the monitoring requirements could be prohibitive for any individual farm.

Perhaps mindful of how jarring these new regulations could be, the

Figure 4.3 — Summary of existing and revised eligibility criteria

Existing Criteria	Revised Criteria	Proposed Changes
Monitoring Tier Determination (Refer to Figure 8) |	High	Med	Low | Cumulative Effects Ratio	>15%	5% to 10%	<10% Drainage Density Index	>100		<100 Soil Disturbance Factor	>2500	2500 to 1000	<1000	**Monitoring Tier Determination** I — <35 % II — 36-45 % III — 46-55 % IV — >56%	**Monitoring Tier Determination** Existing Criteria: monitoring tier threshold formulation uses weighted values through a hierarchical set. Revised Criteria: Tiers based on analysis of statistical sample sites (Table 2). Formulation of submitted inputs assessed through an equally weighted criteria set.
Cumulative Effects Ratio (CER) Q1. Is proposed harvest in a 303(d) listed watershed?** ** "Watershed 303d listed as impaired from sediment or temperature? If yes type "yes" or leave blank. Q2. Acres proposed for harvest or harvested in planning watershed (CalWater) in last fifteen years (includes all acreage in proposed and approved THPs/NTMPs) Q3. Acres to be harvested as part of proposed THP/NTMP Q4. Total Acres in planning watershed	**Cumulative Effects Ratio (CER)** Q1. Number of harvest acres Q2. Planning watershed number (Calwater2.2) Q3. Planning watershed is listed for sediment under 303(d)* Q4. Silviculture listed as a source for sediment under 303(d)* "Response automatically references the "Planning Watershed Stats" to determine yes or no response. Q5. Are winter operations proposed? Q6. Is a source of domestic water supply within or connected to the plan? Q7. Are there in-lieu practices to WLPZ canopy retention? Q8. Are streams within the harvest subject to ASP rules?	**Cumulative Effects Ratio (CER)** Existing Criteria: Calculates rate of harvest for last 15 years from submitted data. Revised Criteria: Average harvest rate, calculated by planning watershed, is derived from up to date agency maintained GIS data. Added questions to address: a) Potential impacts based on 303d sediment impaired watershed conditions b) Potential impacts based on the presence of domestic water supply c) Potential impacts to stream temperature based on in-lieu practices to canopy retention in the WLPZ d) Potential impacts to salmonids based on immediate proximity to habitat
Drainage Density Index (DDI) Q1. Linear feet of Class I stream Q2. Linear feet of Class II stream Q3. Linear feet Class III stream Q4. Plan area acres	**Drainage Density Index (DDI)** Q1. Linear feet of Class I stream a. in slope class < 30% b. in slope class 30-50% c. in slope class >50% Q2. Linear feet of Class II stream a. in slope class < 30% b. in slope class 30-50% c. in slope class >50% Q3. Linear feet Class III stream a. in slope class < 30% b. in slope class 30-50% c. in slope class >50% Note: Plan Acres automatically references Plan Acres input from CER.	**Drainage Density Index (DDI)** Existing Criteria: weights class 1 stream highest and class 3 streams lowest. Revised Criteria: Based on proportion of combined risk factors: extent of WLPZ/ ELZ acres, proportion of stream side slope class greater than 30%, and proportion of class II and III streams.
Soil Disturbance Factor (SDF) Q1. Silviculture a) Harvest area (ac): group and selection b) Area in THP (ac) Q2. Roads a) Linear feet of existing and proposed: seasonal/temporary and All weather/permanent. b) Number of: Class I, Class II, and Class III streams crossed c) Number of feet In-lieu/alt rule in WLPZ d) Number of feet in high or extreme EHR Q3. Skid Trails a) Linear feet of existing and proposed b) Number of: Class I, Class II, and Class III streams crossed c) Number of feet In-lieu/alt rule in WLPZ d) Number of feet in high or extreme EHR Q4. Landings (existing proposed) a) Ground-based b) Helicopter c) No. of In-lieu/alt rule in WLPZ Q5. Winter operations proposed? Yes or No (Yes = Automatic Tier III)	**Soil Disturbance Factor (SDF)** Q1. Roads (existing and proposed) a) Linear feet of : seasonal/temporary and all weather/permanent b) Linear feet in stream protection zone: Seasonal and All weather c) Class I, Class II, and Class III streams crossed: seasonal and all weather. Q2. Skid trails (existing and proposed) a) Linear feet total and in stream protection zones b) Number of feet in high or extreme EHR and number of feet in high or extreme EHR in stream protection zones. c) Number of Class I, Class II, and Class III streams crossed and number of Class I, Class II, and Class III streams crossed under in-lieu/alt rule of FPR. Q3. Landings (existing and proposed) a) Number of landings and number of landings under in-lieu/alt rule of FPR. b) Number of landings in high or extreme EHR and number of landings in high or extreme EHR in stream protection zones. Q4. At present, are all appropriate road surface materials in place? Q5. Are any roads to be regraded before, during, or after the proposed harvest? Q6. Are there debris slides associated with sidecast or fill constructed roads? Q7. Are there in-sloped road drainages hydrologically connected to stream crossings? Q8. Is traffic restricted on plan roads?	**Soil Disturbance Factor (SDF)** Existing Criteria: multiplies inputs for roads, skid trails, and landings by various multipliers to formulate a numerical total. Existing Criteria automatically sets Tier I and Tier II plans into Tier III monitoring requirements if the timber harvest includes winter operation. Revised Criteria: Assessment of inputs based on a proportion of combined risk factors, primarily proximity of compacted surfaces to stream channels, erosion hazard rating, and current road conditions. Removes automatic Tier III for winter operations.

Figure 4.3 Summary of existing and revised eligibility criteria

108

Water Board opted for a modest program. Growers would need to enroll in the agricultural waiver program, complete 15 hours of water quality training, prepare a succinct farm water quality management plan, implement water quality best management practices and do some monitoring. At first, farmers were worried that even modest monitoring requirements would take up a lot of their time and scarce funds. Shortly after the waiver was adopted, a new nongovernmental organization, Central Coast Preservation, Inc., was formed by farmers to cooperatively carry out monitoring for any agricultural operation that wished to participate (see Dowd, Press and Los Huertos, 2008, for a review of the original agricultural waiver).

Growers expressed palpable relief when the Water Board adopted the 2004 waiver program. The water quality short courses were not onerous, nor expensive, and the existence of a third-party organization ready to do most of the water quality monitoring took additional pressure and expense off farm operations. Environmentalists were not especially happy that the Board did not require on-farm water quality data, but knew they had to bide their time until renewal of the waiver program five years later.

The good feelings didn't last long. By the time the waiver was up for its five-year renewal, staff had concluded that they did not know enough about water quality "hotspots" and environmentalists pointed to continuing nitrate contamination in the region's surface and ground waters, sloughs and river mouths. Nitrates were purportedly fouling waterways because farmers used too much fertilizer. Unfortunately, farmers have strong incentives to over-fertilize. After all, they readily see what happens when they put on too few nutrients: their crop yields drop. They tend not to see what happens when their excessive fertilizer usage contaminates waterways.

Although the Water Board should have renewed the waiver in 2009 (orders must be renewed every five years), it lacked a quorum of Board members to proceed. Then, in 2012, came the "Harter Report." Prompted by a request from the California State Senate, University of California Cooperative Extension faculty member Thomas Harter conducted a very thorough assessment of groundwater in two of California's agricultural regions, including the Salinas Valley and the Tulare Basin. The Salinas Valley, while much smaller than the agricultural regions of California's interior valleys, is known as the nation's salad bowl. It is the most important agricultural valley in California's Central Coast.

Drawing on over 100,000 samples from drinking water wells, and covering a period from the 1940s to 2011, the Harter study rocked the state with shocking news about groundwater pollution. Of the 2.6 million people in these two regions who relied on wells for their drinking water, as many as 254,000 were currently at risk for nitrate contamination. Environmentalists who had challenged the Water Board's original agricultural waiver program based principally on water quality concerns now found strong allies from environmental and rural justice groups concerned about public health. Although the Harter report authors readily acknowledged that much of the groundwater nitrate contamination they found had accumulated over decades, they also implicated current farming practices for exacerbating the problem.

Environmental justice organizations affiliated with agricultural communities quickly picked up on the Harter report and started attending regional board hearings. In short order, public discourse shifted from making incremental changes to a regulatory order addressing surface water to a dramatic re-orientation toward drinking water. Faced with a perceived public health crisis and a mandated renewal, staff and board members felt great pressure to adopt a revised order with more teeth. Whereas the 2004 waiver program blamed nitrate contamination on a few bad actors responsible for creating a few "hotspots," these new findings suggested a far more widespread problem involving the whole industry.

Reprising the approach they had used with the timber waiver program, staff developed a three-tiered regulatory system; each successive tier associated with more stringent remedial requirements. As with the timber program, staff developed replicable, transparent criteria for sorting farms into the different tiers, in this case according to the kinds of inputs and cultivation practices used on a given farm as well as the property's relative proximity to impaired or vulnerable surface waters. Based on staff's best estimate of the more important factors driving water quality in agricultural settings, Table 4.1 summarizes the criteria distinguishing each tier. Tier 1 status applies to remedies whose individual farm operations meet all of the criteria in the Tier 1 column below.

Table 4.2 summarizes the different requirements applicable to farm operations in each tier. Some major differences between the 2004 and 2012 waivers included mandatory groundwater monitoring and reporting, use of backflow prevention devices and the addition of a third tier. Most farmers objected to groundwater monitoring, worried that reporting groundwater well data would reveal to the public sensitive information that could be used for suing farmers, even though California state water laws do not provide "citizen suit" provisions like those in the federal CWA. Staff initially proposed monitoring once a year, but under pressure from agricultural stakeholders, the Water Board required groundwater monitoring only twice per permit cycle (effectively, twice every five years) (Young, 2013).

The most controversial changes involved requirements for Tier 3

Table 4.1   Criteria distinguishing farm operations in three tiers, Central Coast Agricultural Order, 2012

Tier 1	Tier 2	Tier 3
Discharger **does not** apply chlorpyrifos or diazinon at the farm/ranch	Discharger **does** apply chlorpyrifos or diazinon at the farm/ranch	Grows crop types with high potential to discharge nitrogen to groundwater **and** farm/ranch total irrigated acreage is *greater than or equal* to 500 acres
Is located **more than** 1,000 feet **from** a surface waterbody listed for toxicity, pesticides, nutrients, turbidity or sediment on the 2010 List of Impaired Waterbodies	Is located **within** 1,000 feet of a surface waterbody listed for toxicity, pesticides, nutrients, turbidity or sediment on the 2010 List of Impaired Waterbodies	Discharger **does apply** chlorpyrifos or diazinon at the farm/ranch **and** discharges irrigation or stormwater runoff to a waterbody listed for toxicity or pesticides on the 2010 List of Impaired Waterbodies
Grows crop types with high potential to discharge nitrogen to groundwater **and** the farm/ranch total irrigated acreage is *less than* 50 acres, **and** is *not* within 1,000 feet of a well that is part of a public water system that exceeds maximum contaminant levels for nitrate	Grows crop types with high potential to discharge nitrogen to groundwater, **and** the farm/ranch total irrigated acreage is greater or equal to 50 acres and *less than* 500 acres, **or** the farm/ranch is *within* 1,000 feet of a well that is part of a public water system that exceeds the maximum contaminant level for nitrate	
Sustainability in Practice (SIP, certified by the Central Coast Vineyard Team) or other certified programs approved by the Executive Officer		

Source: Central Coast Regional Water Quality Control Board, 2013.

Table 4.2　Summary requirements of the Central Coast Agricultural Order, 2012

Regulatory Requirement	Tier 1	Tier 2	Tier 3
Enroll in the Order by Filing an electronic-Notice of Intent (eNOI)	✓	✓	✓
Develop and Implement a Farm Plan	✓	✓	✓
Implement Management Practices to Protect Water Quality	✓	✓	✓
Conduct Surface Water Receiving Monitoring and Reporting (Cooperatively or Individually)	✓	✓	✓
Conduct Groundwater Monitoring and Reporting	✓	✓	✓
Install Backflow Prevention devices	✓	✓	✓
Submit Annual Compliance Form		✓	✓
Conduct Individual Discharge Monitoring and Reporting			✓
Develop and Implement Certified Irrigation and Nutrient Management Plan			✓
Develop and Implement Water Quality Buffer Plan			✓

Source:　Central Coast Regional Water Quality Control Board, 2013.

farms and ranches, including more detailed monitoring and potentially complicated nutrient budgets calculations. Farmers with large holdings responded to the three-tiered regulatory system by enrolling their farms in multiple, smaller parcels, each with its own tier 1 or 2 waiver and less stringent requirements. This resulted in a sharp decrease in the number of tier 3 farms from about 100 in late 2012 to 64 in late 2013. Tier 3 acreages correspondingly dropped from ten percent of the region's total to seven percent (McCann, 2013).

Many growers bitterly fought the monitoring requirements for tier 3 farms and ranches, arguing that these would be onerous and expensive without producing meaningful data. Even farm managers in tiers 1 and 2 objected, worrying that they could someday be moved to tier 3. Unlike electric power utilities, with their access to guaranteed revenues from "captive" ratepayers, farms often operate with razor-thin profit margins. Fresh fruit and vegetable growers in California are thus always looking over their shoulders at competition from Mexico, Chile and, increasingly, Asian agricultural commodity exporters.

Critics argued, first, that nothing in the agricultural waiver (also known as "the order") ensured that water quality sampling would be done consistently across farms or during the same area storm events. Comparing across farms and ranches and over time would thus be nearly impossible. To make matters worse, it's not clear exactly how a farm could measure nitrate leaching under the very best of circumstances. To be sure, farm managers can prepare a nutrient management plan, depicting how much fertilizer they use and estimating how much gets taken up by their crops. That estimate, however, always occurs within large margins of error. Moreover, determining the fate of excess nutrients and when this excess reaches groundwater or surface water is extraordinarily challenging. Finally, establishing the relationship between "legacy" pollution and current applications is also very difficult. Excess nutrients can take a decade to reach deep groundwater and only days or hours to make their ways to surface water.

Requiring a large farm to prepare a nutrient management plan as a part of a nonpoint source water quality control program thus rests on a critical article of faith: regulators must assume that farmers will change their behavior by virtue of having gone through the exercise of writing nutrient management plans. The behavioral assumption is that farmers pollute waterways with nutrients because they don't know enough about their fertilizer use. Either they don't understand how much their crops need or how much they use or what is left after harvest to leach into surface or ground waters.

Maybe nutrient management plans will provide regulators with better information. In principle, regulators could look at all the nutrient management plans from each regulated farm and look for outliers, either growers using much less or much more fertilizer than average for similar crops. It's doubtful that variance in the small set of tier 3 farms means much. Nor is it clear how staff could act on information gleaned from nutrient management plans.

Almost as soon as the ink was dry on the newly adopted 2012 agricultural order, stakeholders appealed against it to the State Board, which quickly issued a stay, ordering the Regional Board to estimate the costs of the most controversial provisions. The Central Coast Board was also asked to provide more and presumably better findings demonstrating the environmental and public benefits that would be gained by implementing the revised order. In summer 2013, about a year after issuing its stay, the State Board upheld the Central Coast's order.

The 2012 agricultural waiver resulted in greater Water Board scrutiny and more compliance (e.g., in the form of nutrient management plans), but not in more usable information. Many states are not faring any better. The Tennessee Department of Agriculture's Non Point Source (NPS) program is typical of most states, as it "is non-regulatory, promoting voluntary, incentive-based solutions. It is a cost-share program, paying for 60 percent of the cost of a project" (TDA, 2010). Nonetheless, even "strong" states limit their efforts. Maine, Oregon and Washington spend relatively more on BMP adoption incentives and also require that nonpoint source concerns receive sustained attention in state and local policymaking (Hoornbeck, 2005), but they do no better than other states in requiring evidence that BMPs work. Like California did until recently, Maryland exempts most agricultural operations from liability for waste discharges if farmers receive water quality education, plan for BMP adoption and pay modest monitoring fees. Farmers objected even to these weak requirements, citing concerns over "rights of entry" onto their lands (Maryland) or posting spatially-explicit water quality data on the Internet (California). Such objections resulted in much lighter regulations than initially proposed (McElfish et al., 2006; Dowd et al., 2008). In 2012, Minnesota rolled out its new Agricultural Water Quality Certification Program, in which volunteer farmers in any of four pilot areas agree to implement best management practices under a great deal of scrutiny. Time will tell if this program helps practitioners and regulators determine just how beneficial BMPs really can be and under what conditions.

URBAN STORMWATER POLLUTION PREVENTION

Since the late 1990s the Water Board has also taken up stormwater pollution prevention, prompted by the federal CWA rather than changes to state law. Urban stormwater refers to water runoff in any setting modified by human activities, during and immediately after rainstorms. Stormwater flows over ground surfaces, which is then collected by natural channels and pipes or gutters and released to rivers, lakes, wetlands or oceans. Some stormwater also reaches surface waters within a day or so of rainfall by saturating soils lying over seeps, springs and other channels.

Urban storm runoff is tough to manage. It comes from every part of developed landscapes, whether pavement or rooftops, but it is produced and delivered very episodically in ways that are difficult to attenuate. It also accumulates and transports tremendous and varied wastes from the urban environment (National Research Council, 2009). And yet, although urban stormwater runoff contributes mightily to the nonpoint source problem, it is actually more tractable than the burdens caused by timber logging and irrigated agriculture. That's largely because Congress shoehorned stormwater pollution into the NPDES permit process developed for point sources. To see how, we need to look at the last amendments Congress made to the Clean Water Act, back in 1987.

Due to its nonpoint source nature, stormwater was not something EPA wanted to regulate in the years immediately following passage of the landmark 1972 Act. In the mid-1970s, the Natural Resources Defense Council successfully brought suit against the EPA. In NRDC vs. Costle (568 F.2d 1369 (D.C. Cir., 1977)), the DC Circuit Court of Appeals rejected EPA's attempts to exempt urban stormwater pollution, arguing that the Act did not grant EPA the authority to exempt whole classes of wastewater discharges. Still, it would be another ten years before Congress would give EPA more guidance and authority in this area.

In a 1987 amendment entitled the Water Quality Act, Congress added to the NPDES permitting process with new requirements for controlling stormwater discharges from 11 categories of industrial sources, large municipalities and other significant sources such as large construction sites. The new section 402(p) required EPA to promulgate standards mandating use of best available technology [42 U.S.C. §1342(p)(3)]. As such, Congress treated stormwater discharges exactly like sewage treatment plants and factories, creating a regulatory fiction that nonpoint stormwater sources could be handled as if they were point sources. Congress would have its cake and eat it too: legislators acknowledged that stormwater was different from sewage and thus required its own part of the CWA, but not so much that it warranted exceptions and waivers to clean water permits or standards.

Section 402(p) eased stormwater dischargers into the EPA's regulatory scope in two phases. The first phase regulated stormwater discharges from the entire manufacturing sector, construction activities occurring on five or more acres and storm sewers in municipal areas serving 100,000 or more people [40 C.F.R. § 122.26(a)(3) (1990); 40 C.F.R. § 122.26 (b) (14) (1990)]. Each of these stormwater dischargers, many of them having some pre-existing responsibilities under the Act, would likely be better equipped to tackle new requirements than much smaller sources, such as little towns. The municipal sources are now commonly referred to as "MS4s," which is the abbreviation for Municipal Separate Storm Sewer Systems.

The second phase brought smaller MS4s and construction sites down to one acre under the regulatory umbrella. Perhaps not wishing to leave too much to chance or undetermined, EPA and Congress required six minimum control measures or program elements of all MS4 stormwater management programs. These included:

- Public Education and Outreach on Stormwater Impacts;
- Public Involvement/Participation;
- Illicit Discharge Detection and Elimination;
- Construction Site Runoff Control;

- Post-Construction Stormwater Management in New Development and Redevelopment;
- Pollution Prevention/Good Housekeeping for Municipal Operations.

For each minimum control measure, MS4s had to specify and implement BMPs tailored to the specific stormwater problems in their jurisdictions, although in practice, many smaller MS4 stormwater management plans read like federal boilerplate. Because of their effects on the built environment, controls on construction and post-construction activities naturally draw the most controversy and cost. They also have the potential to truly transform urban stormwater management.

One of the first nonpoint source issues I encountered during my service on the Water Board was sediment pollution from construction sites. Here was the typical scenario: a developer or contractor and their attorney arrive at the Water Board's nondescript public hearing hall to dispute administrative civil liability charges against them for sediment pollution. With varying degrees of patience, the landowner or developer sits through hours of regularly scheduled agenda items, the public comment period and the lunch break, not knowing precisely when their item is up for deliberation. Finally, the time comes and all parties rise, swearing under oath to tell the truth, much as they would in regular court proceedings. Water Board staff present the prosecution's case: the defendant violated the Clean Water Act by discharging sediments into navigable bodies of water of the United States. Usually, they did so because they didn't implement best management practices that would have prevented erosion of their construction sites, assuming the practices were scrupulously designed and installed.

There then ensue claims and counter-claims, with the accused sometimes trying to show that no harm resulted from their activities. But the beauty of a construction BMP stems from the implied compliance with a management practice. Use the BMP, properly, and you are in compliance. Focusing on the absence or presence of properly installed BMPs greatly simplified the regulatory and judicial processes. Instead of trying to detect the sediment pulse from a construction site, a state inspector can simply look and see whether the site has silt fences, fiber rolls, jute netting and the like.

In addition to regulating construction activities, the Water Board reviewed and approved MS4 stormwater plans, beginning with the region's largest city, Salinas. The 2012 Salinas NPDES permit for stormwater runs to nearly 200 pages, having gone through many drafts and challenges. The toughest negotiations between the City, environmentalists and Water Board staff centered on municipal ordinances covering development activities. The City wanted the Water Board to approve its stormwater plan in advance of new ordinances imposing discharge limits on development. It took years of hearings, city council legislation and even a few permit denials before all the required elements were in place.

Salinas was soon joined by other cities up and down the Central Coast. But a decade after MS4s first began securing their NPDES stormwater permits, the Water Board and its permittees have yet to tell whether new ordinances, public education and best management practices will deliver on their promise to transform urban runoff.

New Technologies, New Approaches?

Traditionally, cities tried to convey stormwater away as fast and far as possible. Big storms brought risks of flooding and often mixed stormwater with sewage unless the two systems were very well isolated from each other. Huge concrete vaults, storm drains and outfalls can indeed move stormwater away from impervious streets, sidewalks, rooftops, parking lots and driveways, but almost always at great environmental cost. These heavily engineered systems concentrate pollutants and deliver them in huge pulses to the nation's rivers, lakes, estuaries and oceans.

A newer approach, now being adopted throughout the country, is called low impact development (LID). LID mimics nature by either retaining stormwater onsite or greatly slowing it down as it moves from the cityscapes to surface waters. Some low impact management practices include creating trenches, planters, grassed pavers and other pervious surfaces, cisterns, green roofs and rain gardens.

The Clean Water Act's urban stormwater programs are succeeding better than the TMDL process, because they don't suffer from the compliance-abatement-mitigation problems that plague other nonpoint source programs. Urban stormwater pollution, though widespread and caused by millions of individual actions, responds quite well to technological requirements. Low-impact development and best management practices work superbly to reduce stormwater volume and infiltrate runoff onsite, if properly designed and implemented.

Besides having a section of the Clean Water Act dedicated to it, several factors make stormwater more tractable than other nonpoint source water problems. First, the regulated community (municipalities and developers, especially) is highly visible. Stormwater-creating activities are easy to spot and attribute to particular activities, sources or dischargers. Second, cityscapes regularly transform themselves, as buildings, sidewalks, streets and subsurface infrastructure get maintained or replaced, although this is less true of residential than commercial areas. All this maintenance and redevelopment creates regular opportunities for replacing traditional stormwater conveyances with more natural, low-impact technologies that keep water in place. Third, low-impact development promises to greatly reduce stormwater management costs as expensive, engineered culverts and storm systems become replaced with vegetated buffers, bio-swales, pervious surfaces and the like.

Representing the Construction Industry Coalition on Water Quality, a trade group seeking to proactively enable developers and builders to influence the stormwater regulatory process, to their advantage, Mark Grey and his colleagues calculated the expenses of LID. Writing in the lead stormwater trade journal, Grey and his coauthors noted how LID technologies vary widely in type, effectiveness and cost. Costs to implement LID BMPs vary greatly. For example, installing vegetated or grassed swales costs $1/ft^2$, but installing a green roof can cost up to $522/ft^2$ (Grey et al., 2013).

The monetary benefits of green infrastructure compare favorably with conventional stormwater controls (Kloss and Calarusse, 2006). Studies in Maryland and Illinois comparing new development either with LID BMPs or conventional stormwater controls found that development with green infrastructure controls saves $3,500–$4,500 for each quarter to a half acre lot (Kloss and Calarusse, 2006). LID sites cost less because they required fewer "hardscape" infrastructural elements such as concrete vaults, drains and pipes.

A comparison of the long-term costs to manage one gallon of stormwater shows that the conventional stormwater controls of retention basins are the least expensive stormwater management tool. Detention and retention basins can control one gallon of stormwater for 3–4 cents, whereas the least expensive LID BMP costs $1/gallon. However, at $1/gallon, the LID BMPs are more cost effective than the conventional methods of surface storage ($3.5/gallon) and deep tunnels ($4.4/gallon). Green roofs seem to be the most expensive option at a low estimate of $22/gallon control (Grey et al., 2013).

As an added bonus, low-impact development approaches can be quite aesthetically attractive, providing much-needed green spaces, frequently throughout urban areas. While urban stormwater pollution prevention can be viewed as imposing large new costs on municipalities, at a time when urban infrastructure is decaying and tax receipts are plummeting, such projects can also keep developers and re-developers, along with their subcontractors, busy for years.

All is not rosy with LID, however. Older residential areas don't redevelop that often, so opportunities for transforming impervious surfaces into vegetated buffers and retention basins are limited. Moreover, LID mimics nature in that it tries to retain and treat stormwater on-site; it does not do anything about limiting inputs. The stormwater equivalent of dirty input limits is called "true source control" and refers to preventing toxins such as metals, oils, sediments and landscaping chemicals from ever reaching impervious surfaces in the first place. Even the very best stormwater programs will always be limited by what the compliance-abatement-mitigation approach can accomplish.

Scott Taylor, a water quality engineer in southern California, points out that "current water quality criteria and regulations were established for a NPDES program intended to address continuous wastewater discharges, and are not appropriate for episodic and highly variable stormwater discharges" (Taylor, 2011). So instead of monitoring mass emissions of pollutants into receiving waters, local regulatory bodies should focus on determining whether beneficial uses are impaired. If so, using dirty input limits in the form of local ordinances banning ". . .the sale and use of consumer products that are shown to be contributing to the exceedance of receiving water standards" would achieve much more than merely controlling stormwater volumes and keeping runoff on site (Taylor, 2011).

By late 2013, the US EPA was under great pressure from environmentalists to push stormwater policy much further. Would private interests become covered by stormwater rules? Would existing properties need to tear up their parking lots and install retention basins and pervious surfaces? How would new rules pass cost-benefit criteria ". . .given the intermittent nature of the stormwater, the various rainfall patterns that exist across the country, and the many different types of technology and site design approaches that could be used to meet the performance standards?" (Snider, 2013). Most profoundly, will new rules consider what Taylor calls true source controls? The answers to these questions will determine whether stormwater pollution prevention stalls or takes a great leap forward.

CONCLUSION

The TMDL program, wetland and conditional waiver programs all look like the sort of nonpoint source controls Congress and administering agencies would devise if they had no real intention of controlling these discharges and taking on the interests – notably, large farms, timber and mining operations, CAFOs and developers – that release them.

Why is that? Simply put, ignorance, followed by disbelief. Ignorance on the part of legislators, who wrote a Clean Water Act to address what they could see, namely municipal and industrial sewage outfalls. And disbelief on the part of constituents, who have a hard time acknowledging that diffuse, episodic and unintentional releases truly warrant the regulatory response environmentalists and governments seek. As Oliver Houck says, the information burdens for programs like TMDLs are enormous, adding to dischargers' incredulity. Very few of the links in the policy causal chain can be established in the case of nonpoint source water pollution. Unlike a power plant or a sewage treatment facility, it's exceedingly difficult to know, in real time or in a reasonable timeframe, how much discharge is caused by a particular source, like a farm or a timber harvest. Proceeding further along the causal chain, it's difficult to establish that any kind of ambient water quality is directly related to a discharger or dischargers. As a consequence, we may be able to tell that a particular best management practice helps reduce effluent loads, but it's hard to say how that translates to water quality improvements. Given these evidentiary problems, tomorrow's nonpoint source regulatory programs will need to use dirty input limits or source controls rather than relying so heavily on voluntarism, minimal compliance and mitigation.

In 1972, Congress acted boldly and invested wisely. For a few years, legislators, agencies and states could point to remarkable improvements thanks to wastewater treatment investments, all while turning a blind eye to the overwhelming threats posed by nonpoint sources. Forty years into the modern era of water quality policy, the nation needs a new commitment, equal in ambition and resolve to the one that reformed the dangerous wastewater practices of yesteryear.

REFERENCES

Alsharif, K. (2010). "Construction and Stormwater Pollution: Policy, Violations and Penalties." *Land Use Policy* 27: 612–616.

Andreen, W. L. (2004). "Water Quality Today – Has the Clean Water Act Been a Success?" *Alabama Law Review* 55: 537–591.

Aulenbach, B., H. Buxton, et al. (2007). "Streamflow and Nutrient Fluxes of the Mississippi-Atchafalaya River Basin and Sub-Basins for the Period of Record through 2005." United States Geological Survey.

Bianchi, T., S. DiMarco, et al. (2010). "The Science of Hypoxia in the Northern Gulf of Mexico: A Review." *Science of the Total Environment* 408(7): 1471–1484.

Brown, J., L. Sprague, et al. (2011). "Nutrient Sources and Transport in the Missouri River Basin, with Emphasis on the Effects of Irrigation and Reservoirs." *Journal of the American Water Resources Association* 47(5): 1034–1060.

California Department of Finance (2009). "California Timber Production 1998 to 2007 (in thousands of board feet)." California Statistical Abstract.

California State Water Resources Control Board. "The California Water Boards'

Annual Performance Report – Fiscal Year 2011–12." Accessed at http://www.waterboards.ca.gov/about_us/performance_report_1112/plan_assess/11112_tmdl_outcomes.shtml.

Central Coast Regional Water Quality Control Board (2013). "Timber Harvest." Accessed at http://www.waterboards.ca.gov/rwqcb3/water_issues/programs/timber_harvest/index.shtml.

Central Coast Regional Water Quality Control Board (2013). "Agricultural Regulatory Program." Accessed at http://www.waterboards.ca.gov/rwqcb3/water_issues/programs/ag_waivers/index.shtml.

Copeland, C. (2013). "Mountaintop Mining: Background on Current Controversies." Congressional Research Service. Washington, DC.

Dahl, T. E. (2011). "Status and Trends of Wetlands in the Conterminous United States 2004 to 2009." United States Department of Interior Fish and Wildlife Service. Washington, DC.

Diaz, R. J. and R. Rosenburg (2008). "Spreading Dead Zones and Consequences for Marine Ecosystems." *Science* 326: 926–929.

Dorfman, M. and K. S. Rosselot (2009). "Testing the Waters: A Guide to Water Quality at Vacation Beaches, 19th edition." Natural Resources Defense Council. Washington, DC.

Dowd, B. N., D. Press, et al. (2008). "Agricultural Nonpoint Source Water Pollution Policy: The Case of California's Central Coast." *Agriculture, Ecosystems and Environment* 128(3): 151–161.

Drelich, D. (2007). "Restoring the Cornerstone of the Clean Water Act." *Columbia Journal of Environmental Law* 34: 267–331.

Duhigg, C. (2010). "Toxic Waters: A Series About the Worsening Pollution in American Waters and Regulators' Response." *The New York Times*. New York, NY.

Gardner, R. C., J. Zedler, et al. (2009). "Compensating for Wetland Losses Under the Clean Water Act (Redux): Evaluating the Federal Compensatory Mitigation Regulation." *Stetson Law Review* 38: 213–249.

Garovoy, J. B. (2003). "A Breathtaking Assertion of Power? Not Quite. Pronsolino vs. Nastri and the Still Limited Role of Federal Regulation of Nonpoint Source Pollution." *Ecology Law Quarterly* 30: 543–568.

Grey, M., D. Sorem, et al. (2013). "Low-Impact Development BMP Installation and Operation and Maintenance Costs in Orange County, CA." *Stormwater* (March/April): 26–35.

Helfield, J. M. and Robert J. Naiman (2001). "Effects of Salmon-Derived Nitrogen on Riparian Forest Growth and Implications for Stream Productivity." *Ecology* 82(9): 2403–2409.

Hitt, N. P. and M. Hendryx (2010). "Ecological Integrity of Streams Related to Human Cancer Mortality Rates." *EcoHealth* 7(1): 91–104.

Hoornbeck, J. A. (2005). "The Promises and Pitfalls of Devolution: Water Pollution Policies in the American States." *Publius* 35(1): 87–114.

Houck, O. A. (2002). "The Clean Water Act TMDL Program V: Aftershock and Prelude." *Environmental Law Reporter* 32: 10385–10419.

Howarth, R. W. (2008). "Coastal Nitrogen Pollution: A Review of Sources and Trends Globally and Regionally." *Harmful Algae* 8: 14–20.

Keller, A. A. and L. Cavallaro (2008). "Assessing the US Clean Water Act 303(d) Listing Process for Determining Impairment of a Waterbody." *Journal of Environmental Management* 86: 699–711.

Kloss, C. and C. Calarusse (2006). "Rooftops to Rivers: Green Strategies for Controlling Stormwater and Combined Sewer Overflows." NRDC.

McCann, L. (2013). Watershed Planning and Protection Section Manager, Central Coast Regional Water Quality Control Board, personal communication.

McElfish, J. M. J., L. Breggin, et al. (2006). "Inventing Nonpoint Controls: Methods, Metrics and Results." *Villanova Environmental Law Journal* 87: 87–216.

Milazzo, P. C. (2006). *Unlikely Environmentalists: Congress and Clean Water, 1945–1972*. Lawrence, KS, University of Kansas Press.

Moreno-Mateos, D., M. E. Power, et al. (2012). "Structural and Functional Loss in Restored Wetland Ecosystems." *PLoS Biology* 10(e1001247. doi:10.1371/journal.pbio.1001247).

National Research Council (2009). *Urban Stormwater Management in the United States*. Washington, DC, National Academies Press.

Natural Resources Defense Council (2013). "Testing the Waters: A Guide to Water Quality at Vacation Beaches, 22nd edition." Washington, DC, Natural Resources Defense Council.

Norton, D., A. Olsen, et al. (2009). "Sampling TMDL Implementation Rates and Patterns in the North Central US. Water Environment Federation." Accessed at http://water.epa.gov/lawsregs/lawsguidance/cwa/tmdl/upload/16A.pdf.

Palmer, M. A., E. S. Bernhardt, et al. (2010). "Mountaintop Mining Consequences." *Science* 327: 148–149.

Rabalais, N., R. Turner, B. Sen Gupta, D. Boesch, P. Chapman, M. Murrell (2007). "Hypoxia in the Northern Gulf of Mexico: Does the Science Support the Plan to Reduce, Mitigate, and Control Hypoxia?" *Estuaries Coasts* 30(5): 753–772.

Robertson, G. P. and P. M. Vitousek (2009). "Nitrogen in Agriculture: Balancing the Cost of an Essential Resource." *Annual Review of Environment and Natural Resources* 34: 97–125.

Robertson, M. and P. Hough (2011). "Wetland Mitigation under the US Clean Water Act," in *Wetlands: Integrating Multidisciplinary Concepts*. B. LePage (Ed.). New York, NY, Springer.

Rose, C. (2013). Senior Environmental Scientist, California Central Coast Regional Water Quality Control Board, personal communication.

Seaburg, K. (2007). "Murky Waters: Courts Should Hold That the 'Any-Progress-is-Sufficient-Progress' Approach to TMDL Development under Section 303(d) of the Clean Water Act is Arbitrary and Capricious." *Washington Law Review* 82: 767–794.

Snider, A. (2013). "Why is EPA Taking So Long to Write a Stormwater Rule? It's Complicated." *E&E News*.

Snider, A. (2014). "EPA Promise of 'No Net Loss' Based on Faulty Assumptions – IG." *E&E News*.

Taylor, S. (2011). "The Next Step for the Stormwater Program." *Stormwater Magazine* 1 October.

Tennessee Department of Agriculture (2010). Nonpoint Source Program, EPA Section 319. Accessed at http://www.tennessee.gov/agriculture/water/nps.html.

Turner, R., N. Rabalais, et al. (2007). "Characterization of Nutrient, Organic Carbon, and Sediment Loads and Concentrations from the Mississippi River into the Northern Gulf of Mexico." *Estuaries Coasts* 30: 773–790.

United States Department of Interior (1969). "The National Estuarine Pollution

Study." Federal Water Pollution Control Administration, United States Department of Interior. Washington, DC.

United States Environmental Protection Agency (2000). "Progress in Water Quality: An Evaluation of the National Investment in Wastewater Treatment." Washington, DC.

United States Environmental Protection Agency (2006a). "Wadeable Streams Assessment: A Collaborative Survey of the Nation's Streams." Washington, DC.

United States Environmental Protection Agency (2006b). Supplemental Environmental Projects. Washington, DC.

United States Environmental Protection Agency (2008a). "Clean Water State Revolving Fund Programs: 2008 Annual Report." Washington, DC.

United States Environmental Protection Agency (2008b). "Clean Watersheds Needs Survey, 2008 Report to Congress." Washington, DC.

United States Environmental Protection Agency (2009). "National Lakes Assessment: A Collaborative Survey of the Nation's Lakes." Washington, DC.

United States Environmental Protection Agency (2010a). "National Summary of Impaired Waters and TMDL Information." Washington, DC.

United States Environmental Protection Agency (2010b). Environmental Compliance History Online (ECHO). Washington, DC.

United States Environmental Protection Agency (2011). "The Effects of Mountaintop Mines and Valley Fills on Aquatic Ecosystems of the Central Appalachian Coalfields (2011 Final)." Washington, DC.

United States Environmental Protection Agency (2013a). "Northern Gulf of Mexico Hypoxic Zone." Accessed at http://water.epa.gov/type/watersheds/named/msbasin/zone.cfm.

United States Environmental Protection Agency (2013b). "Impaired Waters and Total Maximum Daily Loads." Accessed at http://water.epa.gov/lawsregs/lawsguidance/cwa/tmdl/index.cfm.

United States Government Accountability Office (GAO) (2013). "Changes Needed if Key EPA Program is to Help Fulfill the Nation's Water Quality Goals." 14–80. Washington, DC.

Vijay, S., J. F. DeCarolis, et al. (2010). "A Bottom-Up Method to Develop Pollution Abatement Cost Curves for Coal-Fired Utility Boilers." *Energy Policy* 38: 2255–2261.

Wilkinson, J. and J. Thompson (2006). "2005 Status Report on Compensatory Mitigation in the United States." Environmental Law Institute.

Young, J. (2013). Chairman of the Central Coast Regional Water Quality Control Board, personal communication.

Zedler, J. B. and S. Kercher (2005). "Wetland Resources: Status, Trends, Ecosystem Services, and Restorability." *Annual Review of Environment and Resources* 30: 39–74.

5. Failure before the end of the pipe: missed opportunities in American paper recycling

INTRODUCTION

"Reduce, reuse, recycle." Millions of Americans encounter this slogan daily. It exhorts us to minimize environmental damage long before goods become wastes – that is, before there is a pipe releasing pollution that must be abated, mitigated or neutralized. Given the economic importance of engineered materials like cement, steel, plastics, glass and paper, the copious resources needed to manufacture these from virgin raw materials and the negative impacts associated with their life cycles, reduction and reuse certainly ought to serve as guiding principles in industry and commerce as well as domestic life. But how well does American environmental policy reflect our environmental sloganeering?

If "reduce, reuse, recycle" were more than a catchy phrase, public and private forces might avidly pursue multiple aspects of what Julian Allwood and his colleagues refer to as "materials efficiency." These would include inducements or requirements for industries to 1) make longer-lasting products (instead of planning for obsolescence), 2) modularize and remanufacture goods (emulating Germany's Green Dot programs for packaging materials), 3) re-use components (a practice that includes various forms of recycling) and 4) design products that require less material (Allwood et al., 2011).

Of these, relatively recent federal efforts historically focused chiefly on recycling, but most US policies are consistent with a linear, ecologically-naïve notion of materials use. In this resource model, non-renewable resources flow as raw materials from extraction to processing to waste management (Geiser, 2001, p. 198). Thus, over a century of concerted federal effort promoted minerals prospecting and development, materials stockpiling and pollution abatement; much less has been done to increase reduction, reuse and leaner overall input use in manufacturing (Geiser, 2001, p. 161).

The federal government, through at least two blue-ribbon panels and commissions, has occasionally considered more comprehensive materials policies. These included the Paley Commission of the early 1950s and the National Materials Policy Commission of 1970, both of which advocated for transformative approaches to the nation's resources. Despite the commissions' sensible analyses and urgent rhetoric, congressional action and executive orders consisted chiefly of promoting materials markets and regulating materials as environmental pollutants (Geiser, 2001; Smith, 1997). The nation's main federal waste management law, the 1976 Resource Conservation and Recovery Act (RCRA), and various executive orders thus focus on landfill waste diversion (e.g., by curbside recycling) and procurement policies (e.g., President Clinton's order requiring federal agencies to buy 30 percent post-consumer recycled paper).

Recycling as waste diversion is widely considered a success story, and for good reason. Over the last forty years, Americans went from nearly zero municipal recycling to collecting impressive amounts, especially of beverage containers, steel, aluminum and paper. Viewed from a waste management perspective, this achievement has given us much to celebrate: landfills are reaching capacity less quickly and there is money to be made in valuable recyclables. From materials efficiency and industrial feedstock perspectives, we have accomplished far less – less even than many other industrialized nations. During the first half of the 1970s, Congress actually considered amendments to RCRA that would have mandated production standards – codifying either minimum content of desirable inputs or maximum permissible quantities of undesirable raw materials (Smith, 1997). For an industry like paper manufacturing, this could have meant rules dictating the use of recovered fibers in different paper grades – not just for papers purchased by the federal government, but for all papers sold in the US. But Congress blinked, caving to intense lobbying by waste managers and haulers (Szasz, 1986).

The global trends in commodity recycling discussed in Chapter 1 should not be confused with the most efficient materials reuse. Technical and economic factors make most modern recycling destructive: materials are broken down so that they can be used as feedstocks in conventional production or are down-cycled into lesser-valued commodities and purposes (Allwood et al., 2011). The soda-bottle washers that dotted the 1950s landscape became obsolete when beverage manufacturers moved to centralized production and filling, made affordable by lightweight plastic and aluminum containers. Now, instead of re-using perfectly sound bottles and jars, we must collect and sort these items and re-melt them in industrial furnaces.

There is also a tension between the value of recyclables and the complexity of obtaining them. Products like cars, refrigerators and computers have high material values, but over time they feature more complex mixtures of materials, which adds greatly to recycling costs (Dahmus and Gutowski, 2007). Moreover, most commodities have "best practices frontiers": limits beyond which recycling is nearly impossible, given thermodynamic and physical limits as well as quality limits on recycling by-products (Tyteca, 1996; Reuter et al., 2006).

American paper recycling, to which I now turn, shows how today's half-hearted or misguided public policies reduce consumption only by negligible amounts, barely promote materials reuse and stimulate less recycling than the best-performing industrialized nations. The paper industry is particularly emblematic of eco-industrial paradoxes: it relies on a renewable raw material whose harvest and use burden energy systems as well as air and water quality; its end-product is widely collected in the US, but used in production here far less than it could be; its factories have the potential to reach unprecedented levels of industrial symbiosis, but policy and market forces prevent the industry from realizing significant labor gains, economic value-added and resource efficiencies.

THE GLOBAL PULP AND PAPER INDUSTRY

By any measure, the global pulp and paper industry is huge and consequential. Only three industries – chemicals & petrochemicals, iron & steel, and cement – consume more energy globally than this sector (International Energy Agency (IEA), 2006). In 2010, the US pulp and paper sector used about nine percent of the country's total manufacturing energy consumption (2.4 quadrillion BTU, or "quads"), but produced only about two percent of its CO_2 emissions, thanks largely to its heavy reliance on biomass for energy (Farahani et al., 2004; Schipper, 2006; US Department of Energy, 2011).

Total global paper production rises steadily from year to year, falling only when recessions make a big dent in demand for cardboard boxes, newspapers, magazines, packaging materials and writing papers. Paperboard for cartons and packaging dominate world production, followed by printing and writing papers. Most (about 75 percent) of all mills making paper from wood fiber do the pulping and papermaking under one roof in what's called an "integrated" mill.

Collectively, the top 100 pulp and paper companies in the world produced some two-thirds of all paper and board manufactured in 2010, about 200 out of 300 million tons (Rushton et al., 2011). Paper manufacturing is heavily concentrated in Europe, North America and Asia, with China rising as the fastest-growing producer and since 2008, the world leader (UNECE/FAO, 2010). This global picture may make it sound as though production and consumption are widely distributed, but in fact just a handful of countries account for most of the consumption (with the US leading, by far) and production (the US, China, Scandinavian countries, Germany and Japan) (Environmental Paper Network, 2011; Rushton et al., 2011). Consolidation and concentration also characterize this industry within, not just across, countries. Over the course of two decades, the average size of pulp mills in Europe went from about 135,000 metric tons annually to about 300,000 metric tons annually (1991–2009). The number of mills shrank dramatically, from almost 250 to about 175 (Confederation of European Paper Industries, 2009).

By the second decade of the 21st century, packaging paper became one of the highest growth segments of this industry, with companies converting existing mills (largely away from newsprint) and relocating equipment or mills from non-growth to growth areas. Very narrow profit margins and tough competition drove the industry to reduce capital investments and operating costs. Simultaneously, environmental consciousness among consumers has led to increased interest in diverting more paper from waste streams (PPI, 2014).

Despite China's dominance and the rise of other Asian producers, Europeans foresee substantial growth in the pulp and paper sector– from 96 million tons in 2005 to 116 million tons in 2020. Technological advances, proximity to markets and efficiency gains allow European producers to compete. Very efficient Scandinavian mills exhibit some of the highest technology investment rates in the world, which allowed them to post 1.2–1.5 percent productivity gains in the 1990s (Karvonen, 2001; Hseu and Shang, 2005). Between 2010 and 2020, European analysts expect that recovered paper will provide the bulk of fiber for new European production (COST, 2010, p. 118).

Until very recently, the US dominated the global pulp and paper industry in just about every way imaginable. Not only do Americans consume more paper than anyone else, the US also produced more paper products than any single other country until China overtook the number-one spot in the first decade of the 21st century (Paperloop, 2006; Rushton et al., 2011). In 2008, the US paper industry's shipments totaled almost $180 billion, declining with the recession to approximately $160 billion in 2009 (US Census Bureau, 2011; US Department of Energy, 2011).

Papermaking in the US

Despite its enormous size, the US paper industry only employs some 350,000 workers. The industry is highly mechanized and capital-intensive.

In the US, these are good jobs, generating over $19 billion in payroll (in 2011) and good average salaries (US Census Bureau, 2011). Overall, manufacturing jobs have high direct employment multipliers, meaning that a factory worker supports workers in other industries. In 2006, the overall employment multiplier for manufacturing was 2.4, meaning that the 14 million people then employed in manufacturing were holding up another 20 million with their salaries and purchases (Luria and Rogers, 2008, p. 251). The paper industry is not much different, with an average direct employment multiplier of 1.9. It's thus reasonable to say that, in 2011, the industry's 350,000 workers supported another 665,000 employees. That's because paper manufacturing necessarily involves many people, from raw material suppliers and their transporters to primary equipment manufacturers and their maintenance services to general goods and services in the communities hosting major factories (US Census Bureau, 2011; US Bureau of Economic Assessment, 2011).

US paper companies employ sophisticated technology, but their mills are getting old. Because of enormous capital and labor costs, new mill construction slowed in recent decades, so much so that American paper mills are now the oldest in the world, on average (35+ years), followed by Europe (29 years) and China (15 years). One consequence is that American pulp and paper mills use considerably more water to make a sheet of paper than their newer, more water-efficient European counterparts (Denasiewicz and McCarty, 2011).

Moreover, Americans no longer manufacture major papermaking components, resulting in expensive equipment (because of a strong euro) and balance-of-trade problems. By 2009, US demand for paper machinery reached $2 billion, three-quarters of which was for complete machines – an order which no US company can now fill – and the rest in parts and attachments (Freedonia, 2010).

Although old paper machines throughout the US still bear domestic manufacturers' nameplates (see the picture below), a trade deficit in papermaking equipment grew to $264 million in 2010, due in large part to imports from northern Europe (Germany, Austria, Sweden, Finland, France) and Japan. Until 2005, the US actually had a modest trade surplus with China for paper machinery, but it now imports more than it exports even within that industry (US Census Bureau, 2011). This has been worsening for years, especially since the demise of the Beloit Corporation, which dominated American paper machinery manufacturing for most of the 20th century before it was purchased in the 1980s and liquidated when its parent company, Harnischfeger Corporation of Milwaukee, filed for Chapter 11 bankruptcy in 1999 (Beloit Corporation History Forum, 2011).

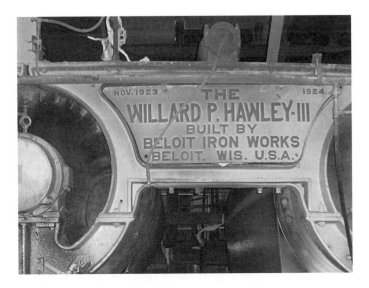

Source: Photo by Kate Pearl.

Figure 5.1   Beloit paper machine at Blue Heron Paper Company, Oregon City, Oregon

PAPER PRODUCTION AND RECYCLING TODAY

Americans were thus big users of cotton, hemp and other grasses for paper-making until about 100 years ago. Blessed with abundant forests and fresh water supplies near major transportation corridors imports, the nation turned to wood pulp for paper fiber. Moreover, as pulp mills grew, they needed large, consistent fiber sources (Thompson, 1992). But based on cellulose content alone, one would never pick wood as a source for paper fiber. A fifth to a third of the carbon atoms in wood are made up of lignin, the glue that holds cellulose in a very rigid, robust structure. Therefore, making paper from wood requires removing the cellulose from lignin – a process that demands a lot of heat or chemicals or both. Moreover, even once removed from its lignin "housing," cellulose from wood must be bleached to achieve the whiteness necessary for printed newspapers, magazines and writing. Without bleaching, these papers would look like cardboard. Unfortunately, the intense cooking required to break the lignin-cellulose bond also produces a lot of fairly noxious wastewater and air emissions.

Fortunately, paper can be recycled quite easily, though not indefinitely. The fibers in a brand-new sheet of paper will degrade and shorten to the point where they can't hook together if recycled too often. There are also inherent supply limits to paper recycling (for example, tissue papers cannot be recycled). Most paper engineers and analysts believe that 80 percent recycling of annual paper production is probably the maximum and that the remaining 20 percent or so will be lost as tissue or papers in permanent applications like books. However, many countries are far from that technical maximum (Miranda et al., 2010; Bobu and Gavrilescu, 2010; Environmental Paper Network, 2007).

Clean, well-sorted recovered paper can be made into new products fairly easily, with a fraction of the energy, water and chemical inputs needed for virgin fiber papers. Today, papermaking technology has evolved to the point where recovered paper can be made into new papers that are almost always as good (i.e., for printing upon) as their virgin fiber counterparts. Moreover, most Americans live in relatively dense urban areas, so collecting paper for recycling can be done with relatively low transportation costs. That's good, because paper is cheap but heavy.

Paper recycling terminology can be tricky. At a minimum, the following distinction must be made: paper *recovery* refers to how much paper gets collected rather than sent to a landfill or burned. Recovered paper *utilization* generally refers to how much paper is used as an industrial feedstock for new paper production.

For example, Germany, whose economy provides the best US comparison, achieved a paper recycling rate of 74 percent in 2008 while the US accomplished only 63 percent. More importantly, the German utilization rate was 68 percent while the US rate was only 37 percent (Confederation of European Paper Industries (CEPI), 2008 and Paper Industry Association Council, 2011). What this means is that Americans diverted nearly the same percentage of paper from the waste stream as their German counterparts; however, German paper industries used much more of their recovered wastepaper to make new products while Americans shipped nearly half of their recovered wastepaper to China for reprocessing mostly into new packaging materials.

For most of the time people have been making paper, they have used plant fibers high in cellulose. That's because a sheet of paper is basically one big felt mat. Given the right mix of cellulose and water, oriented in the right direction, fibers hook together to produce a sturdy but flexible lattice. Historically, good fiber sources included cotton, various grasses and even crop residues. These were good for papermaking because they have a lot of cellulose and relatively little in the way of non-usable materials that would have to be separated out before a sheet of paper could be made (Thompson, 1992).

Since 1990, US new paper and board production oscillated between 85 million and 105 million tons annually, although the industry contracted

Source: Photo by Nicole Nakagawa.

Figure 5.2   Cardboard bales at CoraEnso, Wisconsin Rapids, Wisconsin

by 6 percent between 2008 and 2010 (AF&PA, 2011a). After a big jump in waste paper recovery in the 1980s and early 1990s, American paper and board mills consumed 30–35 million tons of scrap paper every year, about 70 percent of which, by weight, yielded new paper. Thus, new paper products made in the United States contains some 20–25 million tons of recovered fiber in them in any given year. The use of recycled pulp in new production varies widely between paper grades, from an average of 45 percent recycled content in tissue products to a low of 6 percent across all printing and writing papers (Environmental Paper Network, 2007, p. 17).

Remarkably – and despite huge gains in waste paper recycling – the absolute amount of waste paper consumed barely changed between the mid-1990s and the present. In 2010, the US recovered about 51 million tons of waste paper. Most organizations call this a 63 percent recycling rate, but it is only recycling in the sense that an amount of scrap equal to 63 percent of new production was diverted from the waste stream. It does not mean that 63 percent of all paper production used recovered waste paper.

Most of the recovered paper used for new production was consumed in Southern and Midwestern mills in an arc starting in Wisconsin, moving down through the Ohio Valley to North Carolina, and ending in Alabama.

Mills used mostly (61.3 percent) old corrugated cardboard materials, though in recent years, the use of high-grade deinking grade (typically white, sorted office paper) slowly increased (to about 9 percent), perhaps reflecting its substantial value (AF&PA, 2011b).

Despite all this collection, paper is still one of the most common materials going to municipal landfills (about 26 millions tons or 16 percent of total discards in 2009) (US EPA, 2010). Common sense suggests that, in addition to lightening our landfill burden, recycling paper should have tremendous environmental benefits. Not surprisingly, detailed studies confirm this expectation. Because most recycled paper requires few chemical inputs, toxic releases and wastewater burdens differ dramatically between chemical (especially Kraft sulfate) and recycled pulps. When manufacturers replace virgin fiber with recycled pulp, total wastewater releases can go down by 50 percent (Environmental Paper Network, 2007), chemical oxygen demand drops between 40 and 95 percent (Gavrilescu and Bobu, 2009, p. 1131) and total toxic releases decline by as much as 78 percent (Press, 1996).

Energy savings demonstrate the most impressive differences between virgin wood fiber papers and their recycled counterparts. An approximately 50 percent energy saving seems to be the consistent, average advantage of recycled over virgin wood fiber (Environmental Paper Network, 2007; Gavrilescu and Bobu, 2009; Laurijssen et al., 2010). Chemical pulp manufacturing consumes, on average, around 25 gigajoules (GJ) per ton; recovered papers average 6–9 GJ/ton (Gavrilescu and Bobu, 2009), though Dutch recycled paper consumes as much as 14 GJ/ton.

Moving beyond individual mills and processes, Figure 5.3 confirms these differences, showing that countries with high recovered paper utilization rates tend to consume less overall energy to produce all of their paper grades than countries relying heavily on virgin wood fibers.[1] This partly explains why the Finnish industry – although it is very efficient and technologically advanced – averaged 25 GJ/ton in 2008. With a small population consuming and collecting relatively little paper and a large source of domestic wood fiber, the Finnish utilization rate was only 5.5 percent. Contrast that with the Germans, who averaged a little under 11 GJ/ton, partly thanks to their nearly 68 percent utilization rate. Spain has a high recovered paper use rate, but is also a large net importer of recovered paper.

᠎

---

[1] The R^2 value for the regression line in Figure 5.3 is 0.47, with a p-value < 0.005.

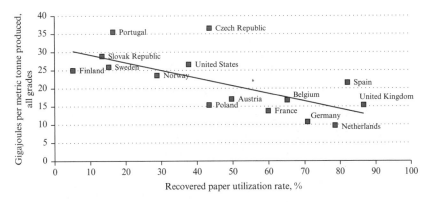

Source: CEPI, 2011.

*Figure 5.3   Energy use vs. recovered paper utilization, selected countries,
2011*

PAPER ON THE HIGH SEAS

Americans recovered 20 million *more* tons of scrap paper in 2008 than in 1990 (51.8 million tons in 2008 versus 29.1 million tons in 1990) (AFPA, 2008); if all that paper wasn't consumed in US mills, where did it go? The answer is exports.

In 1990, the US exported 22 percent of its recovered waste paper; by 2008, that figure rose to 37 percent. After a drop during the 2008–2009 recession, exports picked up again so that by 2010, exports accounted for almost 40 percent of US recovered paper usage (Freedonia, 2010).

Nothing quite says globalization and consumption like a Supramax ship piled high with containers. Large American ports, especially on the West Coast, host vessels capable of carrying 10,000 or more of these containers. Naturally, we assume that those multi-colored metal boxes harbor the finished products of sophisticated manufacturers and their highly skilled employees. And while it is true that American manufacturing is still an economic juggernaut, the US trade imbalance with China means that many of those containers must necessarily go back empty. But no one in the business of transporting anything likes retrieving an empty vessel after delivery. Whether it's a tractor-trailer, railcar or ship, it's in a firm's interest to avoid an empty "back haul," especially if fuel represents a big part of the costs. Container ships delivering goods from China typically return with only 15–20 percent capacity (if not zero), but bunker fuel (the low-grade, syrupy oil used to power large freighters) can account for 50–60 percent of operating costs (Corbett, 2011; Notteboom and Cariou, 2011, p. 223).

Source: Photo by William Livingston.

Figure 5.4   A container ship at the port of Long Beach

Increasingly, those containers now bring American scrap to countries hungry for paper fiber sources. A decade ago, US iron and steel scrap, waste paper, other metals and plastics criss-crossed the globe, landing in Canada, China, Mexico, South Korea and other countries.

Today, China dominates this trade, single-handedly consuming one-fifth to nearly two-thirds of all American scrap exports. In 2010, that amounted to 11.3 million metric tons of recovered paper shipped to China (US ITC, 2011) at an average price of $155 per ton.[2] Waste paper represents the largest tonnage of scrap shipped overseas from the US; a weak dollar, abundant scrap – and thus lower prices – especially benefit waste paper exports (Lyons et al., 2009). In essence, China ships consumer goods to the US, the US returns containers filled with waste paper and other scrap, and the cycle repeats. Chinese mills re-pulp our recovered paper and turn it into new boxes filled with another round of exports.

Maybe there are good reasons for shipping recyclables overseas instead of re-using them at home. Pieter Van Beukering, an experienced observer of global recycling patterns, suggests that developed and developing countries rationally pursue paper recycling and utilization strategies depending on their comparative trade advantages. Developing countries lack either

---

[2]   These are shipments of waste paper, harmonized system code 470790, provided by the US Department of Commerce.

fiber or waste paper recovery infrastructure; moreover, they depend heavily on trade. Consequently, their industrial policies, labor costs and trade opportunities encourage them to purchase waste paper where large supplies are available (van Beukering and Bouman, 2001).

Berglund (2002), along with his colleague Patrick Söderholm (Berglund and Söderholm, 2003) offer different explanations for waste paper utilization rates, emphasizing how much recovered fiber is available domestically rather than focusing on trade patterns. Abundant forest resources help keep wood fiber prices low. In countries where consumption is significantly higher than production, there will be high levels of waste paper available. Berglund refers to this ". . .as the *structural effect* or the *trade effect*, as it ultimately indicates the way in which comparative advantage of the domestic paper and board industry affects waste paper use" (Berglund, 2002, p. 182, italics in original). Countries that demand a lot of newsprint and paper board will likely see higher utilization rates; this is a quality demand function (Berglund, 2002, p. 182).

The US paper industry and some recyclers argue that if recovered paper is consumed abroad, it's all still a closed, sustainable loop, with just a larger circle (Kinsella, 2011; Benamara et al., 2011, p. 20). Lyons et al. (2009) echo this sentiment. In their view, increases in the weight of exported scrap make closing the recycling loop at a purely local level unrealistic (p. 296).

Different scrap circuits operate for exports and import, resulting in low-quality wastepaper exports from the US and small amounts of high-quality imports from the EU (Lyons et al., 2009, p. 297).

Lyons et al. (2009) as well as Benamara et al. (2011) argue that it's cheaper and much less energy-intensive to ship scrap by sea (rather than shipping over land to domestic markets); however, they don't offer empirical evidence or literature to support these claims. The British Waste & Resources Action Programme (WRAP) completed a study supporting the argument in favor of shipping recovered paper long distances. It found that

. . .emissions from shipping recovered paper from the UK to China are less than 1/3 of savings from recycling, and less than 1/10 if the ship carrying the waste would otherwise have returned empty (COST, 2010, p. 109).

Environmental Impacts from Shipping Recovered Paper Overseas: A Distance Penalty

Mile for mile, shipping by sea always compares favorably in terms of cost and energy-efficiency with hauling the same freight in 18-wheeled

*Table 5.1   Emissions from shipping recovered paper from Long Beach,
California to Guangzhou, China, 2010*

Ports	Nautical Kilometers	CO_2 metric tons	NOx metric tons	HC metric tons	CO metric tons	PM metric tons
Long Beach to Guangzhou	11,938	126,545	2,373	124	249	124

tractor-trailers. However, in a small country like the UK, recovered paper wouldn't have to go far to be reused as a domestic source of industrial feedstock – assuming there were enough mills still around to use that feedstock, something the WRAP study authors readily point out. So WRAP's conclusion only makes sense if the UK's recovered paper is landfilled or burned domestically instead of shipped for recycling.

Every ton of recovered paper that we don't use domestically represents a missed opportunity to conserve the virgin fiber, energy and other inputs required for new paper manufacturing. We know that using recovered paper as a feedstock prevents significant waste releases and saves substantial energy and inputs. What can we say about the energy and emissions associated with transpacific shipments? What is the "distance penalty" to shipping recovered paper halfway around the world?

The Swedish Network for Transport and Environment makes available an emissions calculator for analyzing the air pollution and energy consequences of shipping materials via different transport modes. By way of illustration, we can estimate the air emissions associated with the recovered paper shipments for China that left from the port of Long Beach, California (from which 1,046,919 metric tons were shipped in 2010). Assuming these shipments all arrived in Guangzhou (a distance of 11,938 nautical miles), Table 5.1 presents the emissions footprint from this trade.

If all US waste paper shipments to China in 2010 had left from Long Beach, the CO_2 emissions alone would have totaled 1,366,531 metric tons.[3]

Of the approximately 51 million tons of paper recovered in the US in

---

[3] Transportation and location also make a big difference in paper mills using virgin wood fiber. Robert Vos and his colleague Josh Newell compared energy and CO_2 emissions from mills making coated paper in China with the New Page Corporation's mills in Wisconsin. The emissions of CO_2 from sourcing pulp plus shipping new product were enormously different between the two countries. CO_2 emissions from the Chinese coated paper industry were about eight times higher than for New Page's mills (Vos and Newell, 2009).

2010, about 20 million went overseas or abroad to Canada and Mexico (American Forest and Paper Association, 2011). About 31.5 million short tons were consumed by American paper and board mills (American Forest and Paper Association, 2011). Since there are only a tiny number of mills using recovered paper to make new printing and writing paper, most of this consumption goes towards lower grades like newsprint and corrugated cardboard.

Why doesn't more recovered fiber stay in the US? Industry officials and analysts frequently argue that the Midwest is at a disadvantage for using recovered paper. Industry insiders frequently report that they cannot get enough high-quality recovered paper in the Midwest, possibly because Chinese demand drives prices up (Jansen, 2011; Johnson, 2011; Yordanov, 2011).

The pulp and paper industry frequently invokes Chinese competition for fiber. When Manistique Paper (Michigan) filed for Chapter 11 bankruptcy in August of 2011, the country lost another of its few paper mills making high-quality printing paper from recovered materials. As reported in *Pulp and Paper Week*, an industry trade journal,

> Since January 2011, the cost of raw material has increased $1,000,000 per month, severely impacting the bottom line. At the same time, soft market conditions resulted in a significant drop in orders. The result of this unanticipated decline in orders created excess inventory and lost revenues (Pulp & Paper Week, 2011).

The report went on to say that the facility used more than 175,000 tons of recovered paper per year, sourcing it from as far west as Minnesota and as far east as Pennsylvania.

Could Chinese demand for recovered paper really reach all the way into the Midwest? Despite the anecdotes, it seems implausible that paper could be recovered in the Midwest and then shipped to the coasts for export. Whatever the route, the transport costs should be prohibitive. Does recovered paper leave the upper Midwest by barge down the Mississippi to Gulf Coast ports? Apparently not.

In 2009, the latest year for which data were available, only negligible amounts of recovered paper were shipped by domestic waterways. That is, through-freight on, for example, the Mississippi River does not amount to a lot of fiber. Waterborne Commerce Statistics Center data showed that 912,462 short tons of waste paper were shipped in the Gulf Coast/ Mississippi River/Antilles system, but the vast majority of those were shipments from Gulf Coast or Florida ports to overseas markets. Only a little over 4,000 tons traveled down the Mississippi from northern cities to the Gulf (United States Army Corps of Engineers, 2011).

Just to be sure, what about the state-to-state and region-to-region waterborne commerce data for the whole country? Once again, the vast majority of the wastepaper shipments were not between states and regions, but between particular states or regions and foreign export.

Nor does it appear that wastepaper is traveling overland by rail, for example, from the upper Midwest metropolitan areas to ports on the coasts, according to data by the federal government's Surface Transportation Board. The Board samples shipments to estimate which commodities the railways handle, in what quantities, and how they criss-cross the country. The "Public Use Waybill" data for 2009 allow us to examine the estimated recovered paper shipments by rail. Drawing on their sample and projection of how their samples scale up (i.e., the "expanded tons"), the Board estimates that 765,520 tons of recovered paper were shipped by rail in 2009 (United States Department of Transportation, 2011).[4] Clearly then, American recovered paper doesn't travel far from where it is collected.

Mitko Yordanov, statistical program manager at the American Forest & Paper Association, had another hypothesis: perhaps the Midwest paper mills faced chronic recovered-paper shortages because that's not where a lot of paper is collected. The largest markets for paper products are in the big metropolitan areas of the coasts; naturally, a lot of paper will thus be used and then recycled in the cities of the eastern seaboard and the West Coast. But that's not where the paper mills are. The mills are concentrated in the upper Midwest and Southeast.

If Yordanov's hunch is correct, then Midwestern mills are using more recovered paper than their regions collect. The opposite would be true of the eastern seaboard states of the Mid Atlantic and New England. The data to test this idea are not perfect, but here's what we can surmise:

Using the GAA's MRF yearbook for fiber collection data and the AF&PA's statistical summary on recovered paper utilization, the East North Central region (Indiana, Illinois, Michigan, Ohio and Wisconsin) collected about 2.8 million tons of paper in 2008, but consumed about 6.2 million tons in its various mills, for a ratio of 0.45 tons collected to a ton used. For the Mid Atlantic states of Pennsylvania on up through New England, the picture is just the opposite. About 6.1 million tons of paper were collected, but only about 5 million tons were used as fiber in pulp and paper mills, for a ratio of 1.2 tons collected to a ton used.

---

[4] Most of these shipments were medium hauls from metropolitan areas to cities with large mills using significant amounts of recovered paper, e.g., Kansas City to Shreveport, Louisiana, home to large mills owned by International Paper and Pratt Industries. Mexico was the longest haul destination, but accounted for only about 11 percent of these rail shipments (USDOT, 2011).

It's important to caution, however, that the recovered paper data are likely incomplete. The data on paper collection come from the GAA's MRF Yearbook. If we are to believe the AF&PA's numbers on total recovered fiber use in the US, then the GAA probably misses around half of all the paper fiber collected. But even if we double the amount of paper collected, the ratio for the East North Central region becomes 0.9 while that of the eastern seaboard becomes about 2.4. In other words, the Midwest still doesn't have enough recovered paper while the eastern seaboard has far too much.

Similarly, paper mills in the Midwest and Southeast can handle a lot of recovered paper; in recent years, they have not likely been operating at or near capacity. Figure 5.5 shows the materials recover facility (MRF) paper collection capacities alongside of the paper mills that handle some amount of recovered paper. Once again, we see a mismatch between paper collection and mill capacity, especially since Figure 5.5 under-represents total collected paper volumes. In reality, the recovered paper collected outside of the MRF system probably doubles the amounts presented in Figure 5.5.

Of course, paper flows don't respect US Census Bureau regions. Paper mills that rely heavily on recovered paper somehow managed to maintain their raw material sources. There may be "leakage" of recovered paper from other regions, and as noted, we don't have perfect information on the patterns of paper recovery. But clearly it's a tight market for high-quality recovered fiber in some producing regions.

These ratios of paper collection to recovered paper utilization make a strong social and environmental case for developing paper mill capacity in the large metropolitan areas of the coasts. There are lots of obstacles to doing so, to be sure; however, lacking large volumes of fiber sources and markets for finished products are not chief among them. The overall business case has been weak, given structural barriers and an uneven playing field (relative to foreign mills); however, public policy could vastly improve the business case, as we will see in Chapter 6.

OBSTACLES TO FURTHER RECOVERED PAPER USE IN THE UNITED STATES

Paper recycling in the US is paradoxical. Americans have vastly increased their paper recycling rates without actually increasing their recovered paper utilization rates. Reasons include poor sorting, volatile recovered paper prices, a lack of mill capacity near large sources of recovered paper (as I discussed in the previous section) and the related high cost

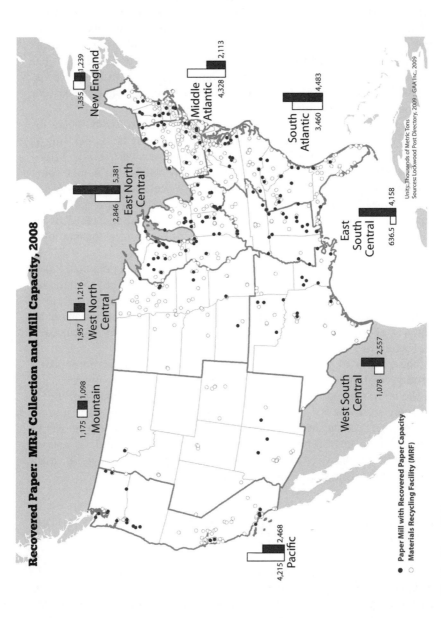

Recovered Paper: MRF Collection and Mill Capacity, 2008

New England
1,355 | 1,239

Middle Atlantic
4,328 | 2,113

South Atlantic
3,460 | 4,483

East North Central
2,846 | 5,381

West North Central
1,957 | 1,216

Mountain
1,175 | 1,098

East South Central
636.5 | 4,158

West South Central
1,078 | 2,557

Pacific
4,215 | 2,468

Units: Thousands of Metric Tons
Sources: Lockwood Post Directory, 2009; GAA Inc., 2009

• Paper Mill with Recovered Paper Capacity
○ Materials Recycling Facility (MRF)

Map by Aaron Cole.

Source: Map by Aaron Cole.

Figure 5.5 Recovered paper: MRF collection and mill capacity, 2008

of transporting raw material. Any viable strategy for increasing recovered paper use at US mills will have to address these obstacles.

Poorly Sorted Recyclables

By the mid- to late-1990s, states and municipalities around the country were looking for ways to increase recycling rates while lowering costs. Public support for recycling was high, but taxpayers were not very interested in paying extra for more or better recycling programs (Cuyler, 2002). Municipal landfills were never very popular to begin with, and the NIMBYism that had characterized opposition to dangerous or high-risk facilities now began extending to ordinary city dumps. Many states adopted waste diversion mandates, some of them quite aggressive. California's AB 939 gave cities and counties in that state just 10 years to reduce their solid waste streams by 50 percent. Curbside recycling would play a big role in meeting the state's mandate.

But curbside recycling in the 1990s asked a lot from participants, while simultaneously allowing industry to divert attention from producer responsibility initiatives. Many municipalities required that residents sort their recyclables, often into multiple bins. Only the most committed citizens carefully sorted the proper (and clean) items into the right boxes, then hefted them one-by-one to the curb. Waste haulers and sanitation workers didn't like this system either. Injuries were common as workers had to step off their trucks and lift bin after bin on collection runs.

The solution to this untenable situation was "single stream" or "commingled" recycling rather than being creative about implementing clean, multi-stream sorting at the curbside (as has been more successful in Germany). Municipalities quickly found that the public likes to put everything into one wheeled cart or bin; when they did so, participation increased substantially (Cuyler, 2002; Berenyi, 2008). Waste haulers prefer having their trucks pick up a single bin with a hydraulic arm. Automating the pickup results in fewer injuries and worker compensation cases, as even late-comers to single-stream systems have found. The city of Minneapolis, Minnesota reported a drop in worker injuries from a dozen to just one when it adopted single-stream in 2013. The city saved $250,000 in workers compensation costs and increased its collection rate from 17.4 percent in 2012 to 23.3 percent in 2013 (Elliott, 2014).

Most of these commingled recyclables end up at materials recovery facilities (MRFs), of which there are about 560 operating in the US (Berenyi, 2008). Not surprisingly, single stream facilities represent the fastest-growing segment of the MRF industry, with over a quarter of the firms designed to handle commingled recyclables exclusively. Many

MRFs are upgrading their equipment with sensors and optical scanners, thereby allowing them to automate sorting, but paper is not especially well suited to these technologies, in part because they sense only the surface of the material. Thus, a plastic bag filled with newsprint would be read as plastic instead of paper (Kinsella, 2011; Birett, 2011; Berenyi, 2008; COST, 2010). Devices that rely on physical properties work better; these include ". . .screen systems (disk, star, drum screens), ballistic separators (rotating screens), gap techniques (acceleration of materials over or into a gap between conveyor belts)" (COST, 2010, p. 50).

By the early 2000s, recyclable-materials processors were becoming more consolidated and regionalized. As the volume of recyclables increased, haulers and processers could engage in long-term contracts; moreover, processers could dictate the terms of those contracts. Previously buyers, such as paper mills, were in a better position to demand particular quality and price factors (Cuyler, 2002).

As Geiser puts it, "[T]he key to high-value markets for secondary materials is quality, not quantity" (Geiser, 2001, p. 231). But as collection rates increased, it became clear that higher rates decrease the quality of the material collected. That's because 1) high quality, easy-to-collect sources (i.e., the low-hanging fruit) are already exploited (e.g., high volumes of clean and uniform paper from individual sources like large printers) and 2) commingling recovered paper with other recyclables in single-stream collection systems increases the amount of contaminant that arrives at the pulp mill. (Birett, 2011; Miranda et al., 2010; Morawski, 2009; Sacia and Simmons, 2006; Cuyler, 2002; Biddle, 1998).

Sadly – given their high recyclability – waste beverage containers present the biggest contamination challenge for MRFs and paper mills, so much so that, by 2008, one fifth of all US MRFs stopped accepting glass (Cuyler, 2002; Themelis and Todd, 2004; Berenyi, 2008). In a single stream recycling system, a lot of glass is bound to be broken, most of which will then be discarded in a landfill rather than re-melted and used again. If the glass isn't initially broken in the recycling bin, it stands a good chance of being broken during handling at the MRF – and MRFs can barely sell broken glass shards and dust. Shockingly, "On average, 40 percent of glass from single-stream collection winds up in landfills, while 20 percent is small broken glass ("glass fines") used for low-end applications. Only 40 percent is recycled into containers and fiberglass" (Morawski, 2009, p. 6). The beverage container industry and a group of secondary processors have addressed the sorting problem with beneficiation plants. These facilities use sophisticated equipment and hand-sorting to provide very clean, uniform and "furnace-ready" cullet to glass plants (Hudson Baylor, 2011).

In a widely cited study, two Weyerhaeuser employees tracked the effects of changing scrap paper quality at the company's NORPAC newsprint mill in Longview, Washington. Over a two-year period, eight different suppliers converted to commingled collections. Within a few years, the company's pulper rejects increased by 800 percent, the mill was forced to spend $2.5 million more on fiber inputs, and maintenance costs increased more than three-fold (Sacia and Simmons, 2006).

Ruben Miranda and his colleagues at the Complutense University of Madrid have reached similar conclusions from their studies of commingled recycling. In an elegant study of recovered paper inputs for a Spanish newsprint mill, Miranda et al. (2013) focused on the company's use of fiber imported from the UK. Taking advantage of a kind of natural experiment, the authors analyzed unusable material content in two time periods. In the first period, commingled recyclables from the UK supplier were poorly sorted, with unusable material content averaging an astonishing 11.9 percent (ranging from 1 percent to 29 percent). Within two years, a new, large Materials Recovery Facility (MRF) had been built with superior sorting capabilities. Drawing on the same commingled recyclables stream, the new MRF achieved a drop to an average of only 7.9 percent unusable material – still unacceptable over the long term, but a remarkable achievement in just two years (Miranda et al., 2013).

In other instances, time is not so kind to recycling. The Blue Heron Paper company, in Oregon City, Oregon, saw its contaminant rate rise to 8 percent (much of it plastics) over a 15-year period that coincided with increased plastics recycling in its region. Fortunately, the trend in contamination led the company to seek grant funding and a partnership with Agri-Plas, a plastics recycler specializing in the recovery of used nursery pots, tarps and baling twine. Blue Heron found that removing the plastics was viable partly because it had a ready buyer in Agri-Plas (Malloch, 2009).[5]

Spain's dramatic recycling experience in recent years mirrors the firm-level problems encountered by Blue Heron Paper. Spain's aggressive efforts to increase its collection rates between 2005 and 2008 worked very well – collection rates country-wide increased from 58.5 percent to 68.6 percent – but quality declined dramatically, with unusable materials growing by 50 percent (Miranda et al., 2011).

Municipalities, which pay for their curbside recycling programs by selling what they collect, also find it increasingly difficult to get the best

---

[5] The mill went out of business in 2010. As Mike Siebers, Blue Heron's former CEO put it, "Blue Heron was eventually forced out of business by dramatically escalating waste paper prices and an imperfect recycling system that forced excess sorting costs, taxes and fees on to the paper consuming plant at Blue Heron" (Siebers, 2011).

prices for their materials, in part because of quality. For example, cities in the province of Ontario, Canada, experienced a twelve-fold increase in the percentage of "outthrows" (contaminated or dirty recyclables) and "prohibitives" (non-recyclable materials) in their curbside mix from 2002 to 2010. At the same time, easy-to-recycle old-newsprint volumes have declined by five percent per year (Birett, 2011).

Susan Kinsella, Executive Director of Conservatree (an environmental NGO specializing in paper sustainability) and a veteran of efforts to green the American paper industry, concluded that paper recycling in the US fails to live up to its promise because the waste management and paper industries each claim that good materials sorting is not their core business. Recyclers don't see themselves in the business of producing industrial feedstocks, while paper companies don't think they should be burdened with the cost and trouble of cleaning up sorted materials (Kinsella, 2011). Ann Jansen, an engineer and analyst at the recycled paper company, FutureMark, echoed this sentiment, pointing out that American attitudes about recycling are "component rather than systems-oriented." As a result, each component of the paper-recycling trade optimizes its own transactions. Waste brokers have little incentive either to improve waste-paper sorting or preferentially sell their product to nearby paper mills (Jansen, 2011).

Europeans complain of the same mentality, even though they have achieved generally better collection and utilization rates. A recent, major study pointed out that:

> Paper recycling in Europe has been faced with an identity crisis ... recovered paper has become an essential raw material – whereas for policy makers used paper has simply been a waste problem. This has. . .culminated in the classification of recovered paper as waste as opposed to secondary material. The very rigid legislation defined waste as 'any substance or object. . .which the holder discards or intends or is required to discard' (COST, 2010, p. 101).

Quixotically, European countries require complex or expensive permits to haul materials classified as waste. The pool of waste transporters is thus naturally smaller than the pool of haulers available to carry secondary materials (COST, 2010, p. 102). Further challenging Old World reuse efforts, European contaminant rates now average 2.5 percent (about ten times what most mills deem acceptable); one Spanish study found an average of over 7 percent unwanted materials (COST, 2010, p. 63; Bobu et al., 2010, p. 465).

Unlike the US, however, the EU will try to resolve its waste identity crisis. A 2008 European Waste Directive, to take effect in 2015, will

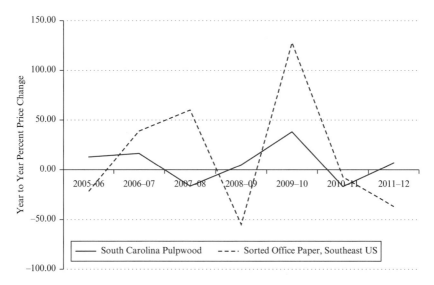

Sources: Official Board Markets, 2005–11; South Carolina Forestry Commission, 2005–11.

Figure 5.6 *Price changes, sorted office paper vs. pine pulpwood,*
southeastern US, 2005–12

require separated collection for paper, metal and plastics (Miranda et al.,
2010).[6]

Recovered Paper Prices

Raw materials can easily rise to 50 percent of a mill's operating costs, so
high prices, quality variations and price volatility add considerable risk to
any paper-making enterprise. Recovered paper grades – especially sourced
from curbside recycling programs – commonly vary widely in quality.
Consequently, the cleanest, most valuable recovered papers are the most
scarce. The soft- and hardwoods typically used for pulp manufacturing
exhibit less variability in both quality and prices. Figure 5.6, above, compares price changes, year-to-year, in the southeastern US. The data are
for sorted office paper from the southeast and pine pulpwood from South
Carolina.[7]

---

[6] The rule is Directive 2008/98/EC of the European Parliament and of the Council of 19
November 2008 on Waste and Repealing Certain Directives.

[7] Although it takes two or more tons of pulpwood to make one ton of finished paper
product, fiber costs for a mill using pulpwood are commonly lower than recovered paper

Lack of Mill Capacity

No amount of paper recycling will change the waste paper industrial utilization rate in the US – however clean and sorted it may be – if mills don't have the capacity to handle it (Andersen, 1997; Kinsella, 2008; EPN, 2007, 2011). Despite record waste paper recovery, the US has not built a new plant dedicated to making printing and writing paper from scrap since the mid-1990s. The 15 mills that produced about 1.7 million tons of deinked pulp for printing and writing grades in 2010 are much the same as those in existence over a decade ago (Environmental Paper Network, 2011).

Building a new deinking mill in a large metropolitan area such as New York or Los Angeles would cost a half billion dollars, assuming one could get the permits (Jansen, 2011). If it's the case that recycled paper must compete on both quality and cost bases, carrying the debt load for major capital expansion makes building a new plant unthinkable.

Historically, large factories that make industrial commodities like paper have seen raw materials prices fall, energy prices stay relatively flat and labor costs rise sharply. One obvious way to save money is to reduce the amount of labor needed per unit manufactured; that may mean replacing labor with more materials use but less sorting (Allwood et al., 2011, p. 374). Older manufacturing facilities have a lot of "legacy assets" – complex, expensive equipment that has long since been amortized. In the paper industry, older mills wrote off their black liquor recovery boilers (an essential energy source in Kraft mills) long ago, so building new mills or purchasing the new kinds of equipment necessary for recycled paper sorting, deinking and re-pulping might be very unattractive (Kinsella, 2011; Alwood et al., 2011).

As Maureen Smith (1997) put it so well, using public policy to successfully spur new manufacturing capacity is extraordinarily complex, relying on information rarely available to policy "generalists," like members of Congress or a state legislature:

> [P]rospects for effective intervention. . .are substantially enhanced if one also has some grasp of the ways in which pulp production is integrated with timber and other forest products production, the locational and skill barriers that attach to alternative materials used, the R&D capacity of the industry, the central technological themes, and the strong, long-standing economic linkages between the pulp and basic chemicals sectors. The environmental

---

costs. For the data in Figure 5.6, pulpwood ranged from $7–11 per ton while sorted office paper ranged from $90–205 per ton (Official Board Markets, 2005–11; South Carolina Forestry Commission, 2005–11).

problems are related by the sector's internal structural characteristics, which in turn are heavily mediated by its relationship with other sectors (Smith, 1997, pp. 232–33).

High Transport Costs – An Economic Form of the Distance Penalty

Earlier we saw that those regions with the most paper collection don't necessarily have the most paper mill capacity. Common sense and prior research tell us that transportation costs loom large for any commodity that is relatively cheap and heavy. That's why low-sulfur Western coal, which can sell for as little as $12 a ton at the mine mouth in Wyoming, will cost a power plant in Georgia twice that (Considine, 2009, p. 14). Recovered paper is no different, and transportation costs may even affect collection rates, as Christer Berglund and his colleagues point out: ". . .the lower the cost of waste paper collection and recovery, in terms of transport etc., the higher the recovery rate" (Berglund, et al., 2002, p. 186).

Even though railroads offer the cheapest surface freight rates, it's easy to see how moving recovered paper around the country is prohibitively expensive. According to the Surface Transportation Board data, the relatively small amount of recovered paper moving around the country by rail in 2009 cost a lot to ship. The Board's 2009 railcar sample revealed about 375 recovered paper shipments, ranging from just a few miles in length to over 2600 miles. The average freight revenue for these shipments was $50 per ton (United States Department of Transportation, 2011). At that price, only the most valuable recovered paper grades – those selling for well over $100 per ton – would be worth shipping long distances. Indeed, for most of 2009, average prices for low-grade recovered paper were lower than the shipping costs!

These obstacles to increasing recovered paper use as an industrial feedstock would look insurmountable were it not for several companies that have reconciled the economic, spatial and environmental paradoxes inherent in US paper recycling. The Chicago-area FutureMark Paper provides one of the best examples.

AN ALTERNATIVE VISION FOR AMERICAN SUSTAINABLE PAPERMAKING: FUTUREMARK PAPER

Sometimes, sustainability takes on a decidedly modest, gritty and urban look.

To see one of the cleanest paper mills in the country for myself, I drove south from Chicago to Alsip, Illinois, about 15 miles away, on a hot August day. As I approached the FutureMark mill from the north, I passed through industrial neighborhoods filled with boxy buildings that looked more like warehouses then factories. Just a few hundred feet further down on South Pulaski road lies the Calumet-Saginaw Channel, a canal built in the 1910s to connect the Little Calumet River and the Chicago Sanitary and Ship Canal. Today, FutureMark is the only paper mill in the United States that makes coated paper (used in glossy paper magazines and catalogs) almost entirely from recovered paper collected regionally.

The mill got its start in 1966 as a joint venture between Field Enterprises and Garden State Paper. At that time, Field Enterprises owned the Chicago Sun-Times and wanted a source of 100 percent recycled-fiber newsprint (Watson, 1988; Mokry and Winkels, 2003). Known as the FSC paper mill, the plant steadily produced about 100,000 tons of newsprint per year over the next couple of decades.

In 1988, FSC tried a new approach to sourcing recovered paper and selling its newsprint. The mill rolled out what it called its Total Recycling program and offered it to communities within about a 100-mile radius. A mill's semi would leave the plant with a load of newsprint for local news-paper printers, unload the newsprint, then head to the closest municipal recycling facility. Dropping off the empty trailer, the truck would pick up a trailer full of old newspapers, thereby allowing the company to have full use of its trucks on both the front- and backhauls. By the late 1980s, nine communities in three states participated in the program (Watson, 1988).

In 1993, senior management at the FSC plant purchased the mill and began investing in plant improvements that would "enable the mill to produce brighter, stronger and cleaner 100 percent recycled paper, which would be suitable for business papers such as forms, envelopes and tablets; commercial printing papers such as inserts; book papers; and newsprint" (Mokry and Winkels, 2003). In a move that would foreshadow the mill's current market niche, the new owners quickly spent $30 million for an on-machine coater that would eventually allow the company to enter the magazine and brochure market (Pulp and Paper, 2000).

Things did not go so well for the company in the late 1990s, perhaps because of lackadaisical marketing. Early in 2000, FSC filed for bank-ruptcy. A few months later, the Myllokoski Corporation of Finland bought the company, some say for less than it was worth (Pulp and Paper, May 2000). Recognizing the mill's marketing potential as an innovative recycler, the new owners set out to convert the facility to lightweight coated printing papers, which would ultimately require another $100 million for new and replacement equipment (Mokry and Winkels 2003; Business Wire, 2001).

By late 2002, the mill's new equipment and processes were up and running, allowing it to produce 125,000 tons of lightweight coated (LWC) paper per year (Mokry and Winkels 2003). The LWC furnish – or raw material – contained "80 percent DIP (deinked) fiber" (Mokry and Winkels 2003). One reporter described the Alsip mill prior to its transformation as "an outdated producer of commodity newsprint grades" (Paterno 2004). It then became "a high-tech mill using cutting-edge papermaking and finishing technology to produce value-added graphic papers . . . [and] was the first mill in the US to use recycled fiber and new online coating and calendering technology to make the coated No. 5 grades commonly used in catalogs, magazines, and inserts" (Paterno 2004).

Despite spending $200 million on the Alsip plant, Myllykoski felt that the mill under its management had never done very well. The company threw in the towel and put the plant up for sale in 2007, although it did not attract buyers for a full two years (Johnson, 2010; Rodden 2011). Late in 2009, deep in a dreary recession, the Lexington, Massachusetts-based Watermill group announced that it had acquired the Alsip paper mill for an undisclosed sum that was nevertheless "a bargain" (Johnson, 2010).

FutureMark owed its turnaround miracle to ordinary marketing. Yes, the facility made excellent engineering and process design choices, both under its current management and the previous group, but that was clearly not enough to make the mill profitable. After all, coated paper is technically difficult to make and sells very much like an ordinary commodity– you make your money on volume and by lowering costs. Moreover, using recycled paper to make coated grades commits a plant to extra capital and operational costs. A mill making newsprint from recovered paper would not need as much equipment and processing to collect, store, transport, clean and de-ink the recovered fiber. To make matters worse, an average mill using recovered fiber for coated paper has to expect lower yields (Metafore Inc., 2009).

Myllykoski and potential buyers concluded that trying to sell recycled paper to glossy magazine and catalog publishers in a down economy was a risky, bad match – so much so that the owners actually downplayed the recovered paper content when making sales (Waste & Recycling News, 2010). Watermill's genius was in pivoting from a product with a liability to a niche market with no competitors, in the sense that no other mills were pushing 100 percent recovered fiber *coated* paper. In an interview for a trade journal, FutureMark's CEO Stephen Silver pointed out that "the mill. . .was 'never marketed. . .as the environmental sustainability pure play that it is. Most paper companies aren't good marketers,' Smith said. 'The other thing we make a big deal out of is who we do business with,' Silver said" (Johnson, 2010). In 2010, the mill picked up 50 accounts that quickly made up more than 50 percent of its capacity. Clients included household names like WalMart, Staples, American Airlines, Dell, Macy's, Scholastic, U.S. News & World Report and Whole Foods Market (Rodden, 2011).

Environmental Performance

Six innovations account for the FutureMark's unusually light environmental footprint. As with any good real estate deal, the first is location. The mill benefits from being close to large recovered paper supplies as well as huge printing enterprises like Quadgraphics.[8] It only takes about two-dozen broker/collectors operating within a 300-mile radius of Chicago to supply most of the mill's needs.

Figure 5.7 illustrates the mill's locational advantage, using two months of supply data from 2010. Fifty-six percent of the shipments came from within 200 miles' distance or less; only about a quarter of them came from over 300 miles away. Recovered fiber shipments to the plant averaged about 0.43 gigajoules per ton, or about 4 percent of what the mill requires to make a ton of coated paper – a very favorable energy burden compared to overseas shipments, which likely average *four times as much* (about 1.75 gigajoules per ton) for a transpacific shipment (based on the NTM transport emissions calculator).

How does this compare to a Midwestern mill making coated paper from virgin wood fiber? Once again, the bottom line is very sensitive to distance. A mill making all of its coated paper from locally-sourced wood fiber (i.e., within 100 miles) could source the same amount of raw material for less energy (about 0.28 gigajoules per metric ton). If that same mill sourced half of its fiber from local providers and purchased half of its market pulp from far-off Canadian sources over 1500 miles away (in Nova Scotia), the transport energy demand would rise to over 1 gigajoule per metric ton.

Second, FutureMark uses primarily old magazines, printer trim (supplied by some of the same printers who buy their coated paper) and other high-quality, clean grades – but not much old newsprint and no cardboard, so the firm does not compete much for fiber going to the big newsprint and boxboard recyclers.

Third, the mill gets much better yields (i.e., new pulp) from its recovered

---

[8] The Quadgraphics printing plant in Sussex, Wisconsin alone produces 4500 tons of scrap paper *per month*. Paper mills eagerly seek out such volumes of high-quality recovered paper and the printers are willing to oblige, provided they have equipped themselves with good trim paper recycling systems to collect the paper and bale it for sale as feedstock (Cagle, 2006).

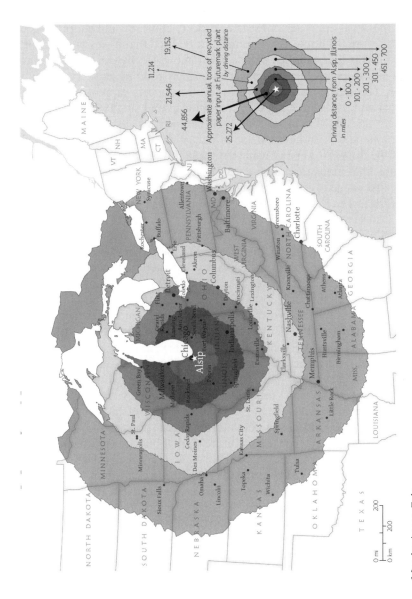

Source: Map by Aaron Cole.

Figure 5.7   Recycled paper source by driving distance from Alsip, Illinois FutureMark paper recycling plant

paper than most of its competitors, as much as 90 percent versus the usual 70 percent recovery in the production of recycled printing and writing grades (Rodden, 2011). The plant's kinder, gentler approach to pulping ensures this impressive yield. When deinking and re-pulping recovered fiber, the usual approach consists of quickly churning and chopping the paper in warm or hot water. FutureMark realized that it was breaking up contaminants that could be more easily removed if they remained whole, so the mill suspends the wastepaper in a slowly rotating, cold-water drum pulper. Through long trial-and-error, mill engineers capitalized on their water's natural hardness, added some cationic sand, and found they could manage "stickies" far better than their competitors. Whole CDs, plastic bottles, metal bits and even strips of magazine binding glue steadily fall out of the drum's lower end while the valuable paper fibers remain in suspension. That innovation, along with others downstream, allows the mill to use an average of only 27 m³ of water per ton of finished paper, which is on the far low end of the US paper industry water consumption (Johnson, 2011; Denasiewicz and McCarty, 2011).[9]

Fourth, in 2010, the mill started using a cornstarch-based binding agent for its coatings rather than the usual petroleum-based latex. The "Ecosphere biolatex" performs as well as synthetic latex, but arrives in pelletized form rather than pre-mixed with water. FutureMark thus saves truck space and shipping costs while enjoying the bragging rights that come with being the first North American paper manufacturer to incorporate a coating ingredient derived from 100 percent renewable feedstock in its commercial production process (FutureMark, 2010).

Fifth, the mill significantly reduced its solid waste production and costs by turning its deinking sludge into a soil amendment. By pulping with just cold water, the plant produces deinking sludge with no hazardous or harmful constituents – what it does have is a lot of calcium, similar to agricultural lime, which is a common fertilizer supplement. After years of testing and agency reviews, FutureMark obtained approval to sell some 30,000 tons per year of its "High-Calcium Paper Lime" to farms in Illinois and Indiana. The company thereby saves a lot on tipping fees (waste disposal costs) and can move these materials from its waste ledger to its product line, a significant plus for the firm's green bottom line (FutureMark, 2010).

Sixth, FutureMark's low chemical usage and its dissolved-air flotation system for deinking allows the mill to send its wastewater to the local Calumet Water Reclamation Plant. ". . .The resulting wastewater is clean

---

[9] American paper mills average between 30 m³ and 150 m³ water per ton of paper (Denasiewicz and McCarty, 2011).

enough to be returned to the municipal water recovery district treatment plant that discharges [about seven miles] upstream of the mill's intake into the Calumet Saginaw Canal". Therefore, says [CEO Stephen] Smith, "In a sense, we are closed cycle" (Johnson, 2011; Rodden, 2011).

Can the FutureMark Model be Replicated?

FutureMark is not the only mill of its kind in the world. Two German mills also make high-quality coated paper from recycled materials, the Steinbeis mill in Glueckstadt (near Hamburg) and the Leipa mill in Schwedt, northeast of Berlin. And in May 2012, the Watermill Group, FutureMark's owner, bought the struggling Manistique Paper Company that had filed for Chapter 11 bankruptcy a year earlier. Pouring $13 million into the Manistique mill allowed it to become the sole North American producer of exclusively 100 percent recycled high-bright printing papers (FutureMark, 2014).

Veterans from the recycled-paper wars of the last 20 years can attest to the nearly heroic efforts it takes to get investors, environmentalists, labor unions and economic development officials together on new manufacturing facility proposals. But US industry can be dynamic and opportunistic, especially when it works towards a profitable and appealing goal. What might a vision for new mill capacity look like? Drawing on the lessons and data of this chapter, we can imagine siting new mills with the greatest environmental, transportation, labor and market opportunities. This hypothetical should not be confused with comparisons between domestic recovered paper use and virgin wood fiber use – many virgin fiber mills compare quite favorably with recycling because they use so much biomass for their energy sources and their cogeneration systems push their mills' overall energy efficiencies quite high.

Suppose a company like FutureMark designed a new deinking mill, with a modest capacity of about 450 tons per day, to use recovered high quality deinking paper for making new printing and writing papers. The confluence of environmental, transportation, labor and market advantages could lie in an East Coast or California metropolitan area. Thus, if our proposed mill were sited somewhere in the New York City metropolitan area, how would its transport air emissions and transport energy consumption compare with what actually left East Coast ports in 2010?

The AF&PA's statistical summary of recovered paper consumption provides the actual tonnage of recovered high-grade deinking paper shift from mid-Atlantic and New England ports, i.e., the shipments total 234,000 tons (see Table 5.2). Assuming fairly modest conversion efficiencies (70 percent) from recovered paper to finished product, these should be

Table 5.2   Sorted office paper shipments from the East Coast of the US, 2010

Origin	Short Tons	Distance to New York City, miles
St. Albans	68,000	360
Boston	2,000	220
New York City area	78,000	50
Ogdensburg, NJ	31,000	50
Buffalo, NY	7,000	375
Baltimore and DC area	13,000	200
Norfolk, VA	35,000	360

Source: AFPA, 2011d.

Table 5.3   Comparison of container ship and tractor-trailor truck emissions for paper shipments

Options	Nautical Kilometers	CO_2 metric tons	NOx metric tons	HC metric tons	CO metric tons	PM metric tons	SOx metric tons	Energy (GJ)
Sea shipments from East Coast ports to Guangzhou, China	15,946	34,290	643	34	68	34	508	372,354
Truck shipments from East Coast ports to NYC	From 50–375	5,207	43	1	8	1	0	67,549

enough fiber for our 450-ton-per-day mill. Annual production would be about 164,000 tons of finished paper.

Converting all of these into ton-kilometers, we then use the Swedish Environmental Institute's transport emissions and energy calculator to come up with Table 5.3 that compares sending all these shipments through the Panama Canal to China versus shipping them by truck (the least efficient surface transport mode method) to the New York City area.

Considering only transport energy, using the recovered paper domestically would require 0.41 GJ per ton of finished product. Contrast that with overseas shipments, which require 2.2 GJ per ton, over five times as much.

On transport energy and emissions alone, using recovered paper in the US is preferable, by far, over shipping overseas.

American labor unions, notably in the Blue Green Alliance, would like to see more domestic recycling for the substantial new jobs it would bring (Blue Green Alliance, 2011). Although the national average direct employment multiplier for the paper industry was 1.9 in 2008, it varied regionally. Those states that already had a lot of paper mills (i.e., a dozen or more, which includes Wisconsin, Alabama, Georgia, Ohio, New York, Michigan) had an average employment multiplier of 2.27, almost 20 percent higher (US Bureau of Economic Assessment, 2011).

Provided the supply and distribution chains remain short, domestic recovered paper use will always have a lighter energy and pollution footprint than shipping fiber many thousands of miles for use in distant factories. Whether the distance penalty will become too severe thus depends on energy prices. However, even if fossil fuel costs soar, willing entrepreneurs and investors may still need a lot of help or coaxing before they open new mills; market forces alone will not likely create many new recycling mills.

Maureen Smith looked at the late-1970s-to-early-1990s generation of paper production and surmised that the US could have reached its production targets with more recovered wastepaper:

> Given the large supplies of virgin newsprint coming in from Canada, essentially all the substantial expansion in domestic newsprint production – a 2.6 million ton increase in annual production between 1970 and 1988 – could have been based on recovered materials. But that less than a third of it was, and that domestic manufacturers were still expanding virgin newsprint production capacity by the late 1980s, represent further complications in the argument that basic market forces provide the strongest and most efficient stimuli for recycling. (Smith, 1997, p. 193).

A vigorous industrial policy aimed at recycling would necessarily enlist many different stakeholders in industry, at all government levels and in the NGO sector. Collection and sorting improvements can't be secured without active participation by municipal governments. Tax policies encouraging new capital investments could be pursued by state governments, but federal involvement would likely be most effective. Chapter 6 will present a suite of policy interventions designed to stimulate US recycling, transforming it from sub-optimal waste management to industrial feedstock.

REFERENCES

Allwood, J., M. Ashby, et al. (2011). "Material Efficiency: A White Paper." *Resources Conservation and Recycling* 55(3): 362–381.

American Forest and Paper Association (AFPA) (2008). 2008 Statistical Summary for Paper, Paperboard and Wood Pulp. Washington, DC, AF&PA.

American Forest and Paper Association (2011a). 51st Annual Survey of Paper, Paperboard and Pulp Capacity. Washington, DC, AF&PA.

American Forest and Paper Association (2011b). Monthly Statistics of Paper, Paperboard and Wood Pulp. Washington, DC, AF&PA.

American Forest and Paper Association (2011c). 2011 Annual Statistical Summary of Recovered Paper Utilization. Washington, DC, AF&PA.

American Forest and Paper Association (AFPA) (2011d). 2011 Annual Statistical Summary of Recovered Paper Utilization. Washington, DC, AF&PA.

Andersen, S. (1997). "The Outer Limits of Paper Recovery and Recycling." *TAPPI Journal* 8(4): 59–62.

Beloit Corporation History Forum. (2011). "Beloit Corporation History Page." Accessed 27 October 2011 at http://paperindustryweb.com/belhistory.htm.

Benamara, H., J. Hoffman, and V. Valentine (2011). "The Maritime Industry: Key Developments in Seaborne Trade, Maritime Business and Markets," in *International Handbook of Maritime Economics*, Kevin Cullinane (Ed.), Edward Elgar.

Berenyi, E. (2008). *Materials Recycling and Processing in the United States, Yearbook and Directory, 5th edition.* Westport, CT, Governmental Advisory Associates.

Berglund, C. and P. Söderholm (2003). "Complementing Empirical Evidence on Global Recycling and Trade of Waste Paper." *World Development* 31(4): 743–754.

Berglund, C., P. Söderholm, et al. (2002). "A Note on Inter-Country Differences in Waste Paper Recovery and Utilization." *Resources Conservation and Recycling* 34(3): 175–191.

Biddle, D. (1998). "MRF Designs around Single Stream Recycling." *BioCycle* 39(8): 45–49.

Birett, M. (2011). "It's in the Mix." *Resources Recycling* April 2011: 20–26.

Blue Green Alliance (2011). Accessed 24 October 2011 at www.bluegreenalliance.org.

Bobu, E., A. Iosip, et al. (2010). "Potential Benefits of Recovered Paper Sorting by Advanced Technology." *Cellulose Chemistry and Technology* 44(10): 461–471.

Bränlund, R., R. Färe, et al. (1995). "Environmental Regulation and Profitability: An Application to Swedish Pulp and Paper Mills." *Environmental and Resource Economics* 6: 23–36.

Business Wire (2001). "Madison Paper Company Announces Modernization of Alsip, Illinois Mill: Facility to Produce Lightweight Coated [Paper] with High Recycled Content." *Business Wire.*

Cagle, E. (2006). "Trim Waste Recycling – Repurposed Dollars." *Printing Impressions*, June.

Confederation of European Paper Industries (CEPI) Annual Statistics, 2001–2011. Brussels, Belgium.

Considine, T. J. (2009). "Powder River Basin Coal: Powering America." Final report presented to the Wyoming Mining Association.

Container Recycling Institute (2011). Accessed September 2011 at http://www.container-recycling.org/facts/all/data/recrates-depnon-3mats.htm.

Corbett, J. (2011). Professor of Civil and Environmental Engineering and Professor of Marine Policy, University of Delaware, personal communication.

COST (2010). "The Future of Paper Recycling in Europe: Opportunities and Limitations." B. Stawicki and B. Read. Bury, Greater Manchester, UK, The Paper Industry Technical Association (PITA). E48.

Cuyler, A. (2002). "Residual Reality with Single Stream Recycling." *BioCycle* June: 62.

Dahmus, J. B. and T. G. Gutowski (2007). "What Gets Recycled: An Information Theory Based Model for Product Recycling." *Environmental Science and Technology* 41(21): 7543–7550.

del Río Merino, M., P. I. Gracia, et al. (2010). "Sustainable Construction: Construction and Demolition Waste Reconsidered." *Waste Management & Research* 28: 118–129.

Denasiewicz, A. and J. McCarty (2011). "Reduce, Reuse and Recycle." *Pulp and Paper International* 53(7): 30–33.

Elliott, B. (2014). "Single-Stream Collection leads to Fewer Injuries in Minneapolis." *Resource Recycling*.

Environmental Paper Network (2007). "The State of the Paper Industry." Accessed at www.greenpressinitiative.org/documents/StateOfPaperInd.pdf.

Environmental Paper Network (2011). "The State of the Paper Industry: Steps toward an Environmental Vision." Accessed at www.environmentalpaper.org/state-of-the-paper-industry-2011.php.

European Aluminium Association (2011). Accessed 30 September 2011 at http://www.eaa.net/en/about-aluminium/recycling/.

Farahani, S., E. Worrell, et al. (2004). "CO2-Free Paper?" *Resources Conservation and Recycling* 42(4): 317–336.

Freedonia (2010). "Freedonia Focus on Paper Industry Machinery." Cleveland, OH, Freedonia Group.

Freedonia (2011). "Freedonia Focus on Wood Pulp and Waste Paper." Cleveland, OH, Freedonia Group. May.

FutureMark (2010). "Press release: FutureMark Makes New Strides in Reducing Environmental Impact of Paper Production."

Gavrilescu, D. and E. Bobu (2009). "Driving Forces and Barriers for Sustainable Use of Recovered Paper in Papermaking." *Environmental Management and Engineering Journal* 8(5): 1129–1134.

Geiser, K. (2001). *Materials Matter: Toward a Sustainable Materials Policy*. Cambridge, MA, MIT Press.

Hekkert, M., J. van den Reek, et al. (2002). "The Impact of Material Efficient End-Use Technologies on Paper Use and Carbon Emissions." *Resources Conservation and Recycling* 36(3): 241–266.

Hseu, J. S. and J. K. Shang (2005). "Productivity Changes of Pulp and Paper Industry in OECD Countries, 1991–2000: A Non-Parametric Malmquist Approach." *Forest Policy and Economics* 7(411–422).

Hudson Baylor, Inc. (2011). Glass. Accessed 14 October 2011 at http://www.hudsonbaylor.com/section/23/Products/Glass.

American environmental policy

International Energy Agency (2006). "Energy Technology Perspectives – Scenarios and Strategies to 2050." Paris, France, OECD Publishing.

International Energy Agency (2007). "Tracking Industrial Energy Efficiency and CO2 Emissions." Paris, France, OECD Publishing.

Jansen, A. (2011). Director of Marketing and Sustainability, FutureMark Paper Company, personal communication.

Johnson, G. N. (2011). Manager of Technical Services, FutureMark Paper Company, personal communication.

Johnson, J. (2010). "A Mark of the Future." *Waste & Recycling News* December.

Kara, S., S. Manmek, et al. (2010). "Global Manufacturing and the Embodied Energy of Products." *CIRP Annals-Manufacturing Technology* 49(1): 29–32.

Karvonen, M. (2001). "Natural versus Manufactured Capital: Win-Lose or Win-Win? A Case Study of the Finnish Pulp and Paper Industry." *Ecological Economics* 37(1): 71–85.

Kinsella, S. (2008). "Recovered Fiber Planning Project: Potential Strategies." Report prepared for the Environmental Paper Network.

Kinsella, S. (2011). Executive Director, Conservatree, San Francisco, California, personal communication.

Laurijssen, J., M. Marsidi, et al. (2010). "Paper and Biomass for Energy? The Impact of Paper Recycling on Energy and CO2 Emissions." *Resources Conservation and Recycling* 54(12).

Luria, D. and J. Rogers (2008). "Manufacturing, Regional Prosperity and Public Policy," in *Retooling for Growth: Building a 21st Century Economy in America's Older Industrial Areas,* R. M. McGahey and J. S. Vey (Eds). Washington, DC: Brookings Institution Press.

Lyons, D., M. Rice, et al. (2009). "Circuits of Scrap: Closed Loop Industrial Ecosystems and the Geography of US International Recyclable Material Flows 1995–2005." *The Geographical Journal* 175(4): 286–300.

Malloch, J. (2009). Technical Superintendent, Blue Heron Paper Company, Oregon City, Oregon, personal communication.

Metafore, Inc. (2009). "Recycled Content and Virgin Fiber: Environmental, Economic, and Technical Considerations for Magazine Publishers." Magazine Publishers of America, June.

Miranda, R., A. Balea, et al. (2008). "Identification of Recalcitrant Stickies and Their Sources in Newsprint Production." *Industrial and Engineering Chemistry Research* 47(16).

Miranda, R., E. Bobu, et al. (2010). "Factors Influencing a Higher Use of Recovered Paper in the European Paper Industry." *Cellulose Chemistry and Technology* 44 (10): 419–430.

Miranda, R., M. Concepcion Monte, et al. (2013). "Analysis of the Quality of the Recovered Paper from Commingled Collection Systems." *Resources, Conservation and Recycling* 72: 60–65.

Miranda, R., M. C. Monte, et al. (2011). "Impact of Increased Collection Rates and the Use of Commingled Collection Systems on the Quality of Recovered Paper. Part 1: Increased Collection Rates." *Waste Management* 31: 2208–2216.

Mokry, M. A. and K. Winkels (2003). "Alsip PM 1: Conversion from Newsprint to LWC." *Twogether* 15: 54–57.

Morawski, C. (2009). "Understanding Economic and Environmental Impacts of Single-Stream Collection Systems." Culver City, CA, Container Recycling Institute.

Notteboom, T. and P. Cariou. (2011). "Are Bunker Adjustment Factors Aimed at Revenue-Making or Cost Recovery? Empirical Evidence on the Pricing Strategies of Shipping Lines," in *International Handbook of Maritime Economics*, Kevin Cullinane (Ed.), Edward Elgar.

Official Board Markets (2005–2011). Transaction Paper Stock Prices. Accessed at http://www.packaging-online.com/.

Organisation for Economic Co-operation and Development (2010). *Environmental Data Compendium 2008*. Paris, France, OECD.

Paper Industry Association Council (2011). "Where Recovered Paper Goes." Accessed at www.paperrecycles.org.

Paperloop (2006). "Pulp & Paper Global Fact and Price Book: Covering North America, Europe, Asia and the World." San Francisco, CA, *Pulp & Paper*, PPI, Paperloop.

Paterno, C. (2004). "Madison Paper's Alsip Mills Drives toward New Products with Upgrade." *Pulp & Paper*, August.

Press, D. (1996). "Toxic Releases from Paper made with Recovered Wastepaper versus Virgin Wood Fiber: A Research Note." *Environmental Management and Engineering Journal* 20(5): 725–730.

Pulp & Paper (2000). "FSC Paper Plans Bankruptcy Auction." *Pulp & Paper*. Accessed at http://www.risiinfo.com/db_area/archive/p_p_mag/2000/0005/news.htm.

Pulp & Paper Week (2011). "Uncoated Mechanical: Manistique Papers Ceases Operations; Seeking Chapter 11 Protection and New Owner." San Francisco, CA, *Pulp & Paper Week*.

Pulp & Paper International (2014). "More Fiber, Less Waste, Less Energy: Modern Technology and New Systems Designs are Essential for Improving Packaging Grades made from OCC." *Pulp & Paper International* 56(7).

Reuter, M., A. van Schaik, et al. (2006). "Fundamental Limits for the Recycling of End-of-Life Vehicles." *Minerals Engineering* 19(5): 433–449.

Rodden, G. (2011). "As Green as You get: FutureMark Paper's Embracement of the Growing 'Green' Marketplace has Resonated Strongly with Customers." *Pulp & Paper International* 53(2).

Rushton, M., G. Rodden, et al. (2011). "The PPI Top 100." *Pulp & Paper International* 53(9).

Sacia, W. K. and J. Simmons (2006). "The Effects of Changing ONP Quality on a Newsprint Mill." *TAPPI Journal* 5(1): 13–17.

Schipper, M. (2006). "Energy-Related Carbon Dioxide Emissions in U.S. Manufacturing." E. I. A. US Department of Energy. Washington, DC.

Siebers, M. (2011). "Get Facts on Blue Heron." Accessed at Oregonlive.com.

Smith, M. (1997). *The U.S. Paper Industry and Sustainable Production: An Argument for Restructuring*. Cambridge, MA, MIT Press.

South Carolina Forestry Commission (2005–2011). Current SC Timber Price Reports. Accessed at http://www.state.sc.us/forest/mprice.htm.

Szasz, A. (1986). "Corporation, Organized Crime, and the Disposal of Hazardous Waste: An Examination of the Making of a Criminogenic Regulatory Structure." *Criminology* 24(1): 1–27.

Themelis, N. J. and C. E. Todd (2004). "Recycling in a Megacity." *Journal of the American Air and Waste Management Association* 54(4): 389–395.

Thompson, C. (1992). *Recycled Papers: The Essential Guide*. Cambridge, MA, MIT Press.

Tyteca, D. (1996). "On the Measurement of the Environmental Performance of Firms – A Literature Review and a Productive Efficiency Perspective." *Journal of Environmental Management* 46(3): 231–308.

United Nations Economic Commission for Europe/Food and Agriculture Organization of the United Nations (UNECE/FAO) (2010). "Forest Products Annual Market Review 2009–2010." Geneva, Switzerland, UNECE/FAO.

United States Army Corps of Engineers (2011). Waterborne Commerce Statistics. Accessed at http://www.ndc.iwr.usace.army.mil//wcsc/wcsc.htm.

United States Bureau of Economic Analysis (2011). RIMS II Multipliers for the Paper Industry. Accessed at http://www.census.gov/manufacturing/asm/index.html.

United States Census Bureau (2009). "Annual Survey of Manufacturers, General Statistics: Statistics for Industry Groups and Industries: 2009 and 2008 Summary Tables." Accessed at http://factfinder.census.gov.

United States Census Bureau (2011). USA Trade Online Data. Accessed at https://usatrade.census.gov/.

United States Department of Energy (2011). "Annual Energy Outlook, 2011." Energy Information Administration. Accessed at http://www.eia.gov/forecasts/aeo/sector_industrial.cfm.

United States Department of Transportation (2011). Public Use Waybill. Surface Transportation Board. Accessed at http://www.stb.dot.gov/stb/industry/econ_waybill.html.

United States Environmental Protection Agency (2010). "Municipal Solid Waste in the United States, 2009 Facts and Figures." Office of Solid Waste, United States Environmental Protection Agency. Washington, DC.

United States International Trade Commission (US ITC) (2011). "US Domestic Exports of Waste Paper: Summary Tables." Accessed at http://dataweb.usitc.gov.

Vos, R. O. and J. Newell (2009). *A Comparative Analysis of Carbon Dioxide Emissions in Coated Paper Production: Key Differences between China and the U.S. Center for Sustainable Cities.* Los Angeles, CA, University of Southern California.

van Beukering, P. and M. N. Bouman (2001). "Empirical Evidence on Recycling and Trade of Paper and Lead in Developed and Developing Countries." *World Development* 29(10): 1717–1737.

Waste & Recycling News (2010). "Open Eyes to Success." Accessed at http://www.wasterecyclingnews.com/opinion2.html?id=1291649435.

Watson, T. (1988). "FSC Paper Builds Markets with Innovative Approach." *Resource Recycling* March/April.

Yordanov, M. (2011). Statistical Program Manager, American Forest and Paper Association, Washington, DC, personal communication.

6. Regulation beyond compliance, abatement and mitigation

In this final chapter, I turn to promising reforms for US environmental regulation. As with the critiques described in prior chapters, this exploration of improvements will focus on policy designs along with some promising policy tools. Mirroring the earlier chapters' critiques, these policy reforms emphasize improving environmental program evidence, ameliorating end-of-pipe pollution abatement, rethinking our approach to nonpoint sources of pollution, and designing recycling programs to meet broader goals of industrial policy rather than limited waste management objectives.

To provide a context for the specific laws and associated regulatory programs that will serve as examples of effective reforms, I begin by pointing out how the flawed compliance-mitigation-abatement approach described earlier should compel us to re-think our objectives for environmental regulation. This focus on design objectives parallels that of other recent environmental regulation scholars, many of whom agree on a common set of reform objectives.

The first conclusion to be drawn from a critical assessment of current policy is that better environmental performance must become paramount; public and environmental health results really do matter. As Davies and Mazurek quipped in 1997, "the current system is focused largely on how to control pollution rather than on whether pollution is actually being controlled" (p. 48), and rectifying this state of affairs should be the chief aim of effective policy reform. A second, related conclusion is that we will only know whether pollution is actually being controlled if we have very high-quality information. Chapter 2 showed how regulators accept environmental data too uncritically, so much so that this evidence fails to give us adequate information about the effect of regulations on environmental quality. Any new environmental data requirement should be designed to provide the best evidence possible, within reasonable technical and cost constraints.

Third, polluters should be motivated to continuously improve their environmental performance (Fiorino, 2006). As Chapter 3 showed, this is a near impossibility with end-of-pipe abatement methods, especially if the number of sources grows while further per-unit emissions reductions become impossible. If, instead of trying to squeeze ever more pollution out of more numerous point sources, we were to emphasize precaution and prevention, how might we design pollution control differently? We might question the very premise of pollution control, favoring source reduction and dirty input limits over end-of-pipe abatement and treatment.

Beyond the technical difficulties, classic command-and-control regulation does little to encourage true source reduction. This behavioral flaw leads to a fourth reform element identified by many environmental policy experts (Vig & Kraft, 2012; Davies and Mazurek, 1997; Gunningham, 2007; Sinden and Driesen, 2009; Potoski and Prakash, 2004) and best articulated by Dan Fiorino (2006): regulators should be able to distinguish between leaders and laggards.

Congress did so, albeit awkwardly and halfheartedly, in the 1984 Hazardous and Solid Waste Amendments (HSWA) to the Resources Conservation and Recovery Act (RCRA). In that law, Congress declared that, wherever feasible, hazardous waste generation should be reduced or eliminated as quickly as possible. In effect, lawmakers sought a waste reduction and treatment hierarchy that made source reduction, including product substitution, reformulation and input substitution, the most preferred option. Lower in the hierarchy came hazardous materials management process modifications and recycling, followed by treatment and distantly by disposal (Mazmanian and Morell, 1992). To promote source reduction, Congress offered very tough-sounding language banning landfill disposal of hazardous wastes. What Congress really meant was that it was banning land disposal of *untreated* hazardous wastes, assuming that proper treatment would adequately neutralize hazardous wastes (Mazmanian and Morell, 1992). Thus, in the 30 years since the 1984 amendments, deep-well injection and land disposal of treated wastes have continued unabated, and have, in fact, grown tremendously (US EPA, RCRA Biennial Report, 2011). Source reduction didn't happen as Congress had hoped, largely because incentives to do so were almost completely absent.

Fifth, the compliance-mitigation-abatement approach assumes that industry will improve its environmental performance only under threat of legal sanctions, an assumption belied by many "first movers" and voluntary programs (Fiorino, 2006; Press and Mazmanian, 2009). Emphasizing voluntarism and collaboration still requires getting incentives and assurances right, which hearkens back to the importance of information.

It is time for the US to shift its emphasis from compliance-mitigation-abatement to effective, parsimonious, precautionary and participatory environmental regulations. To do so, new policy designs should answer the following questions:

- What is the ecological effect we are trying to accomplish?
- What are the fewest resources needed to accomplish that ecological effect?
- What change in human activity do we want to accomplish?
- What policy tools can affect human activity and effect change?
- What is the policy system that can design and implement such policy tools?
- Who benefits from, and who pays for, different policy designs?
- What information and data synthesis are needed to rigorously evaluate regulatory effectiveness?

Answering these questions can help policymakers determine whether particular policy tools are advancing the five objectives listed above. This chapter now applies these design objectives to information, end-of-pipe abatement, nonpoint sources and recycling.

INFORMATION REFORMS

The discussion in Chapter 2 of data problems with the Toxic Release Inventory unfortunately characterizes much of the evidence used in US environmental regulation today. Regulators, environmental activists and permit holders alike routinely throw their hands up in frustration over the paucity of environmental evidence that all can share, understand and believe. Consequently, environmental regulatory systems often lack both data and analysis adequate for determining whether particular rules solved or mitigated their target problems (Tyler, 2013; Coglianese, 2012). Regulators and stakeholders alike find it hard to answer the most basic question: does regulation work?

Their frustration is warranted, given how difficult it is to systematically measure and evaluate tremendously complex ecological and social systems, along with their interactions (Keene and Pullin, 2011). Moreover, public officials rarely face truly positive incentives or rewards for connecting the dots between a specific regulatory intervention and some desired environmental outcomes. Yes, water quality regulators genuinely want to demonstrate reductions in sediments or other pollutants in a given watershed, but they face daunting obstacles in doing so. First, what if the environmental evidence shows that current interventions aren't working? Regulators acting in good faith, enforcing existing statutory mandates, may fail to make much of a difference. How much better, then, for regulators to emphasize the evidence of what they *can* control – program outputs such as staff hours devoted to a particular problem or issue, permits written or denied, enforcement actions, hearings held and the like (Tyler, 2013; Keene and Pullin, 2011) – even if these accomplishments have little bearing on intended outcomes?

Second, regulators are usually evaluated based on whether they have faithfully implemented legislation, i.e., duly issuing permits, enforcing penalties, receiving mandated monitoring data. But we should insist on more than just legally valid regulations; the public is entitled to rule-making that makes a tangible difference for public and environmental health. The fault lies not just with risk-averse regulators, since legislatures rarely incorporate post-rule adoption reviews into their rulemaking. Tyler (2013) points out that even a law as obviously oriented to consumer protection as the Food Safety Act ". . .does nothing to require FDA to evaluate the regulations it develops under the law. This despite the fact that improvement in food safety is a measurable phenomenon."

Third, appropriate data are often lacking even under the best of circumstances. Even if the data exist, they may not be compiled in a usable form, perhaps because they are limited to paper records. Some collectible data are not actually gathered or made available. This is often the case with nonpoint source water pollutants, which could be acquired, in principle, but probably at prohibitive cost in terms of time and money. Finally, there are data that are simply uncollectable (Coglianese, 2013). For example, it can be impossible to tell before many years have gone by whether a specific, complex restoration project has achieved sustainability. Of course, ". . .the ideal indicators would be those that are both (a) highly relevant and accurate for serving the purposes of the evaluation and (b) available and already compiled" (Coglianese, 2013, p. 32).

Fourth, modern societies are drowning in unfiltered information, but, to quote Pullin's trenchant observation, ". . .data are not evidence unless presented in relation to a question" (Pullin, 2012).

Three Modest Proposals

Improving environmental data rarely makes it to the top of any political agenda, so policymakers have to look for non-legislative reforms, which, fortunately, do exist. Cary Coglianese, a law professor at the University Pennsylvania and director of the Penn Program on Regulation, is one of the country's most articulate scholars of regulation. Coglianese has long argued that the country needs an agency dedicated to regulatory information and review, but that, in the interim, several modest reforms could go a long way towards improving what we know about regulation and how we design future rules and standards.

First, the federal Office of Information and Regulatory Affairs (OIRA) can, on its own, issue guidelines showing other agencies how they could improve their retrospective regulatory reviews (Coglianese, 2013). Toxics program managers could learn from experience with acid deposition. The contrast between information in the Toxic Release Inventory versus the Acid Rain Program suggests that, whenever possible, policy should require direct measurement, like continuous emissions monitoring systems (CEMS). However, the fact that direct measurements are not currently possible for all processes or media should not be taken as a permanent given. A waiver from direct measurement should be considered temporary, revocable if and when better measures become available. Congress could codify this commitment to better measurement by requiring that agencies develop and adopt a "Best Available Empirical Evidence" standard like that called for by the Center for Evidence-based Environmental Policies and Programs (CEEP, 2013).

Some capacity building is in order for this effort. Congress and the states have funded the development of new environmental indicators for years, but not consistently nor comprehensively. Moreover, simply generating more data is not enough. Rigorous retrospective review will require synthesis, ". . .a kind of stocktaking of data that establishes the current evidence base with a view to predicting outcomes of alternative actions" (Pullin, 2012). Pullin goes on to ask: "Of all the interventions that are employed, which ones work? Which ones are worth the money spent on them? Which ones do more harm than good and should cease?" (Pullin, 2012).

Second, OIRA already has the authority to require that agencies adopt plans for retrospective reviews each time they issue significant regulations. Such plans need to transparently show the public, beforehand, what metrics will be used and when reviews will be conducted (Coglianese, 2013; Tyler, 2013).

Third, the federal government could habituate agencies to practicing retrospective reviews by formally prompting regulatory evaluations on a regular basis (Coglianese, 2013). Again, OIRA has the authority to require this, but Congress and state legislatures may be taken more seriously if measuring substantive regulatory performance is legislatively mandated (Tyler, 2013).

High-quality information, meaningful synthesis and transparency are necessary, even if not sufficient, conditions of good, smart regulation. Moving beyond dysfunctional compliance-abatement-mitigation approaches is simply impossible without first-rate data and synthesis. A half-century of regulatory experience shows that data collection and synthesis are possible, given the right incentives and support. Moreover, legions of environmental scholars, agency officials and citizen scientists now have the needed innovative capacity; all they need is support and demand for their work.

END-OF-PIPE POLLUTION ABATEMENT

To achieve lasting and significant environmental performance, the regulatory goal for point source pollution should be keeping releases below critical loads. This is, in effect, what health-based ambient air standards seek on behalf of public health. Moreover, health-based standards evolve continuously, at least in the air quality arena. Every few years, new public health findings allow federal regulators to ratchet down ambient standards for pollutants like ozone, $PM_{2.5}$ and oxides of nitrogen or sulfur. In turn, modified ambient standards result in new emissions limits for product reformulations. For example, in 2014, the US EPA adopted new rules lowering acceptable sulfur standards in gasoline from 30 ppm to 10 ppm.

When public health does not drive emissions limits, it's much harder to change end-of-pipe abatement rules and targets. For example, when emissions standards are driven by best available technology rather than by health targets, new emissions reductions should not be expected. That's because technology standards adopted to meet a static emissions target need not be revised: by definition, regulatory goals are met when a particular pollution load has been achieved, even if future technological advances could reduce such loads.

End-of-pipe pollution abatement will always have its place in modern environmental regulation. When the pollutants themselves are not especially toxic or become easily diluted by large sinks, such as large, well-mixed airsheds and receiving waters, end-of-pipe abatement can be quite acceptable. Abatement becomes intolerable, though, as the number of polluting sources overwhelms per-unit gains. In the public health context, regulators determine precisely how intolerable pollution loads are through epidemiological studies. As Chapter 3 discussed, the ecological equivalent to the epidemiological study is the critical load assessment. To reprise the Chapter 3 example, determining critical loads of sulfur and nitrogen deposition requires four kinds of scientific information: 1) ecosystem effects and thresholds, 2) empirical chemistry data, 3) model results, and 4) projected changes in climate and the carbon cycle (Burns et al., 2008). Combining these four elements provides researchers with pollutant load targets, the mechanisms by which those targets are exceeded, and predictive abilities for staying below critical loads. New work by US EPA staff is leading to Aquatic Acidification Indices that should be suitable, in the near future, for translating atmospheric

Table 6.1   When to use bans and dirty-input limits

Criterion	Conditions
Diminishing returns	Current end-of-pipe abatement removes 90+% pollutant per unit; new sources already do or will add to the overall pollutant load in absolute terms
Feasibility	It is feasible to reduce dirty inputs
Severity of harm, critical loads	The environmental problems are severe enough to warrant further reductions, i.e., critical loads are exceeded
Substitutability	Substitutes exist for dirty inputs, products and processes that are not more problematic than the original pollutants or products
Multiple outputs	The environmental stressor in question produces multiple outputs that cause environmental damage

Sources: Driesen and Sinden, 2009; Fiorino, 1995; Salomon, 2002.

concentrations of pollutants like NOx and SOx into ecosystem effects expressed as critical loads and acid neutralizing capacity (Scheffe et al., 2014). Assuming critical loads could someday drive regulatory decisions, under what conditions should end-of-pipe pollution abatement be replaced with new policy designs?

Drawing on David Driesen and Amy Sinden's work, as well as other policy analysts, Table 6.1 proposes criteria and conditions favorable to replacing end-of-pipe pollution abatement with dirty-input limits (DILs) or outright bans. DILs limit the use and/or quantity of inputs that constitute the root cause of a given pollution type (Driesen and Sinden, 2009). The difference between a DIL and a total ban is essentially a matter of degree. For example, a total ban on lead in gasoline could be thought of as a dirty-input limit of zero percent. Designed to reduce the state's greenhouse gas emissions, California's low-carbon fuel mandate is an example of a DIL, requiring a ten percent reduction in the carbon intensity of California's transportation fuels by 2020.

There are several advantages to dirty-input limits and total bans. First, DILs and bans offer considerable administrative simplicity, because it's easier to monitor inputs rather than outputs. Far fewer parties and fewer constituents need to be reviewed in the case of inputs. Second, monitoring becomes easier because regulators need only gather information on what inputs were used rather than separately regulating multiple outputs. In the case of gasoline and all of the air-quality impacts associated with its use, a fuel efficiency standard acting as a DIL requires only that a regulator know how much gasoline is used to achieve a certain amount of transportation benefit. A tailpipe standard, on the other hand, requires regulators to monitor several different pollutants (unburnt hydrocarbons, NOx, CO) and to apportion air pollutant loads among vast numbers of mobile and stationary sources. Finally, DILs tend to stimulate much more fundamental innovation than is typically achieved by incrementally changing emissions limits (Driesen and Sinden, 2009). Faced with dramatic limits or total bans, regulated sources have much more incentive to completely reformulate their products or processes.

Forty to fifty years after the US adopted many of its end-of-pipe abatement controls, the conditions depicted in Table 6.1 are increasingly being met in many different parts of the country. Accordingly, many jurisdictions, mostly at the state and local levels, are re-examining the use of these policy tools.

THE RETURN OF THE BAN – THE APOTHEOSIS OF POLLUTION CONTROL?

Nothing succeeds like. . .nothing. An outright ban on some product, input or technology has a powerful way of eliminating environmental harm, provided substitutes aren't just as bad or worse in their own ways. Bans are hugely popular with environmentalists and equally, if not more, held in contempt by industry, for which they are considered the regulatory equivalent of "nuclear options." Consequently, Americans have not used outright bans much, with some notable exceptions. The ubiquitous flimsy plastic bag has been targeted in recent years, especially at the municipal level. Between 2006 and 2014, more than 100 US cities and counties imposed tight restrictions on single use of plastic bags in their jurisdictions (Logan, 2014). Most cities employ either a tax, ranging from 5–25 cents per bag, or an outright plastic-bag ban. Seattle and a few other cities ban plastic bags *and* tax paper bags, thereby promoting reusable, durable alternatives. Cities typically use the proceeds from the bag taxes for public education, environmental restoration or recycling programs (Logan, 2014).

States have also moved aggressively on especially problematic products. In 2010, for example, California and Washington passed legislation phasing in bans on copper brake pads, finding that these are responsible for up to half of the copper finding its way into urban waterways. Like many metals, copper in fairly low concentrations can be quite hazardous to aquatic organisms.

Both states phase in their bans over a long time – a decade or more. Washington's rule bans brake pads containing more than five percent copper by 2021. California gives more time for compliance – up to 2025 – but restricts copper to 0.5 percent, ten times less than Washington (Motovalli, 2012). The legislative victories in these states inspired bills subsequently introduced in Rhode Island, New York and Oregon (Motovalli, 2012).

Federal bans are less common, though not unheard of. In addition to lead in gasoline and ozone-depleting chlorofluorocarbons, the US EPA has banned production and use of about 50 pesticides out of many thousands of potentially dangerous chemicals approved for sale and use in the US since the early 1970s.

An outright ban is not the only way to improve on the limits of end-of-pipe approaches. By adopting a whole-systems and lifecycle approach, environmental policy can be designed to motivate completely new ways of producing and consuming various goods. California's Safer Consumer Products law, also known as the Green Chemistry Initiative, relies on the ban as a heavy-handed tool of last resort. Instead of focusing on specific products, the initiative instructs the California Department of Toxic Substances Control (DTSC) to identify chemicals that are especially harmful *and* present in a wide variety of products.

For example, in March 2014, the DTSC announced that it was taking issue with three compounds in particular: chlorinated trisphosphate (TDCPP), one of the most commonly used flame retardants for foam products used in children's sleeping mats and bassinets; diisocyanates found in polyurethane foam (commonly used in home and buildings for insulation); and methylene chloride, a kind of varnish stripper or surface cleaner. The three chemicals are nearly ubiquitous in foam bedding products, insulation and strippers, respectively. The innovation of the Green Chemistry Initiative is to announce a ban some years off while, in the interim, launching a process of workshops, public comments and analyses. Specifically, the law puts an evidentiary burden of proof on manufacturers who want to sell these products in California. Manufacturer analyses must either justify existing formulations or determine whether safer compounds exist for the same product classes (Finz, 2014). Furthermore, evaluations must determine not only whether chemicals are safe as used, but also what risks they pose during manufacturing and disposal, that is, at each point in their life cycle. Naturally, whether this initiative truly transforms product formulations depends in large part on how regulators ensure thorough and rigorous manufacturer analyses.

REGULATORY REFORM FOR NONPOINT SOURCES OF WATER POLLUTION

> A well-targeted program would direct resources to attaining specific, measurable water quality goals through the most efficient means possible, that is, through activities that realize these goals at lowest cost. Effective targeting would prioritize hot spots (e.g., particular watersheds and possibly locations within them) and BMPs to achieve the proverbial 'biggest bang for the buck' (Shortle et al., 2012, p.1318).

Unlike a generation ago, most of the nation's persistent water quality challenges no longer pose truly daunting technical or engineering challenges. Environmental scientists, ecologists, developers and engineers test technologies and techniques for mitigating nonpoint source water pollution nearly every day. As Howarth writes, "[T]here is some good news in the coastal nitrogen pollution story: technical solutions exist to reduce nitrogen inputs from all potential sources, and generally at reasonable cost" (Howarth, 2008). For nitrogen loading, these include greater uses of selective catalytic reduction systems (to minimize transfers of nitrogen from air pollution to surface water), changes in cropping, better timing of nitrogen applications, alternative tilling practices and improved manure management at CAFOs (Robertson and Vitousek, 2009).

For urban stormwater, low-impact development (LID) retains runoff on-site by using porous pavements, bio-swales and other vegetated retention basins, resulting in as much as 100 percent runoff reduction, often at lower cost than traditional storm-drain and flood protection "hardscapes" (NAS, 2009). Wetlands, too, can be successfully restored and protected, largely through management interventions based on a better understanding of their structures and functions (e.g., hydroperiods, plant communities, soils, hydrological connectivity) (Zedler and Kercher, 2005).

In short, we have technologies and methods to better manage water quality. On the other hand, we lack policy innovations that encourage, require and enable (sometimes all at once) publicly-owned treatment works (POTWs), farmers, other private landowners and public agency officials to implement best management practices and control technologies. Moreover, US regulators and policymakers tend to adopt "pay the polluter" rather than "polluter pays" principles in their approach to one of the most important non-point sources, agriculture (Shortle et al., 2012). This comes in the form of financial and technical assistance to undertake largely voluntary measures whose efficacy remains questionable. Between the mid-1980s and 1990s, USDA Agricultural Conservation Program funds shifted from just 7 percent of the total to 37 percent, reflecting increased federal concern over water quality in the agricultural sector, but no change in policy design (Shortle et al., 2012).

Many scholars and commentators agree on several key reforms necessary to get the CWA back on course (Houck, 2002; Ruhl, 2000; ELI, 2000; McElfish et al., 2006; Hoornbeck, 2005; Andreen, 2004; Drelich, 2009; Shortle et al., 2012). These include:

1. Mandatory – not optional – adoption of best available technology (BAT) for large firms in many industries, including agriculture, parallel to provisions of the CWA and the Clean Air Act for point sources,
2. Market incentives, including product charges on chemical inputs like fertilizers or pesticides, to address overuse by small farms and dischargers, along with generous BMP implementation assistance,
3. Information and monitoring to prioritize "hot spots,"
4. Outright bans on the most harmful practices and pollutants, and
5. Using the proceeds of enforcement actions for environmental improvement.

I elaborate on each of these reforms below in the five sections that follow.

Best Available Technology for Large, Nonpoint Sources

The EPA and the states took decades to launch their Total Maximum Daily Load (TMDL) programs, not least because they encountered fierce resistance from farmers, feedlot operators, loggers and miners, who argued that they should not be regulated because 1) their discharges are diffuse (they have no "pipes") and 2) real controls would be too costly. Consequently, nonpoint sources have been operating in what Ruhl (2000) calls a system of "anti-law", exempting such dischargers from the waste discharge requirements other industries have had for decades.

Of course, the CWA doesn't explicitly give a pass to nonpoint sources. As Drelich eloquently puts it,

> [A] 'point source' is to be found toward the hand of the discharger rather than the bank of the receiving water; the time and place of a person's discharge of a pollutant do not await its entry into a water of the United States; and, most significantly, the Act provides liability even for those who only allow or create a significant threat of water pollution (Drelich, 2009).

Because of this legal doctrine, states and the EPA can either penalize for discharges to waters of the state (after-the-fact enforcement) and/or enforce BMP adoption to prevent pollution. The enforcement paradox set up by the CWA is that *no one* is legally allowed to discharge pollutants to water-bodies of the US without a permit, but enforcement actions on discharges by farms and timber operations (and mines, etc.) are rare and difficult.

They are difficult because of a terrible evidentiary burden. Imagine many contiguous farms, all irrigating their crops, all of them using chemical inputs, all of them potentially discharging pollutants in surface runoff known as tailwaters. Trying to pin a spike in pollutants on any one of these farms would require a level of forensic monitoring that is too complex and costly, unless each grower already provides data on their property's chemical uses and water quality.

Enforcement actions are also rare because the CWA's nonpoint source sections (303, 305, 319) explicitly create assessment requirements and incentives for BMP adoption – enforcement, such as it is, is applied against those state agencies that fail to perform the required TMDL assessments and determinations. Otherwise, the sections are silent on penalties to dischargers.

By way of illustration, consider federal CWA settlements and other compliance actions (which are much fewer than the number of state enforcement actions). The US EPA's Enforcement and Compliance History Online (ECHO) database lists 11,213 CWA enforcement actions and settlements for the years 2001 to the first half of 2010. None of these penalties were associated with nonpoint source sections of the Act (i.e., §303, 305, 319), unless one includes the dredge-and-fill permits under §404, of which there were 1,159 enforcement actions (EPA, 2010b).[1]

A stronger command-and-control approach for urban stormwater control would be to revise construction standards so that LID becomes the new norm wherever there is new or re-development. Municipal separate storm and sewer systems (MS4) operators could implement these most effectively by 1) writing LID standards into local ordinances and building codes, 2) managing stormwater on a watershed basis instead of by municipal boundaries, 3) serving as the first tier of entities regulating stormwater discharges just as we do with pretreatment standards, and 4) denying MS4 stormwater plans and construction permits unless they retain water and pollutants onsite (NAS, 2009).

As for agriculture, some states, like California and Maryland, now recognize that nonpoint sources like agriculture and timber harvesting can and should be regulated under both state and federal water quality laws (Dowd et al., 2008; McElfish et al., 2006). Of course, any un-regulated industry claims that new rules will put it out of business. But it's hard to

---

[1]   State and federal enforcement of point sources leaves much to be desired as well. See Duhigg (2009) for a very critical analysis of Clean Water Act violations nationwide.

imagine that crop nutrient management, conservation tillage, integrated pest management, vegetated buffer strips, cattle fences in riparian zones, and related agricultural management practices that could be more widely and vigorously implemented for water quality protection will ever be as complex and costly as BAT for traditionally-regulated industries, like sewage plants, petrochemical factories or pulp and paper mills.

Clearly, the difference between agriculture and heavy manufacturing industries lies in how each sector is prepared to handle regulation. Smokestack industries have grappled with pollution abatement regulations for decades. Accordingly, they have long experience dedicating staff to environmental management, selecting technologies and even driving abatement costs down through their own innovation. BMPs represent the current technological equivalent to pollution abatement devices and systems; however, far more work must be done to show which BMPs work, how well and under what local conditions. All but the largest growers lack the resources to undertake such improvements to BMPs, thus policy reforms must address farmers' incentives and capacities, which are addressed in the next section.

Market Incentives: Product Charges, Negative Effluent Taxes and Program Assistance

For the many thousands of small farms, timber operations and quarries in the US, a waste discharge (NPDES) permit process is neither practical, effective nor necessary. Instead, state and federal regulators can use market incentives along with capacity- and information-building tools to address their wastewaters.

This approach recognizes that nonpoint sources never legally enjoyed exemptions from releasing water effluent without a permit – but it requires that three serious obstacles be overcome in order to obtain high rates of pollution abatement in this community. First, small dischargers rarely value BMPs as much as regulators, so implementation is often spotty. Second, proper BMP implementation requires technical know-how that farmers, loggers and miners may or may not have. Third, first-rate water quality management requires data rarely available to most dischargers.

All of these obstacles can be addressed with various kinds of positive and negative market incentives. As an example, consider one method of controlling nitrogen fertilizer use in agriculture. The policy goal is to achieve maximum Nitrogen Use Efficiency (NUE) so that farmers only apply fertilizer in amounts that will actually be used by plants instead of washed away as pollutant. The first step is to calculate NUE for various crops and soils. In the next step, regulators set limits on fertilizer applications (e.g., kg/hectare). In a final step, regulators fine producers who apply more than permitted rates (i.e., a negative effluent tax).

To create positive incentives for growers, the tax can be made progressively higher for fertilizer applications above a certain limit. Proceeds from the tax could be used – robbing Peter to pay Paul – to reward growers who use less than the maximum allowable limits, again on a progressive scale (i.e., fertilizer use very much below the threshold would receive more "rebate," per hectare, than those close to the threshold) (Ruhl, 2000). Variants of this approach were adopted for a few years in the Netherlands (the Mineral Accounting System) and in New Zealand, with mixed success, partly because of poor data on NUE and nitrogen or phosphorus thresholds that were set too high (Schröder and Neeteson, 2008).

Beyond negative incentives, growers often need financial assistance to get BMPs implemented. Many states already share these costs, but the percentages paid by states often fall short of what growers need to make such investments, so cost-shares must rise high enough to spur widespread behavioral changes (ELI, 2000; Hoornbeck, 2005; McElfish et al., 2006).

The second obstacle, technical capacity, can be addressed through grower training (e.g., nitrogen management short courses), which is already well developed – but typically under-funded – in many states. The third obstacle, information and monitoring, should be addressed with much greater, concerted and consistent attention.

Monitoring

New policy, whether based on incentives or command-and-control, is only as good as the data it relies upon. If we don't know whether BMPs work, it makes no sense to require them. Similarly, if regulators don't know how BMPs are executed, they can't parse the water quality consequences of BMP *type* versus BMP *implementation*. Regulators end up granting compliance or rewards (like pollution offset credits) ex ante on the basis of effort, not results achieved and measured (Hahn and Richards, 2010). Accordingly, the most critical information needs for nonpoint sources fall into three categories, 1) chemical use on farms and other nonpoint sources, 2) management practices, and 3) water quality near nonpoint dischargers.

The simplest type of chemical use reporting would only require that, for example, farmers, disclose their agrichemical purchases and use. States have much experience with some aspects of this kind of reporting. Since 1990, California requires users to file monthly pesticide use with county agricultural commissioners, who, in turn, report the data to the state Department of Pesticide Regulation (CADPR, 2010). The DPR makes a great deal of spatially-explicit data available on its web site, thereby also

permitting connections to groundwater quality. Most states require fertilizer distributors to register with state agencies and to report sales, thereby
allowing states to compile fertilizer tonnage statistics – though these are
not reported at the farm level, so they cannot support new policy reforms.

On-farm agrichemical use, along with pre-fertilization soil tests, nitrogen mineralization and final crop yields would, together, provide farmers
with enough information to maximize their returns on nitrogen inputs
while minimizing nitrogen runoff (Robertson and Vitousek, 2009). All the
elements are there: the farmers have access to most of these data (and new
training plus assistance can help them fill in gaps); states have agencies to
receive the information; and extension agents and farm bureaus can help
farmers interpret and act on the data. Such data would also permit regulators to discourage excessive chemical use, through the product charges
outlined above.

As for management practices, several states already require farmers,
loggers and some other nonpoint dischargers to adopt BMPs and report
their choices to agency officials (Hoornbeck, 2005; McElfish et al., 2006).
Greater uniformity in data collection, which could come with new federal
as opposed to state-based regulation, along with geo-referencing, would
permit far better trend analysis.

The last monitoring element consists of water quality measurements
made in the water column (i.e., in-stream water quality testing up- and
downstream of timber harvests, in irrigation tailwaters, settlement ponds,
dikes, and so forth). High-quality, long-term monitoring data continue
to elude regulators because reporting requirements and/or funding often
varies from year to year. Such measurements are not cheap, but if they
were made more widely and consistently, costs would come down, just as
they have for continuous emissions monitoring systems (CEMS) used in
smokestack industries.

Outright Bans and Dirty-Input Limits

Phosphate detergent became a prime, highly visible candidate for a
product ban when it was found to cause eutrophication, especially in the
Great Lakes. By the mid-1970s, so many municipalities and states had
passed bans or strict limits on phosphate content in laundry detergents
that large manufacturers re-formulated nearly every one of their products
so that these could be sold nationally (Kehoe, 1992).

Sediment loads provide another example of dirty-input limits in the nonpoint setting. In April 2010, the EPA adopted new water quality standards
(for electrical conductivity, a measure of salt and sediment loads in the
vicinity of mines) for surface mining in Appalachia. The standards prohibit

conductivity levels greater than five times those found in freshwater, prompting EPA Administrator Lisa Jackson to remark that "there are no or very few valley fills that are going to meet this standard" (Reis, 2010).

For some very problematic agricultural chemicals, like atrazine, zero tolerance may be more appropriate than limits or BMPs. Atrazine, a common herbicide used world-wide by corn growers, now contaminates many drinking water systems in the US, as determined by the US EPA's Atrazine Monitoring Program (Wu et al., 2009). Epidemiologists and ecologists have long been concerned about atrazine as a potent carcinogen and teratogen (Wu et al., 2009) as well as its association with developmental and reproductive malformations in wildlife (Hayes, 2002). These concerns were great enough for the state of Wisconsin to create atrazine "prohibition areas" and for Italy to ban the chemical outright (Giupponi, 2001; Wolf and Nowak, 1996). The US EPA began a new atrazine review in the fall of 2009; re-registration – if it occurs – would be completed by 2014 or 2015.

Another Way the Polluter Pays: Supplemental Environmental Projects

Regulatory reform and an invigorated partnership between dischargers, the states and federal agencies will require greater resources. Many states already charge user fees to help bolster their voluntary programs and permit waivers, but much more could be done to finance water quality improvements with the proceeds of enforcement actions.

Injunctions and civil penalties, the principal tools of environmental enforcement, may halt environmental damage and deter future harm, but they do not necessarily reverse any impacts resulting from noncompliance, nor do they necessarily improve the environment. In theory, civil penalties could be structured to achieve both: the penalty acts as a deterrent while the funds themselves are directed towards restoration. In the US, this general approach to civil penalties involves the use of Supplemental Environmental Projects (SEPs). Once accepted by citizen plaintiffs or environmental agencies in a settlement resolving an enforcement action, a SEP allows a defendant to implement a project that would benefit the environment above and beyond what it is otherwise obligated to do. By implementing a SEP, a discharger can reap reputational and political benefit from what is otherwise a purely negative situation.

Polluter-pays policies work best if they are performance based (Shortle et al., 2012, p.1319), a truism implicit in the US EPA's final guidelines governing SEPs, established in 1998. These require that 1) there be a nexus between the discharge violation and environmental benefits arising from a SEP, 2) the SEP improves protection or reduces risks to public health of the environment, and 3) the SEP consists of a project that violators would otherwise not have performed, either as part of their regular responsibilities under the law or because of environmental programs already adopted and funded (US EPA, 2008b).

Generally, the "nexus test" means that violators must address a problem related to the one caused by the discharge violation (e.g., if the discharge was sediment into a creek, then the SEP might entail restoring fish habitat, preferably somewhere close to the discharge). SEPs can be tremendously beneficial in that they provide much more funding for water-related conservation projects than would otherwise be possible. Just as importantly, they keep a portion of settlement fines local rather than sending them to Washington or a state treasury.

The EPA's record with CWA SEPs is quite lackluster. During FY2001–2009, the agency settled 4,133 formal enforcement actions that resulted in an administrative (and financial) penalty, but only 163 included a SEP. The Bush administration used SEPs for only about 2–4 percent of its Clean Water Act enforcement actions every year (US EPA, 2010b).

For the 2,139 federal CWA administrative enforcement cases that had closed between 2001 and 2009, assessed penalties amounted to $5,379,366 but only $1,189,976 was directed towards SEPs. Effectively, dischargers and the EPA left over $4 million "on the table" that could have gone to water quality improvements rather than being lost to the US Treasury (US EPA, 2010b). Nationally, this may seem a pittance, but the states conduct much more enforcement and also have low SEP usage rates, so it's likely that states would have access to nearly a half billion dollars per year if they made greater use of SEPs. Such sums would go a long way to restoring budget cuts to state watershed restoration projects (PLRI, 2007; Press et al., 2010).

RECYCLING AS IF MATERIALS MATTERED

> I am arguing that the municipal solid waste recycling as we know it today is not an earth-saving activity, nor is it a way to stem industrial waste, nor is it the start of a revolution in eco-consciousness, nor does it more than slightly ameliorate the sited burdens associated with transfer stations, truck routes, landfills, and incinerators. But it *is* a responsible civic activity and can. . .promote the public good by freeing up taxpayer dollars (MacBride, 2012, p. 234).

> Recycle or the tree gets it (recycling slogan of the 1980s and 1990s).

Congressman Esteban Torres, from California's 34th district (in Los Angeles), expressed Samantha McBride's sentiment twenty years before

her in a 1992 hearing on paper recycling when he pointed out that
". . . Recycling isn't the act of putting my newspapers on my curb on
Thursdays. No! Recycling has occurred when the paper is turned into
a new product." Torres had earlier introduced a Newsprint Recycling
Incentives Act (HR 873), which would require newsprint manufacturers
to recycle an amount of newsprint equal to at least that amount of newsprint determined by multiplying a manufacturer or importer's totals by a
percentage set by the EPA, which would be not less than 20 percent after
ten years. (It would be two percent the first year, an additional two percent
the next year, and so on.)

HR 873 never mustered many votes, but it was certainly not the first
nor the last effort to require recovered fiber in new paper, paperboard
and cardboard manufacturing, and it reflected the times. Congressman
Torres's bill came at the height of the national debate over logging
in old-growth forests. In earlier decades, policymakers had pursued
recycling out of concern over litter and overflowing landfills; later,
advocates would invoke jobs and trade deficit concerns. As recently as
November 2013, the US Senate adopted Resolution 309 of the 113th
Congress, expressing ". . .support for policies in the United States that
promote using recyclable materials as feedstock to produce new basic
materials and finished products throughout the world" (US Senate,
2013).

Though the Senate resolution was driven mostly by concerns over trade,
for a brief moment in the late 1960s and early 1970s, Americans flirted
with policies that explicitly targeted profligate exploitation of natural
resources and might truly reconcile our appetites with our material reali-
ties. These began with some ideas popularized in iconic works familiar to
environmentalists of a certain age: from Paul Ehrlich's *Population Bomb*
to the Club of Rome's *Limits to Growth*, from E.F. Schumacher's *Small is
Beautiful* to the *Whole Earth Catalog* and *Progress as if Survival Mattered*.
Each of these rejected neoclassical commitments to endless growth; each
offered alternative visions, ranging from the dour and apocalyptic to the
quaint and utopian.

Environmentalists know this part of our history well. What's less
known is how seriously Congress and several presidents took these concerns. Congress and President Nixon empaneled a blue ribbon National
Materials Policy Commission in 1970. Established by Section 203 of the
Resource Recovery Act of 1970 (84 Stat. 1234), the Commission was
charged with crafting a national policy designed to green the nation's
energy and materials usage, conservation, reuse and recycling. Efficiency,
reuse, industrial feedstock and waste management all figured prominently
in the Commission's report. Yet none of its bold proposals to transform

materials management in the private sector came to pass, and materials policy would continue to exist in name only.

When I was in graduate school in the late 1980s, the most radical political-philosophical idea I encountered was neither libertarian nor Marxist. A small group of modern political theorists and economists going back at least to John Stuart Mill had argued that modern economies should take far more seriously the Earth's energy and materials limits. Mill's "On the Stationary State," an essay published in his 1848 *Principles of Political Economy*, deeply shaped Georgescu-Roegen's *The Entropy Law and the Economic Process* (1971), which postulated that the laws of thermodynamics compel us to seek a stationary or steady state of economic activity rather than economic growth dependent on ever greater resource usage. Georgescu-Roegen's doctoral student, Herman Daly, became most associated with the steady-state concept and was a widely known advocate for material restraint. Daly also co-founded the journal *Ecological Economics*, which lists "implications of thermodynamics for economics and ecology" as one of its specific research areas in its statement of aims and scopes. Peter Victor, author of *Managing Without Growth*, exemplifies a small group of ecological economists striving to translate the steady-state idea into policy proposals. Far from being exotic, these proposals include dirty-input limits, pollution taxes and emissions trading (Victor, 2008). Though the policy tools are similar to ones widely in use, Daly, Victor and the steady-statists justify their proposals not on the basis of mere abatement, but rather for the sake of more ambitious curbs on material and energy use throughout modern economies.

But notwithstanding the wisdom of such arguments, the political left and right both continue to accept the economic growth imperative: polities of all stripes should strive to grow their economies, and that means *more* is always fundamentally better. The steady-state economy idea is thus dismissed, ignored or rebuffed by all of the political orthodoxies. It is too radical in the sense that it urges humanity to forgo valuable resources lying in plain view.

RECYCLING POLICY

If steady-state economics represents the extreme fringe of environmental restraint, *materials efficiency* plays the role of the pragmatic, politically palatable cousin. Materials efficiency has long been appealing for its association with self-sufficiency, individual responsibility, stewardship and resourcefulness. Moreover, as a political matter, pursuing material efficiency easily invokes co-benefits for powerful allies, including those in manufacturing, labor and trade.

What does recycling look like if it is driven not solely or even primarily by concerns over landfills, but rather by materials efficiency, what we could even call an environmental philosophy of parsimony? If we sought to diminish the materials flowing into and out of the US (Macbride, 2012), what manufacturing practices would modern societies seek? Would these result in shorter supply and distribution chains, blue-collar job growth, low resource consumption and high materials reuse? Would recyclables still be considered as problems for waste managers, or would they become viewed as valuable industrial feedstock?

Focusing just on US paper recycling illustrates how we can answer these questions with new policy designs and approaches. Three main goals capture much of what needs to be done to make good on the promise of US paper recycling.

Improve Collection and Sorting

As Chapter 5 made clear, we are not collecting enough paper and paperboard; what we are collecting is too often contaminated or outright unusable. As a consequence, high quality printing and writing paper gets "down-cycled," thereby wasting the high embodied energy, emissions and resources that went into producing a strong, bright sheet of paper. And while it's important to move away from defining recycling as a waste management issue and begin seeing it as an industrial feedstock matter, it is still the case that over a quarter of all US municipal landfill waste is composed of paper.

Brokers of scrap and recovered fiber certainly know what they want. Working from the demand side, recycling and scrap trade associations in Europe and the US have provided specifications for recovered fiber grades over many years, and these evolve continually. Late in 2013, the European Committee for Standardization voted to adopt a revision of its European List of Standard Grades of Paper and Board for Recycling (numbered EN 643). Although the standards are voluntary, they were adopted by every European member and compliance is very high, so the new standards are likely to be quite influential (CEPI, 2013). Numbering in the dozens of specifications for various contaminants or percentages of specific papers grades, these European standards would go far in reducing contamination in recovered fiber, *if the specifications were scrupulously observed.*

Alas, the outlook for US compliance with similar recycling specifications published by the Institute for Scrap Recycling Industries (ISRI) is not great. Referring to the ISRI specs as a kind of a "wish list," Susan Kinsella, from the Environmental Paper Network, a green paper NGO, remarked that "[T]hey are still the basis for trade, but too often what is claimed to meet each standard level is far different from what it used to be" (Kinsella, 2014). In her view, contaminants today are more prevalent than ever.

Given the considerable energy and resources embodied in office paper, the US does an especially poor job of collecting these grades. Only about half of all US office paper is ever collected, even though good models exist for vastly increasing collection in large office buildings (Blackledge, 2011). Compelling people to collect and sort paper through classic command and control is certainly an option – one that cities all around the world have pursued, both for residential and commercial waste generators. In 2011, England and Wales changed their waste directive to prohibit co-mingling and require separation of recyclables, provided it is "technically, environmentally and economically practicable," effective 1 January 2015 (Waste (England and Wales) Regulation, 2011). It remains to be seen how "practicable" will be tested and defined in practice, particularly since improved sorting shifts the costs of contamination off the end user (paper mills) and onto generators (residences and businesses) or Materials Recovery Facilities (MRF).

Over the years, technology has made curbside sorting more practicable, especially where split compartment recycling carts are used. Collection vehicles must have corresponding compartments to "mate" the split carts with truck-mounted receiving bins. Retrofitting trucks and substituting bins can require substantial initial capital outlays, but such one-time funds lend themselves to state or federal subsidies and grants. Similarly, newer MRFs can now take advantage of more sophisticated automation and multi-stage star-screens that perform far better than the older trommels (Miranda et al., 2013).

US municipalities, waste brokers, shippers and traders can sell contaminated recyclables only as long as their biggest buyer – China – tolerates poor quality. In early 2013, China announced a profound departure from its prior tolerance for widely-contaminated shipments, launching "Operation Green Fence." This national initiative set a limit of 1.5 percent contaminants per bale of imported recyclables and adopted an aggressive shipping container inspection program. Rejected shipments quickly piled up, with 55 shipments halted and 7,600 metric tons rejected in the program's first three months (Earley, 2013). A year after adopting Operation Green Fence, recovered paper exports from the US to China had dropped to about 14.6 million tons, a 6 percent decline from 2012 (Resource Recycling, 2014). Shippers also saw rising demurrage (unloading) costs as they were forced to pay ports to hold containers until they could be inspected. American Chung Nam, one of the largest US shippers of recyclables, quickly moved to avoid costly penalties for unloading delays by issuing a "Supplier Letter of Awareness" to its many brokers and sources (Powell, 2013). A mix of information and concern, the Supplier Letter included the following highlights:

- Zero tolerance for banned items, such as e-scrap, textiles, green waste, animal/human waste, insects, animals, food waste, medical waste, etc.
- Prohibitive levels (allowable levels of specific contaminants) must be maintained below 1.5 percent on a bale-by-bale basis. Common examples include wood, metal, glass and plastic.
- Material shipped as "waste paper" but incorrectly declared (i.e., actually consisting of other materials) is cause for customs penalty, including shipment of convertible items such as rolls, reels, boxed or plastic-wrapped paper, cut sheets, etc. Wire baling is the only acceptable form of packaging for "waste paper."
- Wet material (exceeding 12 percent "air-dry" standard) creates an environment for degradation where material can pick up dirt, inviting additional scrutiny, regardless of prohibitive level.
- Loading photos for each container must be sent on or before the cut-off date for each booking, so that they may be reviewed in a timely manner. Shipment will be suspended and potentially returned for any failure to do so.
- Make sure each container is clear of foreign matter/debris before loading (items such as those for blocking/bracing and items such as moisture absorbent gel packs left by previous shipper) (Powell, 2013).

Operation Green Fence ended by 2014, but will have lasting effects on the global trade in recycled materials. In the near term, China's market share in purchasing recovered paper is falling (Resource Recycling, 2014a) and other countries (such as Vietnam) may step in to accept poorly-sorted scrap, either for cleaning and shipping on to China or reprocessing on their own soil. American paper mills responded by lowering prices for recovered paper, thereby bumping up US utilization slightly (Powell, 2013). In the absence of state or federal recovered materials requirements, stricter overseas standards could be the principal way US sorting and quality improves.

Increase Recovered Fiber Use in US Mills

Even if Americans improved their paper collection and sorting overnight, there would not be enough domestic industrial capacity to handle all of the high-quality fiber. The supply of good recovered paper must be matched by industrial demand, especially in the form of paper mills that have the requisite deinking capacity. Without such capacity, high quality recovered papers (e.g., sorted office paper) easily run the risk of "down-cycling" to products like cardboard, which don't require deinking.

The US has long offered loan guarantees to specific firms as a way of favoring innovative manufacturing technologies. When the federal government offers a loan guarantee, it is promising to repay a loan if a commercial third party defaults. The result is access to much cheaper credit than would otherwise be available. In his first term of office, President Barack Obama widely publicized his use of loan guarantees to stimulate innovation in the energy sector, singling out renewables and energy efficiency in particular. While the vast majority of the firms receiving his Department of Energy's loan guarantees make good on their loans, the solar energy firm Solyndra defaulted, resulting in a long, loud outcry against this policy tool. If the US wished to reinvigorate its manufacturing sector, it could proffer less-risky loan guarantees for proven technologies, like paper deinking – conferring many of the economic, environmental and labor benefits that policymakers seek.

Loan guarantees are not the only way to spur new factory development. States and municipalities employ many tax and land-use policy tools for encouraging new facility development. Taxation tools can be used to attract firms to particular zones in cities or unincorporated areas that policymakers wish to develop, either for tax revenues or jobs creation or both. These policy tools typically include abatements (forgiving tax liabilities for a specified period of time), property tax reductions, sales tax exemptions or depreciation allowances for particular types of equipment and machinery, and new-job tax credits or grants (Ladd, 1998).

Despite widespread interest in promoting manufacturing, not all states employ these policy tools. California's manufacturing investment credit expired in 2003; it wasn't until ten years later that the legislature passed a new sales and use tax (SUT) exemption of 4.19 percent for equipment used primarily in any stage of the manufacturing, processing, refining, fabricating, or recycling process (BOE, 2013).

Land economists often dis-favor tax abatements and their related policy tools, economic enterprise zones, because these set up artificial scarcity for the fiscal benefits conferred by policy. Firms can then pit states or local jurisdictions against each other, in essence, ransoming them for the best abatement deals (Ladd, 1998). Such a "race of abatement" works when there are relatively few geographic imperatives (e.g., a steel mill can locate or expand in eastern Iowa as well as Mobile, Alabama, because of similar labor factors, power rates, access to markets and the like). However, to seriously address the country's need for deinking capacity while avoiding the distance penalty, tax abatement policies should carefully limit their availability to urban zones close to large sources of high-quality recovered fibers, transportation hubs and skilled labor pools.

Trade associations, federal agencies and NGOs can collaborate productively to estimate expanded deinking mill capacity for the US, as Conservatree and the Environmental Paper Network (EPN) did in 2001 (Gleason, Kinsella and Mills, 2002). Authors of this capacity study pointed out that the US produced enough recovered material to meet far more fiber demand by US mills. Their analysis offered a modest scenario for sharing excess deinked pulp among coated and uncoated grades. Just increasing the post-consumer content to 10–30 percent could result in 2.7 million tons of US paper production. Moreover, many mills that can't offer 100 percent post-consumer recycled content can easily accommodate relatively low post-consumer percentages (Gelason, Kinsell and Mills, 2002).

In contrast to providing new fiscal incentives, reforms could remove subsidies that favor firms using virgin inputs. American firms have long enjoyed a "black liquor credit" of fifty cents to a dollar per gallon, rewarding them for burning spent chemicals used in the Kraft pulping process. Removing that subsidy would be worth at least $2 billion per year and perhaps far more (Mufson, 2013); savings could be used to fund recovered fiber incentives. If it were politically impossible to remove the credit entirely, it could be reduced, or a similar-sized credit could be offered to firms using recovered fiber for their pulping needs.

A serious potential obstacle in the path toward more mill capacity has nothing to do with technology, subsidies or distance: our country's labor woes. As Wall Street executive Steve Rattner has long pointed out, labor is the Achilles' heel of US manufacturing. Recent auto plant openings in the US illustrate the problem best: manufacturers cannot find enough skilled workers, so they have had to re-invent the factory apprenticeship. For their part, new employees are happy to get the internships, but lament the very low wages. At an average of $39.04 per hour per worker in 2012, US auto manufacturing compensation is paradoxically both too low and too high. Wages are too low relative to the US cost of living, but very high relative to rates in other countries such as China, Mexico, India and Brazil (Rattner, 2014). Unless and until the wage paradox can be resolved, US firms will be reluctant to site new factories in the US.

Shorten Distances that Recovered Materials Travel

Chapter 5 illustrated how the current export-led paper recovery model incurs a high environmental and energy distance penalty. Instead of incurring that penalty by shipping recovered materials hundreds or even thousands of miles, manufacturers could enjoy a recycling bonus in the form of energy savings and easier materials transformation. Several policy innovations could help here.

First, as Klee puts it, "you are what you measure" (Klee, 2004). Valuable information on the fuel and cost savings from transportation changes would help firms discover the break-even points for shipping different recovered paper products, depending on transport mode (truck, rail, freighter). These break-even points show to what distance recovered paper can be shipped before transportation costs eclipse energy savings from recycling. A 2007 Oregon Department of Environmental Quality (DEQ) study did just that with greenhouse gas emissions in mind (Allaway, 2007). If one attributes a lot of CO_2e to virgin fiber production, as did the DEQ study, then long-range transport of recycled materials looks favorable compared to production with new feedstocks. The DEQ argued, for example, that the break-even point for shipping recycled office paper was 7,000 miles by truck, 27,000 miles by rail and 31,000 miles by freighter (Allaway, 2007).

To internalize the climate advantages of recycling, tax credits could be provided for low-carbon recovered fiber transport (and these could vary by transport mode). Transport can be characterized as "low-carbon" by virtue of the CO_2e produced for each ton-mile of shipment. Low-carbon transport can be achieved by mode (rail, ship, truck), fuel or even the nature of hauls (e.g., new fiber on the out-haul; recovered fiber on the back haul so that trucks are never empty). Of course, negative tax incentives could also greatly encourage shorter transport of heavy scrap recyclables. If the US ever implements a carbon tax, the distance penalty would automatically become much greater (in monetary terms), thereby rewarding firms with more efficient supply and distribution loops.

Though they were not conceived for mitigating the distance penalty, "Recycling Market Development Zones," an under-used approach, provide technical assistance, low-interest loans, and marketing help for businesses seeking to find and use recovered materials within fairly small regions. Many states employ this clearinghouse role, matching materials brokers to industries, but the programs are only as good as the staffing and budget resources states are willing to provide. On the federal level, the US has long employed procurement guidelines to spur mills towards producing paper with post-consumer recovered fiber content, but the fiber percentages have stalled at 30 percent for many years (see US EPA, 2014).

One Goal, Many Paths

Table 6.2 summarizes the materials recovery proposals I've discussed here. Materials recycling engages an enormous network of private and public actors, so any reform proposal could be viewed as quite unwieldy. This disadvantage is also a virtue: a very broad policy network is available for materials re-design; there's something for everyone, local, state, federal government, NGOs, private sector and schools. Valuable policy options exist all along the chain from the moment paper or glass or plastic is used to the instant it becomes a renewed version of its old state.

The table follows Allwood's (2012) approach for depicting policy options. Some of the table items are "either/or." For example, standards governing recovered paper grades, contaminants, etc. can be voluntary (down in "capacity building") or could be adopted as part of a mandatory recycling requirement. Similarly, some policy initiatives address several of the recycling outcomes we should pursue. For example, returning old magazines directly to coated paper mills could simultaneously improve collection quality and increase recovered fiber in US mills. Frank Locantore, a longtime observer of the recycled paper market, suggested that this kind of take-back program could be easy to set up using peel-off mailing labels (Locantore, 2011). Public policy could help with this, at least initially, by offering postage subsidies to get the program rolling.

THE POLITICS OF REGULATORY REFORM OR THE END OF PUBLIC POLICY?

> Surely there never was such fragile china-ware as that of which the millers of Coketown were made. Handle them ever so lightly, and they fell to pieces with such ease that you might suspect them of having been flawed before. They were ruined, when they were required to send labouring children to school; they were ruined, when inspectors were appointed to look into their works; they were ruined, when such inspectors considered it doubtful whether they were quite justified in chopping people up with their machinery; they were utterly undone, when it was hinted that perhaps they need not always make quite so much smoke (Charles Dickens, *Hard Times*, 1854).

> It's not just that we can no longer pull together to put a man on the moon. It's that we can't even implement proven common-sense solutions that others have long mastered – some form of national health care, gun control, road pricing, a gasoline tax to escape our budget and carbon bind (Thomas L. Friedman, *New York Times*, Sunday 3 November 2013, p. 11).

Anyone observing US politics early in the 21st century could understandably conclude that public policy is dead. The partisan gridlock that

Table 6.2   Policy tools for paper recovery and reuse

	Improve Collection and Sorting	Increase Recovered Fiber use in US mills	Shorten Distances that Recovered Materials Travel
Command and Control	Implement mandatory curbside sorting rather than commingling	Mandatory recycling legislation (for collection) Increase recovered fiber percentages in Comprehensive Procurement Guidelines	Increase fuel efficiency standards for trucks
Incentives	Depreciation deduction allowance for reuse and recovery equipment (e.g., HR 5372 – RISE Act) Postage subsidies for direct returns of magazines Advance Recycling Fees Recycling Market Development Zones	Loan guarantees for new mill construction Tax credits for investing in equipment for manufacturing recycled products Tax credits for using recycled content in manufacturing, including authorizing companies to trade and sell the credits Remove the black liquor credit or offer similar incentives to firms using recovered paper	Tax credits for low-carbon recovered fiber transport, by mode (rail, ship, truck)
Capacity building	Office building sorting and recycling, education, best practices for increasing collection; Improving and adhering to voluntary US scrap standards (ISRI) similar to the European EN 643		Emissions and fuel calculators for recovered fiber freight haul, by mode

Sources: Kinsella, 2008; Allwood and Cullen, 2012; MacBride, 2012.

shut down the federal government and brought the US to the brink of defaulting on its debt surely will prevent regulatory reform for the foreseeable future. Gridlock in the US Congress makes that legislative body more resistant to movement politics. Today, it is exceptionally difficult to assemble sufficient mass demands for new policy initiatives to break through the partisan fences legislators and their campaign funders have erected. Members of Congress will continue introducing new bills, some to strengthen environmental protections, others to weaken them. But the kinds of omnibus, comprehensive efforts characterized by huge statutes like the Clean Water Act, the Clean Air Act and CERCLA almost certainly cannot pass in today's Washington.

With respect to the environment, the US ideological center applies "good enough-ism" to current conditions and a very high scientific standard to proposals for new or strengthened regulation. This is why nearly every industry routinely claims that it is highly regulated already and that agencies have not met standards of evidence for new, stronger requirements. When the Obama Administration's EPA proposed modest reductions in the sulfur content of gasoline, industry representatives called these "illogical and counterproductive" (Plautz, 2014). As Fiona Haines (2011) puts it, today we live with a curious regulatory paradox: crises like oil spills, financial market collapses and mass shootings spur indignant demands for more and better regulation while, at the same time, citizens the world over complain that we are overregulated, living in a "nanny-state" and stifled by inane rules. This paradox makes sense because most people don't think of problems like pollution or product safety until they directly experience danger, rising costs or inconvenience. In short, it seems we all need focusing events in our own personal dramas in order to favor real change.

US environmental policy, however, is alive and well, but not living in Congress. The prospects for better policy designs seem brighter at state and local levels and maybe in Europe as well, particularly in those jurisdictions willing to re-shape the relationships between government and business. Product bans come to mind, such as the prohibitions by Italian provincial governments on the use of the herbicide atrazine (Bottoni, 2013), but also urban transport pricing in cities like Brussels and London (Proost and Sen, 2006) and bike- or car-share programs embraced by dozens of cities.

Although it barely reaches the level of national discussion, cities and states or provinces around the world are quietly transforming the relationships between producers and their goods through "extended producer responsibility" (EPR) laws and rules. Such rules require that manufacturers either take back their products when these have reached the ends of their useful lives or pay for third-parties to accept them. Once received,

Table 6.3   State extended producer responsibility laws and products regulated

Product type	Number of states with EPR	States with EPR
Carpet	1	California
Paint	7	California, Connecticut, Maine, Minnesota, Oregon, Rhode Island, Vermont
Thermostats	10	California, Connecticut, Illinois, Iowa, Maine, Montana, New Hampshire, Pennsylvania, Rhode Island, Vermont
Pesticide Containers	1	California
Batteries (either primary or rechargeable)	10	California, Florida, Iowa, Maine, Maryland, Minnesota, New Jersey, New York, Vermont
Cell phones	1	California
Electronics	24	California, Connecticut, Hawaii, Illinois, Indiana, Maine, Maryland, Michigan, Minnesota, Missouri, New Jersey, New York, North Carolina, Oklahoma, Oregon, Pennsylvania, Rhode Island, South Carolina, Texas, Vermont, Virginia, Washington, West Virginia, Wisconsin
Mattresses	2	California, Connecticut
Automobile switches	11	Illinois, Indiana, Iowa, Maine, Massachusetts, New Jersey, Rhode Island, South Carolina, Utah, Vermont, Virginia
Fluorescent Lamps	3	Maine, Vermont, Washington

Source: Product Stewardship Institute, 2013.

used materials should either be re-processed, dismantled into valuable elements or otherwise recycled. Costs can be entirely borne by producers or shared with consumers through "advance recycling fees," which attach modest fees to new purchases. The funds then support re-processing or recycling. Table 6.3 lists major EPR laws and rules as well as the product types they seek to regulate.

These rules typically cover relatively durable goods that pose difficult and expensive disposal challenges. The most commonly covered goods include paints, electronics, batteries, mattresses and devices containing heavy metals like thermostats and automobile switches. Statutes like RCRA and its amendments (e.g., HSWA, 1984) prohibit land disposal of goods containing hazardous materials. Inevitably, city or county waste management authorities end up bearing the cost for properly handling them, which can rapidly run into the hundreds of thousands of dollars or even millions of dollars per year. In an era of recession and declining local government budgets, EPR bills become associated less with controversial environmental causes and more with responsible, cost-saving good government. Nash and Bosso (2013) point out that Hennepin County (Minnesota) saved $681,982 during the first year of its EPR for waste electronics, because producers started collecting and recycling electronic waste that the county had previously managed on its own.

EPRs have had limited applicability to paper and paperboard, though some municipalities have tried adopting them, citing the enormous amount of paper and paperboard waste associated with packaging. The City Council of Chicopee, Massachusetts, tried to pass a resolution urging the Commonwealth to adopt extended producer responsibility rules for paper and packaging, but the resolution failed, largely because councilors found it vague and overbroad (Chicopee City Council, 2011). The environmental NGO, Recycling Reinvented, used the state of Minnesota as a case study of the potential for EPRs covering packaging and printed paper. The authors concluded that an EPR rule (in which manufacturers paid for their products to be recycled) for paper in Minnesota would increase that state's paper recovery rate from 46 percent to 61 percent (Recycling Reinvented, 2014).[2]

American cities and states continue to creatively and aggressively innovate for environmental restoration and protection. As Barry Rabe has long pointed out, states may be more proactive on issues like climate change, because they see economic growth opportunities in green investments; some states are already feeling effects of climate change, and states that implement policy early stand a chance of affecting future federal policies if/when the federal government gets around to adopting any (Rabe, Ed., 2014, in Nahmias-Wolinsky (N-W)). State efforts are often influential, far-reaching and effective, but there is a limit to what even large states like California and New York can do, not only because issues like climate change require greater collective action, but also because the Constitution constrains many policy options available to the states. Any action that may restrict interstate movement of goods and services is unlawful under the Constitution's commerce clause (Rabe, Ed., 2014, in N-W).

The transboundary nature of many environmental problems ensures

---

[2] That claim was immediately and hotly contested by the National Waste and Recycling Association (NWRA), arguing that paper generation is down while packaging recycling is up, a sign that the current fiber recovery system is working well (Resource Recycling, 2014b).

that nationwide rules will be necessary for a very long time, but climate change adds a new twist. American policymakers of the 1970s designed the compliance-abatement-mitigation approach to damp down the worst pollution excesses. The goal was to return air and water quality *back* to acceptable levels; in essence, to prevent, conserve and restore to pre-lapsarian "beauty, health and permanence," as the historian Samuel Hays would put it (Hays, 1987). Now that we have altered the global climate, the policy goal, at least for many years to come, will increasingly become one of adapting to new conditions. Nations will surely need to continue reducing greenhouse gas loadings and will do so through well-understood abatement and efficiency measures. And humans have long adapted to changing environmental conditions, including anthropogenic ones. But for statutes like the Clean Water and Clean Air Acts, adaptation as an environmental policy goal is unthinkable, a concession and failure. New pollution abatement and land use rules will have to pursue ever-changing environmental quality targets, which will require leadership and creative policy design.

If the US could once claim leadership in environmental policy and regulation, unmatched in scope or sophistication by any other country, what hope is there today for not just good, but great, environmental policy and regulation in the US? As an environmental studies professor, that's a question I hear a lot.

When I tell people that I teach environmental studies, I often get a look of pained sympathy, as if the subject could only be one long dirge, characterized by bad news, intransigence, denial and misanthropy. A necessary subject, yes, but dour and painful. I never try to refute these sentiments; rather, I draw attention to the responsibility of hope I have toward my students and future generations. It would not do to tell a class of 300 students, most between the ages of 18 and 21, that their parents and generations before have hopelessly mucked it up, that their struggle is over before it has properly begun. If progress and renewal seem hopeless, we must conjure up hope, to *will* it into existence. We must improve our approach to solving environmental problems as if the political support was there or would eventually appear.

It's tempting to assume or hope that good policy naturally flows from strong political will to address problems. Certainly, political will is a sine qua non for policy change. Regardless of whether we are waiting for political climates to improve or are enjoying the rare windows of opportunity for progress, we still have to get the policy designs right. If we learned anything from the bold regulatory and legislative experiments of the 1970s, it is that getting it right is a way of life, requiring us to learn and change. A sustainable future demands nothing less.

REFERENCES

Allaway, D. (2007). "Climate and Waste: The Next Frontier in Waste Management Policies?" EPA Resource Conservation Challenge Web Academy, Oregon Department of Environmental Quality.

Allwood, J. M. and J. M. Cullen (2012). *Sustainable Materials with Both Eyes Open*. Cambridge, UK, Cambridge University Press.

Andreen, W. L. (2004). "Water Quality Today – Has the Clean Water Act Been a Success?" *Alabama Law Review* 55: 537–591.

Anthoff, D. and R. Hahn (2010). "Government Failure and Market Failure: On the Inefficiency of Environmental and Energy Policy." *Oxford Review of Economic Policy* 26(2): 197–224.

Baldwin, R. and J. Black (2008). "Really Responsive Regulation." *The Modern Law Review* 71(1): 59–94.

Blackledge, P. (2011). Environmental Paper Network, personal communication, 1 August, 2011.

Bottoni, P., P. Grenni, et al. (2013). "Terbuthylazine and Other Triazines in Italian Water Resources." *Microchemical Journal* 107: 136–142.

Bruijn, T. d. and V. Norberg-Bohm (Eds.) (2005). *Industrial Transformation: Environmental Policy Innovation in the United States and Europe*. Cambridge, MA, The MIT Press.

Burns, D. A., T. Blett, R. Haeuber and L. H. Pardo (2008). "Critical Loads as a Policy Tool for Protecting Ecosystems from the Effects of Air Pollutants." *Frontiers in Ecology and Environment* 6(3): 156–159.

California Board of Equalization (2013). Manufacturing Exemption. Accessed at http://www.boe.ca.gov/sutax/manufacturing_exemptions.htm#page=Overview.

CEEP (2013). Center for Evidence-based Environmental Policies and Programs. Accessed at http://www2.gsu.edu/~wwwcec/ceep/.

Chertow, M. R. and D. C. Esty (Eds.) (1997). *Thinking Ecologically: The Next Generation of Environmental Policy*. New Haven, CT, Yale University Press.

Chicopee City Council (2011). Public hearing of the Public Works Committee. Chicopee, MA. 6 June.

Coglianese, C. (2013). "Moving Toward the Evaluation State." RegBlog. Philadelphia, Pennsylvania, University of Pennsylvania.

Cohen, S., S. Kamieniecki, et al. (2005). *Strategic Planning in Environmental Regulation: A Policy Approach That Works*. Cambridge, MA, MIT Press.

Confederation of European Paper Industries (CEPI) (2013). CEPI Guidance for Revised EN643 Published. Brussels, Belgium. 12 December, 2013.

Confederation of European Paper Industries (2013). "Standardisation Bodies Vote to Improve Quality of Paper Recycling." Accessed at http://www.cepi.org/topic/recycling/pressrelease/en643.

Davies, J. Clarence and Jan Mazurek (1997). *Regulating Pollution: Does the US System Work?* Washington, DC, Resources for the Future.

Davies, J. C. and J. Mazurek (1998). *Pollution Control in the United States: Evaluating the System*. Washington, DC, Resources for the Future.

De Rosa, C. (2010). "The USEPA and the Toxic Substances Control Act (TSCA) of 1976: The Promise, the Reality, and the Reason(s) Why." *Human and Ecological Risk Assessment* 16(6): 1227–1233.

Dietz, T. and P. C. Stern (Eds.) (2002). *New Tools for Environmental Protection: Education, Information, and Voluntary Measures*. Washington, DC, National Academy Press.

Donahue, J. D. and J. Joseph S. Nye (Eds.) (2002). *Market-Based Governance: Supply-Side, Demand-Side, Upside, and Downside*. Washington, DC, Brookings Institution Press.

Downing, P. B. and K. Hanf (1983). *International Comparisons in Implementing Pollution Laws*. Boston, MA, Kluwer-Nijhoff.

Drelich, D. (2007). "Restoring the Cornerstone of the Clean Water Act." *Columbia Journal of Environmental Law* 34: 267–331.

Driesen, D. M. and A. Sinden (2009). "The Missing Instrument: Dirty Input Limits." *Harvard Environmental Law Review* 33(1): 65–116.

Dunn, W. N. (1994). *Public Policy Analysis: An Introduction*. Englewood Cliffs, NJ, Prentice Hall.

Earley, K. (2013). "Could China's 'Green Fence' Prompt a Global Recycling Innovation?" *The Guardian*. London, UK. 27 August.

Environmental Law Institute (2000). *Putting the Pieces Together: State Nonpoint Source Enforceable Mechanisms in Context*. Washington, DC, ELI.

Epps, T. and A. Green (2010). *Reconciling Trade and Climate: How the WTO can Help Address Climate Change*. Cheltenham, UK, Edward Elgar.

Finz, S. (2014). "State Warns Consumers of Three Unsafe Products." *San Francisco Chronicle*. San Francisco, CA. 14 March.

Fiorino, D. J. (2006). *The New Environmental Regulation*. Cambridge, MA, MIT Press.

Geiser, K. (2001). *Materials Matter: Toward a Sustainable Materials Policy*. Cambridge, MA, MIT Press.

Georgescu-Roegen, N. (1971). *The Entropy Law and the Economic Process*. Cambridge, MA, Harvard University Press.

Gerard, D. (2000). "The Law and Economics of Reclamation Bonds." *Resources Policy* 26(4): 189–197.

Gerard, D. and E. J. Wilson (2009). "Environmental Bonds and the Challenge of Long-Term Carbon Sequestration." *Journal of Environmental Management* 90(2): 1097–1105.

Gerard Gleason, S. Kinsella and V. Mills (2002). "Recycled Paper: Plenty Available – Now Let's All Use It!" *Resource Recycling* February: 1–3.

Giupponi, C. (2001). "The Substitution of Hazardous Molecules in Production Processes: The Atrazine Case Study in Italian Agriculture". FEEM working paper no. 35. Accessed at http://papers.ssrn.com/sol3/papers.cfm?abstract_id=278243.

Gleason, G., S. Kinsella and V. Mills (2002). "Recycled Paper: Plenty Available – Now Let's All Use It!" *Resource Recycling*, February.

Gunningham, N. (2007). "Corporate Environmental Responsibility, Law and the Limits of Voluntarism", in McBarnett, D, Voicelescu, A and Campbell, T. *The New Corporate Accountability: Corporate Social Responsibility and the Law*, Cambridge: Cambridge University Press.

Hahn, R. and K. Richards (2010). "Environmental Offset Programs: Survey and Synthesis." Indiana University School of Public and Environmental Affairs.

Haines, F. (2011). *The Paradox of Regulation: What Regulation Can Achieve and What It Cannot*. Cheltenham, UK, Edward Elgar.

Hatch, M. T. (Ed.) (2005). *Environmental Policymaking: Assessing the Use of*

Alternative Policy Instruments. Albany, NY, State University of New York Press.

Hays, Samuel P. (1987). *Beauty, Health, and Permanence: Environmental Politics in the United States, 1955–1985*. New York, NY, Cambridge University Press.

Hayes, T., K. Haston, M. Tsui, A. Hoang, C. Haeffele and A. Vonk (2002). "Atrazine induced Hermaphroditism at .1 ppb in American Leopard Frogs (Rana pipiens): Laboratory and Field Evidence." *Environmental Health Perspectives* 111(4): 568–575.

Hoornbeck, J. A. (2005). "The Promises and Pitfalls of Devolution: Water Pollution Policies in the American States." *Publius* 35(1): 87–114.

Houck, O. A. (2002). "The Clean Water Act TMDL Program V: Aftershock and Prelude." *Environmental Law Reporter* 32: 10385–10419.

Keene, M. and A. S. Pullin (2011). "Realizing an Effectiveness Revolution in Environmental Management." *Journal of Environmental Management* 92(9): 2130–2135.

Kinsella, S. (2014). Executive Director, Conservatree, San Francisco, California, personal communication.

Klee, R. J. (2004). "Enabling Environmental Sustainability in the United States: The Case for a Comprehensive Material Flow Inventory." *Stanford Environmental Law Journal* 23: 131–167.

Ladd, H. F. (1998). *Local Government Tax and Land Use Policies in the United States: Understanding the Links*. Cheltenham, UK, Edward Elgar.

Locantore, F. (2011). GreenAmerica, personal communication.

Logan, M. (2014). "Plastic Bag Regulations Gain Momentum, Face Criticism." RegBlog. Philadelphia, Penn Program on Regulation. 23 January.

MacBride, S. (2011). *Recycling Reconsidered*. Cambridge, MA, The MIT Press.

Malik, A. S., B. A. Larson, et al. (1994). "Economics Incentives for Agricultural Nonpoint-Source Pollution Control." *Water Resources Bulletin* 30(3): 471–480.

Mazmanian, D.and D. Morell (1992). *Beyond Superfailure: America's Toxics Policy for the 1990s*. Boulder, CO, Westview Press.

McElfish, J. M. J., L. Breggin, et al. (2006). "Inventing Nonpoint Controls: Methods, Metrics and Results." *Villanova Environmental Law Journal* 87: 87–216.

Metzenbaum, S. (1998). *Making Measurements Matter*. Washington, DC, Brookings Institution.

Milon, J. W. and J. F. Shogren (Eds.) (1995). *Integrating Economic and Ecological Indicators: Practical Methods for Environmental Policy Analysis*. Westport, CT, Praeger.

Miranda, R., M. Concepcion Monte, et al. (2013). "Analysis of the Quality of the Recovered Paper from Commingled Collection Systems." *Resources, Conservation and Recycling* 72: 60–65.

Mufson, S. (2013). "When it Comes to the Paper Industry and Fuel Tax Credits, IRS Looks like a Soft Touch." *The Washington Post*. Washington, DC. 19 July.

Parto, S. and B. Herbert-Copley (Eds.) (2007). *Industrial Innovation and Environmental Regulation: Developing Workable Solutions*. New York, NY, United Nations University Press.

Plautz, J. (2014). "EPA Unveils Final Rule for Curbing Sulfur in Gasoline." *E&E News*.

Polenske, K. R. (Ed.) (2007). *The Economic Geography of Innovation*. New York, NY, Cambridge University Press.

Popp, D. (2010). "Innovation and Climate Policy." *Annual Review of Resource Economics*, Vol 2, 2010. Palo Alto, Annual Reviews. 2: 275–298.

Potoski, M. and A. Prakash (2004). "The Regulation Dilemma: Cooperation and Conflict in Environmental Governance." *Public Administration Review* 64 (2).

Powell, J. (2013) "Operation Green Fence is Deeply Affecting Export Markets." *Resource Recycling* 12 April.

Press, D., P. Holloran and B. Petersen (2010). "Enforcement-Driven Financing of Water Quality in California: The Case of Supplemental Environmental Projects." UC Water Resources Center Technical Completion Report Project No. WR1022.

Press, D. and D. A. Mazmanian (2009). "Toward Sustainable Production: Finding Workable Strategies for Government and Industry," in Norman Vig and Michael Kraft (Eds.) *Environmental Policy: New Directions for the Twenty-First Century*, 7th edition. Washington, DC, CQ Press.

Proost, S. and A. Sen (2006). "Urban Transport Pricing Reform with Two Levels of Government: A Case Study of Brussels." *Transport Policy* 13(2): 127–139.

Public Law Research Institute (PLRI) (2007). "Supplemental Environmental Projects: A Fifty-State Survey with Model Practices." San Francisco, UC Hastings College of the Law. Accessed at http://www.uchastings.edu/site_files/plri/ABAHastingsSEPreport.pdf on 12 January 2010.

Pullin, A. S. (2012). "Realising the Potential of Environmental Data: A Call for Systematic Review and Evidence Synthesis in Environmental Management." *Environmental Evidence* 1(2): 3.

Reis, P. (2010). "With EPA's Blessing, Army Corps Issues Mountaintop Permit." Greenwire, 6 January.

Resource Recycling (2014a). "China Slowly Losing Paper Recycling Market Power." *Resource Recycling* 19 February.

Resource Recycling (2014b). "Major Association Slams Producer Responsibility Systems." *Resource Recycling* 27 March.

Robertson, G. P. and P. M. Vitousek (2009). "Nitrogen in Agriculture: Balancing the Cost of an Essential Resource." *Annual Review of Environment and Natural Resources* 34: 97–125.

Ruhl, J.B. (2000). "Farms, Their Environmental Harms, and Environmental Law." *Ecology Law Quarterly* 27, 263–349.

Salamon, L. M. (2002). *The Tools of Government: A Guide to the New Governance.* New York, Oxford University Press.

Scheffe, R. D., J. A. Lynch, et al. (2014). "The Aquatic Acidification Index: A New Regulatory Metric Linking Atmospheric and Biogeochemical Models to Assess Potential Aquatic Ecosystem Recovery." *Water, Air and Soil Pollution* 225.

Schwarzman, M. R. and M. P. Wilson (2009). "New Science for Chemicals Policy." *Science* 326(5956): 1065–1066.

Schröder, J. J. and J. J. Neeteson (2008). "Nutrient Management Regulations in the Netherlands". *Geoderma* 418–425.

Shortle, J. S., M. Ribaudo, R. D. Horan and D. Blandford (2012). "Reforming Agricultural Nonpoint Pollution Policy in an Increasingly Budget-Constrained Environment." *Environmental Science and Technology* 46: 1316–1325.

Tyler, R. (2013). "Does Regulation Work?" RegBlog. J. Hobbs. Philadelphia, Pennsylvania, Penn Program on Regulation: Opinion. 14 August.

United Kingdom (2011). The Waste (England and Wales) Regulations 2011. United Kingdom, Rule Number 988.

United States Environmental Protection Agency (2014). Comprehensive Procurement Guidelines: Paper and Paper Products. Accessed at http://www.epa.gov/epawaste/conserve/tools/cpg/products/paperproducts.htm.

United States Senate (2013). A Resolution Expressing Support for Improvement in the Collection, Processing, and Consumption of Recyclable Materials throughout the United States. Washington, DC, Senate Resolution 309, 113th Congress, 21 November.

Victor, P. A. (2008). *Managing Without Growth: Slower by Design, Not Disaster*. Cheltenham, UK, Edward Elgar.

Vig, N. E. and M. E. Kraft (Eds.) (2012). *Environmental Policy: New Directions for the 21st Century*, 8th edition. Washington, DC, CQ Press.

Wilson, M. P. and M. R. Schwarzman (2009). "Toward a New US Chemicals Policy: Rebuilding the Foundation to Advance New Science, Green Chemistry, and Environmental Health." *Environmental Health Perspectives* 117(8): 1202–1209.

Wolf, S. A. and P. Nowak (1996). "A Regulatory Approach to Atrazine Management: Evaluation of Wisconsin's Groundwater Protection Strategy." *Journal of Soil and Water Conservation* 51(1): 94–100.

Zedler, J. B. and S. Kercher (2005). "Wetland Resources: Status, Trends, Ecosystem Services, and Restorability." *Annual Review of Environment and Resources* 30: 39–74.

Index